Conceptual Activism

Conceptual Activism

Radical Sense-Making and the Struggle for Gender

DAVINA COOPER

Duke University Press *Durham and London* 2026

Cover designed by Dave Rainey
Typeset in Garamond Premier Pro by Westchester Publishing Services

Library of Congress Cataloging-in-Publication Data
Names: Cooper, Davina author
Title: Conceptual activism : radical sense-making and the struggle for gender / Davina Cooper.
Description: Durham : Duke University Press, 2026. | Includes bibliographical references and index.
Identifiers: LCCN 2026011402 (print)
LCCN 2026011403 (ebook)
ISBN 9781478039280 paperback
ISBN 9781478034322 hardcover
ISBN 9781478062899 ebook
Subjects: LCSH: Activism | Gender identity—Political aspects | Minorities—Political activity | Trans-exclusionary radical feminism | Sociological jurisprudence | Political participation | Social movements | LGBT activism | Social action
Classification: LCC HM881 .C6675 2026 (print) | LCC HM881 (ebook) | DDC 303.48/4—dc23/eng/20260603
LC record available at https://lccn.loc.gov/2026011402
LC ebook record available at https://lccn.loc.gov/2026011403

Cover art: Helena Goldwater, *Gut Reaction*, 2009. Watercolor on paper, 31 × 41 cm. Courtesy of the artist.

For Didi

Contents

Acknowledgments ix

Introduction 1

1. Materializing the Concept: From Conceptual Engineering to Census Sex 23

2. How Concepts Dance: As Sea Urchins, Mushrooms, and Little, Tiny Angels 45

3. Speculative Imaginaries: Decertification as Economy 67

4. Common Sense and Facing Both Ways: When Public Bodies Do Activism 95

5. Playing with Hazardous Concepts 121

Conclusion: Gender's Conceptual Morphologies, Methods, and Dances 147

Notes 163

References 205

Index 233

Acknowledgments

This book could not have happened without the input of a great many people. I am grateful to all the local government, trade union, regulatory, and NGO staff I spoke with, whose words inform this book. Because they asked not to be named, they remain anonymous in its pages, yet their perspectives form a crucial and central foundation for the analysis of British gender politics provided. Some interview material also comes from the Future of Legal Gender project, funded by the Economic and Social Research Council. The discussions about gender in this book are deeply indebted to work and conversations within that research project, and I would like to thank my fellow researchers, Flora Renz, Liz Peel, Emily Grabham, Robyn Emerton, Han Newman, and Jess Smith, for coming with me on a shared journey to explore whether legal sex status should be abolished in Britain. I am also very grateful to the academics who agreed to be interviewed for this book, and who generously gave their time to reflect on the form and shape of concepts in their research, and to think about conceptual activism with me.

Chen First and Jenny Logan provided excellent research assistance. Lucia King, Helena Goldwater, Reina Lewis, and Yvonne Lawrence asked hard questions that helped me work out the book's contours. Flora Renz, Amanda Perry-Kessaris, Bonnie Honig, Swethaa Ballakrishnen, Margaret Davies, Donatella Alessandrini, Janet Newman, Rebecca Hewer, Sameer Ashar, Katharine Jenkins, Jon Goldberg-Hiller, Sarah Keenan, Marquis Bey, Amy Cohen, Shirin Rai, Mathias Thaler, Danish Sheikh, Suvi Salmenniemi, Sarah Lamble, Amelia Thorpe, Beth Goldblatt, Mihaela Mihai, Ben Golder, and Bronwen Morgan contributed to this book in diverse ways, answering queries, discussing aspects of the book's argument, in some cases giving feedback on draft chapters, and generally sitting in my head as I traveled with conceptual activism. Marianne

Constable and John Clarke read and commented on multiple chapters, helping me to develop the landscape and topography of the book. Sylvia Walby and the two anonymous readers from Duke University Press read and commented on the entire manuscript in the months leading up to its final submission; their immensely thoughtful feedback fueled the last set of revisions.

My thanks go to the Leverhulme Trust, whose Major Research Fellowship scheme gave me the time to write this book, and to the Dickson Poon School of Law, King's College London, for their ongoing support. My thanks are also due to my editor, Courtney Berger. I have worked with Courtney for well over a decade and across three books, benefiting from her clarity of thinking and excellent, kind advice.

Although this book draws on academic lines of thinking developed over decades, the three years of its writing were shaped by many deaths, including those of my mother, Kitty Cooper; sister-in-law Lisa Herman; friend Kal Michael; and mentor since 1985, Michael Freeman. Their perspectives, concerns, and voices reside beneath the words of the text.

My partner, Didi Herman, continues to read what I write and give me feedback. I remain grateful for her capacity to know exactly what is wrong with what I have written, and I continue to benefit from her sharp feedback but also from her sense of play. This book is dedicated to her.

Introduction

The capture of the collective imagination is undoubtedly one of the most fundamental ways in which power is exercised. —MAARTEN HAJER AND WYTSKE VERSTEEG, "Imagining the Post-Fossil City"

Something pulsed in the silver—something alive, something forceful and bold; a gale of wind, a crashing wave; and in that fraction of a second Robin felt the source of its power, that sublime, unnameable place where meaning was created, that place which words approximated but could not, could never pin down; the place which could only be invoked, imperfectly, but even so would make its presence felt. —R. F. KUANG, *Babel*

In R. F. Kuang's speculative novel *Babel* (2022),[1] a student-led group from Oxford's Royal Institute of Translation tries to stop Britain's aggressive nineteenth-century war with China over opium. Their field of action is silver translation bars, a magical energy source that is powering Britain's socioeconomic and colonial dominance. The Oxford translation institute is a lead player in this imagined sector. Here, translators find English words to match selected terms from other languages. The power of the bars resides in those source language meanings not carried into their English equivalents. These "surplus" meanings then act through the bar. So, if two words mean "power," but the original word also contains the meaning "to hold up a building"—unconveyed by the English translation into *power*—this physical capacity enters the silver bar and can be harnessed and deployed.

The allegory of silver bars in Kuang's novel provides an inventive way of exploring colonial exploitation. Here, not only raw materials and colonial subjects but also meanings are extracted and forced to work in the service of imperial government. Politics, power, materiality, and meaning are at the heart of

Kuang's novel. They are also central elements in this book, which, like Kuang's, attends to the work, force, and deployment of concepts. But while Kuang focuses on the oppressive and violent use of concepts to sustain imperial hegemony, this book focuses on progressive and critical conceptual praxis, in the form of conceptual activism.

Struggles over meaning are a common aspect of sociopolitical praxis and have been extensively studied. What this book contributes is a framework and set of thoughtways for exploring them that pay particular attention to the concept as materially organized meaning. Concepts are typically understood as *imagined* meaning, with all the values, understandings, beliefs, ideas, and feelings that this entails. But in this book, I approach concepts also in terms of what is done—what materializes. Conceptual meanings are expressed in words and actions; they are also manifested and realized in laws, policies, buildings, services, and more, infinitely more. These diverse forms of materialization organize meaning, explicitly or tacitly, and as such form an essential part of the terrain of conceptual activism.

To explore conceptual activism, I examine one specific contemporary struggle: the conflict over the meaning of sex and gender, and the categories that make these concepts up. This conflict has been very public and transnational, but this book focuses on one specific place and time—Britain between 2018 and 2025, where intense disagreement erupted over who counts as a woman (and, to a far lesser degree, a man) and over the scope, relationship, and boundaries between the concepts of sex and gender. This period was also pivotal as the high-water mark of a more flexible and plural approach to gender as intense and sustained pushback from opponents, including through litigation, reinstitutionalized sex, rather than gender, as the primary legal and policy term, a sex reaffirmed as binary and individually immutable.[2] In April 2025, the Supreme Court decision in *For Women Scotland Ltd* was handed down.[3] Proclaimed by both supporters and critics as momentous, this decision by the highest court in Britain held that *sex* (at least for equality law purposes) meant biological sex—"the sex of a person at birth" (para. 7).

This book explores the conceptual activism over sex and gender that led to this point. However, the book is not a study of a social movement, nor is it an analysis of the conditions that caused gender-(as)-diversity to bed in and then recede in Britain's institutional spaces during this period.[4] While conceptual activism is a way of exploring the conflict over sex and gender through the stressed enactment of competing meanings by public bodies and others, the emphasis of this book is on how this conflict helps us to understand and think about conceptual activism. Here, the book interweaves and moves between the concept of conceptual activism, the concept in conceptual activism, and a series of partner concepts (including economy, property, activism, and play), which I draw on to explore the conflict over sex and gender. Imagined but also materializing, these partner concepts shape how sex and gender meanings are organized, while also being shaped and reshaped in turn.

Together, they bring the concept of the concept to the fore. Progressive work on concepts, from sex and gender to property, state, and play, typically addresses the substance and meaning of specific concepts, and how this might and should change. However, what often remains insufficiently attended to is the concept itself. This book approaches the concept as the relationship between the imaginary and material (re)organization of meaning, where meaning consists of definition, value, significance, understanding, and sense-making. In foregrounding both epistemic and ontological dimensions—how meaning is understood and felt, and how it is manifested—this book's approach is deliberately heterodox, refusing to treat concepts as abstract ideational devices lodged in the world of thought, whether individual or collective. The impetus for adopting a more material approach to the concept, one that foregrounds how meaning is shaped by social relations, and how meaning is expressed and realized through networks of things and processes, is indebted to Marxist, feminist, and new materialist traditions. It is also shaped by the book's focus on conceptual activism. While we could think of concepts as exclusively ideational—abstract ways of slicing or organizing social life, including into categories such as man, violence, or equality—doing so sustains and reinforces the ontological division between what is imagined and what materializes (see chapter 1). Approaching concepts, in contrast, as incorporating the material organization of meaning, which includes how meaning is expressed, represented, pursued, and realized, a more dynamic relationship emerges between changes in imagining and changes in what is actualized.[5] Here, the concept of the concept confronts and is located at the crux of this inter- (and intra)relationship rather than on one side of it.[6] This makes concepts more exciting, useful, and intricate sites of sociopolitical change.

In the rest of this chapter, I introduce conceptual activism and address its relationship to prefiguration—the anticipatory enactment of sought-after meanings—before turning to the book's methodological ambition. This is a book about studying conceptual activism, about undertaking it, and about the value of reflexively tracing the processes involved in doing both. But it is also a book about a specific conceptual conflict. This conflict matters because of what it is doing to gender, feminist, trans, and queer politics, as well as for the glimpses (and sometimes pathways) it provides of a radically different gender landscape. The struggle over sex and gender also demonstrates the significance of conceptual activism as a mode of social activity and as an interpretive frame.[7] As such, it reveals the force and agility of concepts, their power to reach toward new horizons and reanchor previous ones.

Struggling over Gender: In Flight from and Captured by Sex

Struggles over the meaning of gender and sex, and how to access and exit their categories, have been long-standing in feminist politics, as social movement actors (collectively and as individuals) parse concepts of woman, gender, lesbian, sex, and more, using these concepts to secure competing political projects and to secure competing understandings of oppression, how to undo it, and the character of the group or class whose oppression is to be centered. In Britain, these conceptual struggles continue to mesh with others, over racism, socioeconomic class, queerness, disability, sex work, and trans politics, giving rise to different divisions and different sites of conflict. Taking place in the late 2010s and early 2020s in Britain, the struggle at the center of this book concerns the definition of woman and man, male and female, sex and gender, and the relationship between these concepts.[8] While various opinions got voiced during this period, the primary division to mobilize and solidify across British public arenas was between gender-critical feminism, with its conception of sex as biological, binary, individually unchanging, and central to women's subordination and vulnerability, and a politics of gender-(as)-diversity, oriented to gender as an open-ended series of identity categories that are normatively equivalent and self-authorized.[9] Outside Britain, right-wing forces, including conservative Christians, have been central players in opposing gender's reconceptualization as plural, flexible, and self-identified.[10] However, strikingly, in the British context, they proved much less conspicuous. Instead, public leadership in opposing gender-(as)-diversity came from feminist and other women's organizations.[11]

Older terms like the slur TERF (trans-exclusionary radical feminist), as well as gender-critical, can seem to imply that those named shared a stable common political project. But as this book explores, what coalesced at this time into a sex-based politics involved different conceptual threads. One thread was the long-standing feminist impetus to free people, women in particular, from gender-specific roles and inequalities. However, in the late 2010s, gender-critical approaches proved increasingly responsive to a different pressure, one we might describe as "sex nativism" (Cooper 2024), that was more concerned to revalue and naturalize sex than to dismantle gender as a social structure of unequal difference. While not all gender-critical feminists, at this time, were sex nativists, it formed a significant tendency—sometimes explicit and sometimes latent—among opponents of gender-(as)-diversity. This was a tendency that privileged "first entrants" (those designated female at birth), with a skeptical resistance that often bled into outright hostility toward those joining the category "woman" through other routes. As such, it resonated with ethnic forms of nativism, mobilized in the lead-up to the 2016 Brexit vote and in its aftermath (see also John Clarke 2023). This nativism treats later entrants as always outsiders, whose attempts to belong (socially and culturally) threaten "real" members' well-being, not least, it is claimed, by remaking what the category is and stands for (see also Franklin 2022). Sex nativism captures how the category of woman—and, sometimes, "sex" too—gets deemed to belong. Here national territory threatened with invasion combines with property discourse to characterize access by others, attempting to share the category, as a form of illegitimate seizure, taking over the category and depleting what remains for its rightful members (see chapter 3).[12]

The conservative resonance of sex nativism is strong. Yet, in attending to gender-critical politics in Britain, a distinctive feature has been the presence and active participation of women who self-identify as socialist or progressive.[13] Concerned with the importance of sexed embodiment to women's long histories of subordination and male power, and the need for women to organize as a sex-based class, gender-critical feminists have, at times, vehemently disputed the notion that recognizing the significance of sexed embodiment to women's inequality is inherently antitrans or reactionary.[14] Instead, they emphasize the importance of definitional clarity (in who counts as a woman or man) to equality laws and policies, how treatment as a woman depends on others' perceptions rather than self-description, and the need to recognize the material reality (centered on the reproductive reality) of sex and sex-based subordination against what they perceive as the illusions and delusions of gender. Gender-critical feminism, for the most part, has also relied on a sharp division between meaning and materiality, with concepts approached as ideational tenets, validated by their capacity to depict a material reality that is distinct and separate (see chapter 1). As such, their conceptual ontology diverges significantly from the approach of this book, which understands the relationship between how meaning is imagined and materialized as far more enmeshed and coproduced. Given gender-critical reliance on the material/imaginary division, and the primacy they afford to sex (and given also the fact that others are critical of gender without being gender-critical), I use the term sex realism for this political project, to emphasize its reliance on the perceived reality and truth of sex as binary, individually fixed, and politically foundational.

Trans politics today stands as the protagonist of sex realism, including in ways that can problematically assume that trans and feminism are antithetical.

While the volume of recent writing on trans feminism (and transfeminism) counters this latter assumption, the terrain of this book is one in which trans women have become the very public target and impetus for sex-realist feminism's development, with trans men largely ignored. Defending trans people and trans rights, while opposing the precepts of sex-nativist expression and gender-critical sex realism, is what gender-(as)-diversity politics stands for.[15] However, despite a shared commitment to this defense, as a conceptual constellation gender-(as)-diversity also faces competing pulls—from a multicultural politics of benign variety, committed to extending gender's categories, along with a deconstructive radical politics that, in different ways, seeks to disrupt, dismantle, or abolish the institution of gender and the meaningful distinctions that gender categories articulate.[16] Since the conflict with sex realism has strongly influenced the public parameters of this politics—so that an affirmative, at times realist, approach to gender holds public sway—in this book gender-(as)-diversity refers to a political project that views minoritized and dissident genders as entitled to rights and protection, where equality consists of equal recognition and acceptance of different gender identities and expressions, and where gender diversity is seen to nourish social life and expression, and so is entitled to survive and thrive on its own terms. More generally, gender-(as)-diversity approaches gender as a valuable register of self-expression and social difference. Whether or not gender—as a way of ordering or making sense of difference—should be dismantled in the future remains open. But while gender remains a central aspect of everyday life, political agendas need to support self-definition and address the injuries that people with nonconforming gender identities and expressions face (see also Renz 2024). Sociocultural erasure, discrimination, and violence here form central addressable harms in an account of gender that is also about more than harm. In a social world that places tremendous stock on gender belonging, where personhood continues to be formed through gender, where gender remains a terrain of necessary self-expression and identification, along with pleasure for some (see chapter 5), gender's social affirmation is deemed essential. This point was underscored by a staff member at a trans organization who was interviewed for the Future of Legal Gender Project (introduced later in this chapter): "There is a spectrum, a wonderful spectrum of gender identities, including those gender identities that mean someone who doesn't have a gender as well."

To the extent that gender-critical and gender-(as)-diversity politics (along with forerunners such as sex-positive and queer feminists, and revolutionary and radical lesbians) remained relatively insulated from one another, they could coexist, embedded within different communities of interest. Certainly, there were flashpoints, including over sex work, pornography, and BDSM, when laws, policies, community organizing, and retail strategies propelled proponents of different sex and gender projects into confrontation. But the sustained and public contemporary struggle of this book, with its legal, political, social, and philosophical conflicts and dramas, is distinct—in its scale, visibility, fields and sites of power, enrollment of publics (including parents, children, religious women, sportswomen, sporting bodies, and women prisoners), and continuously escalating duration. Between 2018 and 2025, conflict over whether to informalize or reformalize gender, to render it more institutionally flexible or inflexible, crisscrossed a series of spaces, including government consultations on reforming the Gender Recognition Act 2004;[17] school policies on sex-segregated toilets, sports, residential accommodation, and sex education;[18] adolescents' access to trans-affirming health care;[19] legal freedoms and equality law protections for gender-critical workers and speech acts in workplaces and social media;[20] trans women's placement in women's refuges and prisons;[21] how to talk about the body in health care settings (e.g., "people with penises" rather than "men");[22] trans women's access to positive action initiatives for women (such as all-women parliamentary shortlists);[23] the decennial census (specifically, how to ask about sex and gender, and what guidance to provide; see chapter 1); and trans-inclusive accreditation and benchmarking schemes for women's equality.[24]

At one level, these different conflicts concerned gender transitioning and how it should be treated and regulated, as sex realists mobilized against liberalizing the procedure for formally changing one's legal sex and gender status (by means of a Gender Recognition Certificate), sought to curtail both formal and informal transitioning by young people (including at school), and aimed to limit the contexts in which a change in sex and gender would be treated as determinative, particularly when it came to positive action, sports, prisons, and women's refuges.[25] Thanks to gender-critical actions, a legal distinction, sex, that had been growing increasingly dim was recharged as those committed to excluding trans women from the category of woman mobilized. But, directly and indirectly, the battle was also about the conceptual meaning, more generally, of gender and sex, its categories, foundations, and normative valence; the conceptual relationship of gender inequality to other social relations (particularly race, class, and sexuality); the power and authority of different conceptions of gender and sex when it came to structuring law, policy, and social provision; and ontology, as the reality claimed for gender was pitted against the reality claimed for sex.

This book takes up the conceptual struggle over gender and sex, as a struggle between divergent activist projects that, thanks to media, law, and social movement activism, congealed into two opposing forces, to think about the politics and meaning of gender politics and change, including in relation to gender's affirmation, proliferation, equalization, and abolition. To do so, it also pulls in conceptions of gender marginalized in this publicly staged conflict, particularly of gender as an institution (and so not simply about how other institutions are gendered). Approached institutionally, gender constitutes an assemblage (formal and informal) of practices, roles, procedures, rules, norms, embodied agents, tangible things, spaces and places, relations of power, and self-legitimizing ideologies persisting across space and time (see P. Martin 2004).[26] Institutional thinking has been criticized for being overly monolithic and structuralist, and these critiques are important. There is no single institutional order, such as The Patriarchy, or even a multitude of discrete stable patterns—gender formations and regimes change, subordinate and dissident forms exist, practices and projects push away from institutional norm founding and norm maintenance.[27] However, what an institutional account offers, against the prevailing focus on gender and sex as attributes of individuals, groups, and classes, is a depiction of gender and sex as patterned and societal, with some degree of stability, replenishment, power, and coherence. This pushes toward a politics that refuses current frameworks of interests and rights where identities, such as gender, constitute possessions or property deemed to belong and to accrue value (see chapters 3–5). However, while an institutional account supports society-level understandings of gender, gender's form may exceed even this framing. What if conceptual activism reimagines gender as monstrous—not that specific gender identities are monstrous, but that gender's form is one that cannot be pinned down to an existing and recognized shape?

Conceptual Activism and the Prefiguring of Meaning

The question of how to think about gender's form takes us to the ontology and politics of concepts. Conceptual meanings evolve and fluctuate thanks to the structural processes through which power relations of wealth, race, empire, gender, and more are expressed and formed. At the same time, conceptual meanings can be deliberately advanced and resisted.[28] Recognizing both structural and agentic aspects is important for conceptual activism. Without the former, conceptual activism can appear unlimited and unrestrained, a voluntaristic activity capable of expressing (and enacting) the infinite creative possibilities of human minds. Without the latter, conceptual activism is limited to the play of structural contradictions without the possibility for meaning to be deliberately reshaped, including against and away from dominant meanings. As both structured and agentic, conceptual activism takes a range of forms. It can involve deliberately destabilizing established meanings, which may involve excavating benign-seeming concepts for the "bad" meanings they hold—markets, competition, and individualism, for example. It can involve developing new meanings that are imagined, sought after, and campaigned for; or enacting new meanings, materially, through forms of representation and accomplishment that anticipate or realize the meanings sought. Conceptual activism can involve changes in a concept's register—tying concepts like gender and property to play, for example, to remove some of their gravity and significance (see chapter 5). It can involve practically developing meanings that seem extraordinary or bizarre, and treating them as if they were true; and it can involve recognizing practices through meanings that solidify and mark alternative sociomaterial cuts and joins (for instance, families of choice, or gender divorced from sex).

Conceptual activism is integral to social movement activity and to political projects—on the left and right: feminist, communist, anarchist, ecological, neoliberal, and neofascist, among others. And since development, resistance, and engagement with conceptual meaning are central to the tacit politics of everyday social practices, professional conduct, and state administration, conceptual activism is found in these spaces also. It is tempting to see conceptual activism as being about overt conflict and how meanings are deliberately (re)imagined, but one aim of this book is to expand this envisioning to take in the everyday and not overtly conflictual as well as how conceptual meanings materialize and are realized, whether as laws and policies or in living a nonbinary or agender life.

There are many critical frameworks for approaching the politics of conceptual meaning and the development of alternative understandings, knowledges, narratives, and discourse. Thus it may seem somewhat surprising that this book takes conceptual engineering as its springboard—a flourishing field, associated with analytic philosophy, that studies the deliberate recrafting of concepts (chapter 1)—since this book is not a work of analytic philosophy. Conceptual engineering, however, offers some helpful prompts and lines of analysis for thinking about the intentional recrafting of conceptual meaning, including the difficulties of doing so. It also offers an important foil for the approach to concepts and conceptual activism taken in this book.

Conceptual engineering involves assessing, improving, and replacing concepts for semantic and political reasons (see Burgess and Plunkett 2020), and conceptual activism focuses on the latter. Elizabeth Cantalamessa (2021, 49, 70) describes conceptual activism as taking place when "speakers make claims that they believe to be trivial, overstated, incomplete, or simply false as a means of pragmatically subverting the received use of a term or concept and to encourage their audience to lower their degree of confidence in their current concept or conceptual framework. . . . What matters in these cases is how someone's use of a term or concept aims to change how others use that term." Cantalamessa's (2021) account of conceptual activism focuses on the destabilization of existing meanings, anchored in conceptual engineering's concern with concepts as tools designed by academics and others. In her work, concepts appear as linguistic devices that speakers deploy to affect how audiences think about and use a term (see Cantalamessa 2021, 54; also Sterken 2020 on strategic "linguistic interventions").[29] This book carves some distance from conceptual engineering. It departs from the presupposition that conceptual activism is necessarily about more accurate representations or linguistic action, that it concerns meanings within an ideational realm distinct from material reality, or that it is principally undertaken by academics.[30] Challenging these precepts takes us to the ground of conceptual prefiguration.

Conceptual activism can be critical or hopeful, challenging or protective; it can be explicitly undertaken, or it can be the effects of institutional practices and currents. Yet across these different forms and registers, this book is oriented to conceptual activism informed by prefiguration—a mode of activity that treats conceptual meanings as if they were already otherwise, an otherwise that pulls against the grain of dominant existing understandings. Conceptual prefiguration is a bridge between conceptual activism and prefigurative politics, undertaking the former in ways informed by the latter. Prefiguration has become a revitalized site of political and academic attention in recent years as sociopolitical projects enact in the present the values, practices, and institutions associated with sought-after ends that may be (but don't have to be) distant future ends, such as participatory democracy, ecological care, noncompetitive economic relations, communal property, and consensual nonmonogamy.[31] As such, prefiguration rejects the transactional contract of representative politics, where activists campaign and pressure others—including governments but not only them—to introduce changes on their behalf.[32] Prefiguration also opposes the notion that meaningful change cascades down. Instead, sought-after changes, including in meaning, are introduced and practiced, typically in small-scale, often dissident, ways to rehearse, advance, or experience the norms and practices of desired social life.

Conceptual prefiguration is both a new idea and an old one. Prefigurative politics has long involved the destabilization and dismantling of hegemonic meanings and understandings—countering and refusing the propertied individualism underpinning liberal notions of freedom, for example, or the heteronormative conjugal relationship underpinning imaginings of romantic or sexual intimacy. But in its concern with practice and the materialization of counterhegemonic social processes (from democratic people's assemblies to communes), prefiguration has not given conceptual meaning a central spot. Prefiguring targets new ways of living and organizing rather than their abstract contemplation; yet concepts are not just about abstract contemplation, and prefigurative politics also relies on new conceptual imaginaries. For instance, altered meanings of what democracy and households are help to transform, and provide the impetus for changing, how democracy or domestic households are practically done; while changing how democracy or households are done—reorganizing the materiality of these practices—changes what they mean.[33] This is an interactive process, but it is also more than that. As such, it complicates the tendency within some prefigurative thinking to aim for new forms of correspondence between reimagining and realizing concepts, where the lagging partner in the relationship is obliged (or compelled) to catch up.

Conventional conceptual work assumes that modes of thinking represent (or should represent) the world as it is and so are in a constant game of catch-up to be adequate to what is (where thinking and what is are clearly and stably differentiated). Conceptual prefiguration extends this relationship of correspondence to a hoped-for future, but it also recognizes that meanings which appear (especially to critics) to deliberately misrepresent the world may do politically valuable stuff.[34] Discussing trans-positive conceptions of gender, Robin Dembroff (2018) suggests that transgender politics should explicitly take up novel gender categories and meanings rather than rely on arguments grounded in the "real." For Dembroff (2018) and other critical scholars working in this vein, privileging conceptual alignment in the present naturalizes (and so reinforces) oppressive relations and practices since these tend to be caught or supported by the "best" meaning. Dembroff (2018, 42) writes, "Identifying as having a gender that does not yet exist, even when these claims are false and largely unintelligible, can be a way to advocate for the construction of new gender kinds." If concepts like the state, property, and gender remain tethered to established understandings, change may be possible, but it is limited. If gender, for instance, is held to a conventional meaning-account of woman and man as natural stable categories, progressive politics can reach for gender equality, but this is an equality predicated on the categories remaining in place, where $m > f$ in Janet Halley's (2006) terms becomes, at best, $m = f$. However, if it is recognized, instead, that gender's meanings can and will also change, that they do not correspond neatly and simply to what is "out there"—an out there that, like gender's meaning, is also fractured, changing, uneven, and disputed—political possibilities become far more extensive: New gender identities emerge, new accounts arise about how gender is taken up (and what concept of gender is taken up), and the possibilities for gender as an institutional formation (or as a set of sociolegal categories) to be deproduced or dismantled surface (see chapter 3).[35]

I have suggested that conceptual prefiguration foregrounds the importance of new conceptual meanings, but it also demonstrates the importance of practice to remaking meaning. Conceptual prefiguration does not take shape as a hope or wish for meanings to change, as in, "Wouldn't it be wonderful if gender was understood as a plural, flexible form of self-expression devoid of asymmetrical power?" Nor does conceptual prefiguration operate through forms of activism that campaign for meaning to change. Conceptual prefiguration enacts meaning as if the change *has already happened*. Doing so—enacting new meanings of democracy, care, family, or the state—may be undertaken to anticipate their realization; it may also be done for other ends: to prompt, stimulate, and challenge, for instance, as I explore in chapter 3.[36] Nevertheless, across these different intentions, meanings remain prefigurative to the extent that they have not been ontologically realized, that their materialization remains illustrative, small-scale, or incomplete—out of joint with dominant regimes and, perhaps, out of joint too with prefigurative conceptual imaginaries as both continue to evolve.

Participatory democracy, ecological care, gender diversity: these compound terms can suggest that conceptual prefiguration remakes concepts in ways that stretch them toward positive meanings or versions of themselves. Thus, for leftists, the state might be reimagined as egalitarian, responsible, caring, nonsovereign, and democratic. But conceptual prefiguration also has a critical dimension when subjects act as if the negative meanings of objected-to concepts already formed part of the collective conceptual imagination.[37] Critical prefiguration advances the negative meanings of concepts such as property, individualism, and punishment that it would like to see installed, acting as if such meanings were already in place. Unlike positive conceptual prefiguration, the intention here is not to realize such meanings ontologically (however imperfect and temporary such realization is) but to create conceptual imaginaries that recognize and respond to already existing harms so that they can be identified and addressed. Michelle Dempsey and Matthew Lister (2016), for instance, explore sexual harassment and intersectionality as examples of a critical form of conceptual activism that creates new concepts to capture negative or problematic practices, enabling them to be discussed, analyzed, and framed as targets for legal and social remedies. Critical prefiguration may seek to eliminate concepts whose imaginaries appear irretrievably toxic (racist terms, for instance); or it may replace one concept by another as gender-critical feminists have done with sex and gender—where the cuts and joins organizing gender as a social concept of difference have been displaced by performatively biological ones of sex (see chapter 1). This gender-critical move has been enacted in grassroots publications and social media discourse; it has also been enacted in litigation to reinterpellate trans women as men and trans men as women, and to discount other gender identities.

Prefiguring negative meanings as well as positive ones can be done in the service of progressive or rightist political projects. This book focuses on conceptual meanings that seek to express more equal, freer, caring, ecologically sustainable worlds—or that are, at least, sufficiently expansive to encompass them.[38] Like other forms of prefigurative politics, prefigurative conceptualizing is an invitation. It is a stimulation and prompt—not a directive—of what concepts could come to mean, one that materializes in practices that treat the conceptual meanings in question as already valid (while knowing this may prove contentious). Conceptual prefiguration is part of a wider transformative politics, not a discrete isolated act, and, as an anticipatory change-based praxis, it is forward-facing, sometimes backward-facing (when justice is found in past places and times), and constantly on the move. Meanings may be described as new because they have not yet become institutionalized, but when it comes to institutions, there is no single, ultimate, progressive variant to install.[39] What appears reactionary or progressive keeps evolving (including as seemingly radical concepts—gay pride, rights of nature, for instance—get appropriated by powerful establishment bodies). Thus, while prefigurative talk of enacting sought-after ends may seem to signal ambitious meanings associated with a time ahead, for contemporary secular versions of prefiguration, such meanings do not fly back from a settled future but are "ends" that are thinkable and desired in the present. We do not know what aspirational progressive meanings (if any) will be carried by concepts, such as gender, property, or the state, across the coming decades.

Conceptual prefiguration works from the premise that conceptual meanings are plural and mutating. But does this approach cause problems for progressive politics given the strategic, evaluative, and transformative imperative to pin down relations of power and meaning? In the struggle over sex and gender, there have been several tense pressure points. One is the relationship between meanings that prefigure new possibilities and meanings that support critical understandings of current harms and exploitation. If gender is seen as elective and diverse, for example, can this sit comfortably alongside critical understandings of gender as a socially imposed, oppressive structure subjecting women and others to various forms of inequality? This question surfaced, with heat, during research I was undertaking with colleagues on the abolition of legal sex status ("decertification"), which I explore in chapter 3. Designing decertification as a speculative law reform proposal also had to confront a second pressure point, concerned with (in)stability and (in)consistency of status. Should conceptions of gender and sex, and the categories they give rise to, be standardized and so consistent across different fields and sectors, or can it make sense, from a progressive conceptual activist perspective, for them to vary—so that how a person is hailed or categorized may diverge according to the context, as what it is to be a category member changes?[40] A third tension arising from conceptual plurality and change concerns the place of loose, uncertain, and discrepant definitions. In the conflict over gender, some gender-critical feminists argued sharply for stable common meanings of key terms. Kathleen Stock (2022, 34), for instance, criticized the reengineering tendencies of "ameliorative definitions," "attempts to improve our concepts according to certain corrective visions, and to say what those meanings should be but currently are not."[41] Yet several policymakers and others interviewed for this book spoke in favor of less tied-down concepts, allowing meaning to change and diverge among stakeholders (see chapter 4). The stakes in this dispute over the specificity and looseness of conceptual meaning (whether concepts should be narrowly and explicitly tailored or more expansive and flexible) came vividly to the fore in the conflict over the 2021 Census for England and Wales and how to ask about sex and gender (see chapter 1).

Developing Conceptual Activist Methods

This book approaches progressive conceptual activism from a prefigurative vantage point, concerned with how meaning gets remade. Caitlin Gunn (2019, 16) talks about "radical speculation" within Black emancipatory politics, stating that it "enables us to imagine futures, reclaim histories, and create alternate realities." Prefigurative conceptual activism does something similar. Against the depiction of concepts as arid, siloed, eviscerated abstractions, it retrieves and resituates concepts as lively, evolving, material, and powerful (see chapter 2).

More generally, conceptual activism becomes something to study and undertake (a studying that can also be an undertaking and vice versa). As a site of study, conceptual activism provides a way of understanding political projects and their conflicts that foregrounds change, resilience, and disputes in how concepts are imagined and enacted. By focusing on specific concepts, such as gender, property, play, and economy, studying conceptual activism brings to the fore the networks of meaning that concepts consist of and that they carry. Sometimes these come publicly and vocally to the fore, as with the conceptual relationship of woman to sex, protection, and girls, which gender-critical feminism asserts and, also, has materially advanced (see chapter 1). But conceptual activism can also identify quieter, more tacit practices that fortify conceptual connections, including new ones, and that naturalize them as common sense (chapter 4).

This book addresses the conceptual activism of different bodies, including trade unions, community organizations, local government, and regulatory agencies. It also explores academic conceptual activism, both as a concept adopted to study the meaning-politics of others and as something to undertake. But what does it mean to undertake academic conceptual activism? Does it mean academics engaging in grassroots activism or, conversely, pursuing abstract explorations of concepts? Academics can do conceptual activism on their computers, on the committees they sit on, on marches and protests, in interactions with state officials, and in their food shopping and traveling, among other sites and activities. But the academic conceptual activism on which I focus concerns the development of new conceptual imaginaries and the material processes involved.[42] I want to approach this way of doing academic conceptual activism as a "manner of proceeding" (Holbraad and Pedersen 2017, 41) attuned to what Klag and Langley (2013, 151, 161) describe as "conceptual leaps," where "dialectic tensions: between deliberation and serendipity; between engagement and detachment; between knowing and not knowing; and between self-expression and social connection" pull thinking away from "well-worn" grooves (see also Wicker 1985).

Social justice and progressive scholarship, more generally, have long confronted the challenge of how to imagine concepts against (and beyond) the grain of current hegemonic understandings and away from methods that focus on immanent reparative work (identifying and repairing internal contradictions and slides in meaning).[43] J. K. Gibson-Graham (2008, 620), the pen name of social geographers Katherine Gibson and Julie Graham, suggest "thinking techniques" that include "ontological reframing to produce the ground of possibility; re-reading to uncover or excavate the possible; and creativity to generate actual possibilities where none formerly existed." Gibson-Graham use these techniques to rethink economy, to demonstrate how expansive noncapitalist economies already are, refusing to let capitalism monopolize its conceptual terrain (see chapter 3).

When it comes to academics developing alternative conceptual meanings, small-scale enactments often play an important role. This is where much work on everyday utopias and prefigurative practice sits. While there is a tendency to focus on the meanings that alternative communities explicitly invoke, minor-stream social practices can also prompt new academic imaginaries, including by partnering sites with incongruous-seeming concepts. In *Everyday Utopias*, I adopted this method to study, among other things, equality through nudism, care at a casual sex place for women, and property at a democratic free school (see Cooper 2014). Orthogonal pairings can prove fruitful for reimagining concepts—not least because the concepts in question have not been publicly and explicitly labored over in relation to the space or organization studied. As a result, good-sense and commonsense conceptual grooves have not hardened and deepened (at least not in relation to this specific concept). This makes it easier to consider different cuts and joins, and to stretch or fold a concept into new shapes. This facility also applies to unlikely conceptual pairs. Lack of an immediate and obvious connection draws contact along new pathways—for instance, when concepts of touch and equality connect, or markets and play.

With their practical and imaginative resources for progressive change, including conceptual change, alternative micro-spaces and practices have been subject to a proliferation of studies in recent years. While oversaturation does not appear to be a problem, academic conceptual activism can also benefit from a wider array of research resources, including sites and practices that do not seem, straightforwardly, to support progressive conceptual development. One I turned to, in the late 2010s, was a transnational legal drama then taking place as conservative Christian organizations and businesses withdrew membership, goods, and services from lesbians and gay men, and liberal governmental bodies, in response, withdrew contracts, promotions, subsidies, and recognition from conservative Christians. Drawing on a strikingly large number of legal cases from the US, Canada, and the UK, I considered whether such a legal drama could prompt innovative progressive ways of reimagining the state.[44] This was not through revaluing conservative accounts of the state, nor through siding with conservative Christian anxieties, but by adopting a queer, utopian method that worked with the legal drama and, particularly, the judicial narratives it generated to reimagine what it could mean to be a state, a journey routed through state heterogeneity, plurality, playfulness, and the erotic.[45]

Building on the conceptual methods developed in relation to everyday utopias, on the one hand, and conservative (dissident) minor-stream practices, on the other, this book attends to the practices of academics, policymakers, and others who use their institutional position in mainstream public bodies for progressive praxis (see also J. Newman 2012). In other words, this book is about everyday conceptual activism in spaces that are not normally associated with it (since conceptual activism is more commonly associated with nonstate social movements, or the conceptual creativity of theorists). Conceptual activism by academics, policymakers, trade unionists, and others does not necessarily collide with the bodies that host it. While it may do so, mainstream public organizations, such as universities, local government, and trade unions, often authorize (or at least don't fight) the take-up of progressive meanings that are emerging as new common sense, including in public service provision, positive action initiatives, funding decisions, academic writing, and publicly funded speculative projects. But as this book explores, such authorizations cannot be assumed and may not last. Mainstream public organizations may resist or shut down specific avenues of conceptual activist practice (often alongside or while opening others), particularly when the costs (and not just the financial costs) of a particular conceptual activist project appear too high.

In the chapters that follow, I weave together three primary threads: the concept in and of conceptual activism, gender-based conceptual activism in Britain in the late 2010s and early 2020s, and prefigurative conceptual methods, focusing particularly on the place of partner concepts. These last enter as analytical aids but quickly get lifted, turned around, and transformed as they become sites, themselves, of political reimagining. In this book, I explore the interactions between these partner concepts through the figure of the dance. This figure provides a way of tracing how concepts move in relation to each other, especially when new or unexpected partnerships are introduced, such as between property and play. These introductions may prompt thinking about new dances—new ways of organizing the imagined and material relationship between concepts—but they also trace dances already underway, understood in other terms.

To undertake this conceptual engagement, I draw on a diverse set of academic literatures on gender politics, regulation, concept-making, speculative law, policy practice, cooperative economies, property, and play. I also draw on three sets of interviews with actors studying and engaged in conceptual activism. Between 2022 and 2024, I conducted twenty-three interviews with academics whose work involved (and combined) progressive conceptual analysis, empirical research, and utopian or prefigurative studies.[46] From 2023 to 2024, I also undertook twelve interviews with (mainly senior) staff working in equality governance in local governments, trade unions, and regulatory bodies in Britain. This supplemented a third, earlier set of about seventy interviews with equality governance actors carried out between 2018 and 2021, for a prior collaborative research project, the Future of Legal Gender.[47] This project also generated other data, drawn on in this book, specifically a speculative legislative proposal to "decertify" sex and gender. This imaginary legal proposal sought to abolish the formal legal status accorded to both sex and gender as aspects of legal personhood (while leaving the concepts of sex and, more particularly, gender available for progressive legal uses).[48] In conditions of decertification, people would no longer have a legally imposed or secured sex or gender, something currently experienced through birth certificate registration and, for some people, through formal revision later on. However, it would not stop law and government from using these (or similar) categories for reparative purposes. Role-playing institutional processes is a conventional method for learning how institutions, such as Parliament, the United Nations, or courts, work. Elsewhere, I have explored institutional role-play-with-revisions—where tribunals, legal judgments, and claims to statehood have been politically, sometimes wittily, appropriated to advance social justice projects—a form of institutional appropriation that, daringly but also caringly, tends to an apparatus ostensibly owned by others.[49] Here I consider what designing a speculative radical law might contribute to deproducing gender, and what the limits and challenges of deproducing gender might be.

Chapter Outlines

Chapter 1 begins by locating conceptual activism within the explosion of recent literature on conceptual engineering. Work on conceptual engineering addresses the different ways that concepts can be revised, and the challenges such revisions face. While some work in this field recognizes the impact of material conditions on conceptual engineering—depressing, for instance, the likelihood that new meanings will be taken up—conceptual engineering tends to presume a clear and settled distinction between meaning and materiality, with concepts assigned to the domain of the former. Chapter 1 argues for a different understanding. It unpicks the meaning/materiality distinction to suggest an approach that foregrounds the multifaceted and complex relations between how conceptual meaning is imagined and how it materializes over time, then explores this approach through a study of the conceptual conflict that arose over how to ask about sex and gender in the 2021 Census in England and Wales. This conflict ended up in court, as gender-critical forces challenged the proposed official guidance on answering the sex question, claiming it improperly permitted informal sex identifications to be given. Tracing this conflict, through its escalation over several years, reveals the different conceptual activisms in play, and the contribution that interactions and contexts made to how sex and gender meanings got manifested. In other words, conceptual meanings cannot simply be tracked back to organizational and movement actors holding independent, stable, antagonistic understandings.

Conceptual activism takes shape in and through specific concepts: gender, property, the state, economy, and so on. While attention usually centers on those specific concepts, an important dimension of how concepts are imagined and actualized concerns the imagining and actualization of the concept qua concept itself. Chapter 1 addresses the concept in terms of the relationship between meaning's imagining and materiality; chapter 2 turns to a different conceptual dimension, namely of form, and the work that conceptual form does. Drawing on interviews with twenty-three academics, the chapter considers four forms (or shapes) that concepts assume—of aid, world, current, and cell—and explores how conceptual activism works with these different forms. The concept as aid focuses on what concepts do as instruments of use; the world approaches concepts as spaces of inhabitance, of tending, remaking, and occupation; the current foregrounds the force of concepts as they shape and sustain their environment and affect what actors do; and the cell offers a bounded form that moves and travels within a host environment that it nourishes, protects, and sometimes attacks. These figures can be read as metaphors for the concept, but this chapter offers a different approach. Taking up the idea of dance, it treats these four figures as different moves that the concept in conceptual activism assumes, both concurrently and sequentially. In other words, the concept does not come to these figures already formed but takes its shape and affordances from the ways that these figures are enacted and combine.

While chapter 2 focuses on the solo dance, chapter 3 takes up the figure of the dance as a partnering—here with the concepts of gender, decertification, and economy. It explores this partnership through three different dances that the proposal to abolish legal sex status brings into play: the speculative law reform proposal, imagined regulatory reform, and gender's hoped-for future. Decertification of sex and gender is typically approached as a governmental and administrative concern; this chapter approaches it, instead, as an economic move. Central to this chapter's analysis is an account of economy that reaches beyond capitalist markets to foreground relations of making, allocating, holding, using, and disposing that can be applied to a wide variety of things, including relations, statuses, policies, proposals, and values. Bringing economy in demonstrates aspects of dismantling a governmental mechanism, like legal sex, that can be missed in other conceptual partnerships. The commercial literature on certification is useful here in understanding what the decertification of sex and gender takes away. But the concept of economy does not just offer an analytical vantage point or interpretive tool. It also poses questions and thoughtways for gender politics: What should be done when gender is approached as something that is made, allocated, acquired, and used? In turn, this partnership also poses questions and thoughtways for the concept of economy. Approaching economy through decertification demonstrates a form of conceptual activism that reimagines what economy means through forms of making, allocating, holding, and using not typically thought of as economic. Building on the work of J. K. Gibson-Graham and others, this account extends ways of thinking about economy—and what economic relations could entail—beyond capitalism's exploitative relations of production, exchange, waste, and competition.

Chapter 3 focuses on ways of reimagining gender, decertification, and the concept of economy; chapter 4, by contrast, turns to gender's rematerialization through the policy practice of British public bodies between 2018 and 2025. At the heart of this chapter are the new gender meanings actualized in policies, provisions, and ad hoc initiatives—of gender as self-declared, changeable, and plural—the resistance and opposition that materializing these meanings faced, and the consequences of such resistance, including for trans, nonbinary, genderqueer, and agender subjects. Conceptual meaning is not epiphenomenal. The stakes can be high in how concepts are manifested and in what follows—in terms of what is made available, prohibited, expected, and produced, thanks to the meanings of sex and gender that materialize. To explore this interplay, I approach the purposive activities of public bodies and their staff as a form of activism. Describing public bodies in this way is not uncontentious given the more familiar tendency in critical scholarship to tie activism to partisan grassroots practice, and to see public bodies' emphasis on balance and common sense as diluting activism, especially the activism of radical beyond-the-state projects. Without negating the value of this critique, the chapter considers a more expansive concept of activism. It draws on writing about tacit, quiet, and institutional activisms to explore public bodies' conduct and the different repertoires of resources and techniques that they accessed. My discussion centers on three features of public bodies' activism: reliance on common sense to legitimize and give direction to action, a care-full attention toward contrasting views, and relations of responsible attachment toward the objected-to meanings that also get expressed. This last emphasizes an important aspect of conceptual activism. While conceptual activism can involve advancing meanings that an organizational body or actors are committed to, it can also involve responding to the manifestation of meanings that a body or its actors oppose but that takes place within it, as responsibility is collectively taken for meanings as troublesome attachments. In studying how bodies do conceptual activism and how they respond to the conceptual activism of others, the chapter also turns to slow activism as a form of activism that is hesitant, ambitious, persistent, and care-full against the spectacular, explicitly adversarial character of its faster counterparts.

Chapters 1–4 approach conceptual activism as something undertaken seriously—whether in critiquing and practically dismantling the institutionalization of oppressive meanings or in designing and manifesting more progressive ones. But conceptual activism can also assume other registers, and chapter 5 explores one instance of this with play. The chapter considers what play brings to gender-based conceptual activism, starting with the question of whether play might provide a bounded, contained space within which gender could endure in conditions of its wider overcoming. In other words, if gender were to be severed from institutionalized relations of power, where might it then reside for those who continue to find it pleasurable and meaningful? The notion of gender being cubbyholed by play, however, is problematic on several fronts, as the chapter explores. But if this is the case, what can play offer? To explore this question, the chapter turns to a parallel institutional concept—property. Using examples of property play, from graffitiing and trespassing to PARK(ing) Day events, state free-running, and urban gardening, the chapter explores how play can help to resist property, establish currents that carry property's repurposing, and form cells of activity that validate and animate property's reimagining. In the final discussion, I turn to the prompts that property play offers for thinking about gender play as a form of conceptual activism, attending to the strengths and challenges of play as a polymorphic concept. The concluding chapter draws together the book's main threads: the struggle for gender's future, the morphology of concepts, and methods for undertaking and studying conceptual activism. In doing so, I consider the relationship and tension between conceptual activism oriented to gender's overcoming and gender dissidence; the moves, economies, and metacategories that gender concepts relate to; and the value of solo, coupled, and larger dances for prefigurative conceptual studies.

1

Materializing the Concept

From Conceptual Engineering to Census Sex

Like civil engineering, conceptual engineering is not a matter for discovery but for invention. But also like civil engineering, that does not mean that the choices we make are arbitrary, unconstrained, merely subject to our will, or "subjective." —AMIE THOMASSON, "A Pragmatic Method for Normative Conceptual Work"

When activists have claimed that same sex couples can be married, or that LGBTQ domestic arrangements are families, it wasn't based on what we have meant all along, but on what we should have meant. And what we should mean going forward, at least for now. A new answer, if it is incorporated into our practical consciousness, can be emancipatory and can change our social world, for we shape that world through what we do and who we think we are. —SALLY HASLANGER, "Going On, Not in the Same Way"

In June 2020, I attended a small online meeting, hosted by the Office for National Statistics (ONS). It had been called to discuss a problem: how to frame the guidance for the sex question in the 2021 England and Wales Census for those uncertain about how to answer. Underpinning this question lay a broader controversy: What did sex itself mean for Census purposes? The Census provides a state-controlled decennial snapshot of a national population, based on state-determined categories. While its value, in general terms, has been debated, also debated has been the use and framing of social identity markers, such as sex and gender—what categories should be used, how should they be understood, and what conditions govern their entry (e.g., see Guyan 2022)?

How to understand and ask about sex and gender proved a major site of disagreement in early twenty-first-century Britain.[1] In the 2011 Census, guidance advised those in doubt to "select the answer which you identify yourself as."[2] This was for "sex" since, in 2011, there was no separate question on gender identity. By 2020, activists on different sides perceived this approach as insufficient. Organizations promoting gender-(as)-diversity (see introduction) wanted questions that would recognize people's self-identity, and that would not require transgender people to have to "out" a prior sex. By contrast, sex-realist organizations and activists, including self-identified gender-critical feminists, demanded a discrete sex question (not combined with gender identity), where sex was biological sex, proxied by the category formally registered at birth. With opinion radically divided, mistrust among participants was high.

The June 2020 online meeting brought together academics (holding different perspectives) with representatives from regulatory and nongovernmental bodies to explore possible solutions.[3] The ONS asked all of those attending to briefly introduce their view on the guidance to accompany the sex question. In 2020, I was involved in a research project exploring ideas for radically transforming legal sex and gender categories (see chapter 3). For me, the invitation to participate in the ONS meeting was a welcome opportunity to reflect on how survey questions on sex and gender categories in twenty-first-century Britain might be phrased when there was no shared agreement on concepts or language use, and in conditions where, increasingly, people wanted to self-identify through both established and new terms. I look back now at my preparatory notes offering one possible design that I shared with the group. It involved asking, "What is your sex/gender—please choose whichever apply (so there is an option to have more than one answer)"; what followed was a list of the most likely categories followed by a write-in option. In practical terms, this was a proposal for a future Census, given the limited room for maneuver at this stage in the 2021 Census development. But it was also intended as a response to the conceptual struggle taking shape, to the dilemmas around splitting or joining sex to gender, and to the increasingly evident lack of public consensus about which sex and gender categories properly existed, and how membership in them should be determined.

How to ask the Census sex question, whether to add a gender identity question, and what guidance to provide can be viewed from a data-governance perspective as technical issues that, in Britain in 2020, had become heavily freighted. Intense political disagreement surrounded the meaning of sex and gender, and how this meaning should be manifested in survey questions, as sex-realist, trans-positive, and governmental bodies struggled over (and with) what then seemed to be the new settlement emerging around gender-(as)-diversity—and whether it should be consolidated, revised, or reversed. In the third part of this chapter, I return to the Census conflict to explore conceptual activism in action. While there is much that can be critically said about the production of governmental knowledge where a population is rendered intelligible through official categories, including as categories to act on, my focus is narrower—namely, how category concepts get made and remade. In particular, the chapter focuses on how this making and remaking are enacted materially in conditions of conflict, which here involved the sex-realist positions of gender critics meeting the more liberal approach (at least initially) of the ONS. In tracing this confrontation and the settlement imposed, the chapter provides an account of the concept that departs from its conventional characterization as a mental or abstract frame to develop instead a materialist account of the concept for (and within) conceptual activism. But since this discussion is tied to a description of concepts as plastic and plural, I want to begin by introducing a way of thinking about concepts that foregrounds their deliberate revision.

Feminist, anarchist, communist, antiracist, anticolonial, queer, ecological, and disability activists and writers, among many others, have long addressed the importance of attending to what concepts mean and could mean, and the histories of oppression they too often carry. Major political struggles have iconically condensed into the question of what it is to be a person or woman, who gets to be included and recognized, alongside disagreement about how more explicitly normative concepts, such as property, democracy, equality, and freedom, should be understood. Radical forms of conceptual activism revise concepts to identify underattended-to harms, and to identify underattended-to projects, values, and changes. At different times, this conceptual activism has retrieved and reconceptualized existing terms (such as lesbian, Black, disabled, or queer), introduced new ones (such as nonbinary or agender), and developed compound concepts (such as racialized capitalism or the prison-industrial complex) in ways that expose, stretch, and critically invigorate underattended-to aspects. Framed as abolitionist, utopian, prefigurative, and more, radical conceptual activism seeks to identify harms, dismantle how troubling concepts materialize, and forge new, more progressive alternatives.

Recognizing work across different interdisciplinary fields, and by radical nonacademic practitioners, writers, and others—who are innovating conceptually to advance political projects—is essential. As I explore here and in later chapters, conceptual development and redesign is carried out across many sectors, including in everyday professional and bureaucratic practice. It is not the exclusive purview of academics, let alone philosophers, even as academic fields may give the notion of conceptual development and redesign distinctive meaning. Nevertheless, I start with a set of contemporary philosophical discussions about the remaking of concepts, described as conceptual engineering, since it provides a detailed and thoughtful account of the aims, value, and challenges in redesigning conceptual meaning. Unlike many critical conceptual literatures that attend to specific concepts, conceptual engineering also addresses the concept of the concept—what it is and means to be a concept, how concepts work, and what they can and cannot do—as well as specific concepts, such as gender.[4] This helps in thinking about conceptual activism in its prefigurative mode, where hoped-for meanings are deliberately adopted ahead of their wider acceptance or realization (a future accomplishment that, of course, may never happen or be meant to happen). With its depiction of concepts as coherent, rational, mental, or linguistic frameworks, set apart and differentiated from the material world to which they relate, conceptual engineering also provides a valuable foil for the approach to the concept developed in this book. The discussion that follows addresses four key aspects of conceptual engineering—what it is for, how it is done, its relationship to the world, and the difficulties it faces—before turning to the limits of conceptual engineering as a theoretical method, and to the need to bring materiality back into the concept.

Conceptual Engineering

Conceptual engineering is an overarching term for purposeful activities concerned with conceptual repair, improvement, innovation, and replacement. David Chalmers (2025, 2917) describes conceptual engineering as "the design, implementation, and evaluation of concepts." While undertaken for different reasons, I want to focus here on conceptual engineering for sociopolitical purposes, rather than to correct other problems, such as being "vague, or internally inconsistent, or empty, or in some way incoherent" (Nado 2026, 51)—although engineering for sociopolitical purposes can engage these latter concerns also. Conceptual engineering is sometimes justified as a form of modernization or democratization, to generate more accurate or resonant terms that reflect what the world is like or becoming. For some writers, effectively depicting reality is the overriding purpose of concepts, with concepts as "representational devices" (Cappelen and Plunkett 2020, 3). Other writers treat "political ends" as a primary and sometimes overriding rationale (e.g., Leng 2023). Elizabeth Cantalamessa (2021, 48–49) describes how, for conceptual activism within disability politics, concepts like disability may be remade in ways that are not driven by the pursuit of "truth" as narrowly conceived, but to produce modes of understanding that unsettle conventional thoughtways and conventional notions of what should or can be done. But if concepts are revised for social justice purposes, and particularly when such revisions take concepts away from commonsense or accepted meanings (a criticism that gender-critical feminists have launched at new gender concepts), some writers worry that this may create confusion and uncertainty—not only about the concept being engineered but also about the network of concepts it is part of—impeding communication and understanding as a result.[5] Many conceptual engineers consequently worry about how to rank different purposes, such as social justice, on the one hand, and representing the "real," on the other, when these rationales do not seem to align (see also Belleri 2021).[6]

Yet whether undertaken to better represent social practice or to change it, conceptual engineering takes different forms (see also Cappelen 2023). It can involve creating new concepts or revising and discarding existing ones—as sex-realist feminists have advocated for gender. It can also involve using new or familiar words to characterize the concepts being engineered. Chalmers (2025, 2910–11) writes, "Cases like 'woman' or 'misogyny' and 'truth' are homonymous, at least insofar as they involve conceptual engineering at all. . . . Heteronymous conceptual engineering is different-word linguistic engineering. . . . Using a prefix is a very common strategy in philosophy. The prefix makes it heteronymous, but with a degree of continuity. In other cases there's a new concept and a new word: 'supervenience' and, indeed, 'conceptual engineering' may be cases of this." Homonymous conceptual engineering is a familiar process for normative concepts, such as democracy, freedom, truth, and equality, which are taken for granted as leading contested and political lives (see Connolly 1993; Gallie 1955–56). What conceptual engineering and conceptual activism do is extend this understanding to other concepts, including institutional ones—gender, economy, property, decertification, and activism, for example—to identify primary concepts explored in this book.[7]

Conceptual engineering works and reworks concepts. It may introduce several terms to capture aspects of social life perceived as unhelpfully or improperly merged into a single term. Here the objective is to reengineer well-established terms to differentiate them more clearly. As Jennifer Nado (2026, 49) notes,

"Such a strategy might be employed when the pre-engineering concept conflates categories that we hold to be genuinely distinct, as in for instance the move to recognize the difference between biological sex and gender." Conceptual engineering may also target the component parts that make up concepts and how they relate in making up concepts, thereby affecting the things that come within such concepts (such as who counts as a man). Conversely, changing who or what counts as a member of the concept (such as man) may lead the parts that make up the concept and how they go together to alter.

Engineering concepts to produce specific splits, such as the exclusion of trans men from the concept of man on the basis that lived experience is excluded from the concept of sex and that man is a sex-based term, can be a strategic political act. Committed to the reality of sex as a basic biological division, sex-realist feminists argued in the struggle over the Census questions and guidance for its conceptual distinction from gender. This was not just about having two terms with their own separate definitions; it was also about ensuring that elements associated with gender did not find their way into the concept of sex. For sex realists, woman was a category based on birth sex rather than gender and so distinguishable from gender-based categories of nonbinary, agender, and others (annoyance was particularly acute when these latter categories were defined or described as sex-based ones). As sex-realist forces sought to institutionally embed their preferred split (and the preeminence of sex over gender for the 2021 Census), my proposed menu approach, introduced at the start of this chapter, was a deliberate attempt to counter the assertion of a single authoritative conceptualization—"This is what sex and gender mean"—by suggesting a way of framing the question that would allow for different conceptions of what sex and gender mean (and how they related) to be simultaneously viable. But recognition that terms like sex and gender carried different meanings, and that this diversity should be acknowledged in surveys (as it is, to some degree, in the Census race question), was not accepted by gender critics. Writing on the Census conflict, policy studies scholar Alice Sullivan (2021, 639) remarked, "In postmodernist style, the goal of the gender-identity lobby has been to change reality by redefining the meaning of words. Such Humpty Dumptyism . . . jars rather glaringly with the precepts of good questionnaire design." While the need for "good questionnaire design" may be a shared one (even as views will differ on what it entails), the difficulty in generating Census terms, in conditions of conceptual conflict, proved incontrovertible, as I explore below.

One division to run through the conflict over sex concerns the relationship between ideational meaning and social practice. This division mirrors one that is sometimes drawn in conceptual engineering between world-to-mind concepts and mind-to-world ones. Critics of conceptually reengineering sex treat sex as a world-to-mind representation (see Sawyer 2026). Here the world (as it is) structures what constitutes good, truthful meanings and definitions. Amie Thomasson (2020, 450) writes, "Some concepts seem 'objectively' better than others. For it is plausible that some words serve something like a joint-tracking function—and are best left serving that function. . . . Since these terms have the function of serving in explanatory and predictive scientific theories, which in turn aim to predict and explain, there are worldly constraints on what concepts we ought to adopt." Mind-to-world concepts work differently. Sarah Sawyer (2026, 85) describes this category using the examples of games and juice: "It's not that games and juice aren't real things; it's just that what counts as a game or as juice depends on how we (as a community) use the relevant terms. . . . There is no independent, objective property that either community is trying to characterise and that could serve as an anchor for a single concept around which the linguistic practices of the different communities might vary."

Conceptual engineering in its social justice mode concerns the latter type of concept, or at least concepts with some mind-to-world aspects, even as the world also imposes constraints on what meanings are plausible or possible. Within conceptual engineering discussions, there is some recognition of how material and mental processes interact for concepts that could be too quickly identified as mind-to-world. I will return to this mind/world tension shortly, as it is central to the conflict over sex and gender. But aside from disagreement about which concepts can be engineered for social justice purposes, given the capacity and constraints of both mind and world, effective engineering is not deemed easy or straightforward. Chalmers (2025, 2916) writes, "The hardest part is implementation. First, you have to use an expression in the relevant way yourself. Even that much is nontrivial. Second, you have to get others to use it that way. That's really hard."[8] Chalmers's concerns about operationalizing new meanings have a particular resonance in contexts where new conceptual meanings are advanced by or in support of those lacking social power and authority (see also Bartoli 2025; Finocchiaro 2025), or where meanings appear radically counterintuitive.[9] Reconceptualizing the state, for instance, as a solidaristic, caring, responsible governance formation (Cooper 2019a) illustrates this efficacy challenge. What the new state term describes may already exist (in the sense of identifying cuts and joins in the social fabric), but there seems to be little overlap between the phenomena characterized as states in the reengineered concept and what gets recognized as states in conventional and established uses of the term. Moreover, for those invested in critical uses of the concept of the state, who seek ways of understanding those material cuts and joins that make the state an assemblage of authority, legitimacy, force, and international relevance, new or reimagined meanings may seem uncompelling. Material practices and reforms are required if the state as it is (or something proximate to this structure) is to become more caring and responsible. Addressing this challenge, Allison Koslow (2022, 13) writes, "If the goal is to have certain meanings expressed less, then what is needed may be not conceptual engineering, but something that addresses the desires, something which eliminates part of what drives expression of the problematic meaning." She continues, "To the extent conceptual engineering does not address the underlying forces, communicative and otherwise, that give rise to the target linguistic behavior, there's reason to worry that circumstances engineers hope to change will continue to reproduce themselves, perhaps with the aid of other words" (14).

Koslow's reservations demonstrate how a more expansive understanding of world-to-mind, one that recognizes the social domain as shaping and constraining conceptual meaning, limits the value of a strategy like conceptual engineering to effect meaning change. One context where this is apparent is where the meaning of concepts depends on institutional recognition for success. Sawyer (2026, 96) develops this line of argument in relation to marriage, a term she suggests that requires institutional action if reengineering is to occur: "Using the term 'marriage' in a clearly-defined, non-standard way in a local context so as not to exclude same-sex couples did not count as conceptually engineering the term 'marriage'; a change to the institutionalised practices was also required."[10] Before legal recognition, the informal treatment of gay couples as married took place against a backdrop of unhelpful institutional conditions. Since informal recognition could not procure the legal consequences that the concept of marriage demands, it could not change the meaning of marriage as a concept. Sawyer's conclusion throws doubt on the value of conceptual prefiguration in institutional contexts, where meanings are taken up as if they were otherwise in ways that do not directly reform the formal authorization conditions involved. Informal gender transitioning might also be an example of this. But is the stability and significance of institutional requirements as firm as Sawyer suggests? Prefigurative projects question both. Jessica Clarke (2005) also discusses the efficacy of de facto practices, such as around ownership and parenthood, troubling the assertion that they are inevitably unsuccessful, including in generating legal recognition, simply because prior status as owner or parent is missing. This troubling is important for the analysis in this book. While the discussion that follows attends to the value of formal authorization and recognition when it comes to institutionalized conceptual categories, it also attends to the expressive, affective, and consequential value of acting as if such categories were already otherwise.[11]

Revisiting the Mind/World Distinction

Conceptual engineering, and the account of conceptual activism to which it has given rise, offers a generative account of the rationales, mechanics, and challenges of deliberately recrafting meaning. Writing on conceptual engineering helps us think about the motivations for redesigning concepts, what concepts consist of, questions of conceptual continuity (when is this a revised concept and when a new one), the relationship between concepts and words, the usefulness in cutting the social world into different conceptual shapes (and when it can be properly done), how context shapes meaning, which meanings are to count as good meanings, and the difficulties in popularizing or operationalizing new meanings. But conceptual engineering also has limitations for understanding the concept.

The main problem, from this book's perspective, is that conceptual engineering largely approaches concepts as mental, logical, or linguistic abstractions that are distinct from the biological, physical, political, economic, and social life that such abstractions depict, "capture," or otherwise engage with.[12] In conceptual engineering, words, concepts, and things operate on noninterchangeable planes. Words cannot become things or things become concepts, although, as discrete stable phenomena, relations between them, including causational ones, can be drawn. These divisions surface in world-to-mind and mind-to-world engineering as well as in accounts that foreground the connections between mind and world. Matteo Santarelli (2024, 886), for instance, recognizes the importance of seeing how "existing social practices" shape projects of "conceptual revision" so that ameliorative projects do not "fall[] back into abstract idealism." Nevertheless, "two very heterogeneous domains" remain, "namely our revised concepts and social practices" (Santarelli 2024, 887). Things and thinking, meaning and materiality, are distinct and different ontological registers. While they may be connected, and while conceptual engineering may contribute to the production of something that is materially new or different, it remains itself a logical or ideational practice, not a material one.[13]

Two important aspects of concepts follow from this. First, conceptual engineering's approach to cognition and meaning ties concepts to language and word-meaning pairs. Approached as an exercise in meaning-making that often seems captured by the task of determining boundaries between inside(rs) and outside(rs) for a conceptual category, conceptual engineering takes place with and through texts and speech or, as Paul-Mikhail Catapang Podosky (2024, 1671) puts it, through "thought and talk."[14] Conceptual engineers downgrade—largely by disregarding—nonlinguistic forms of conceptual action, including by frontline service staff, households, workplaces, social movements, and artists.

This affects how the hurdles to conceptual engineering are understood, being narrowed to the obstacles placed in the way of revised conceptual meaning within written or spoken conversation. Focusing on words and the relationship between words and things, conceptual engineering also inclines toward a mechanical account of practice and change. As world-to-mind and mind-to-world framings suggest, either the world imposes limits and constraints on how a concept can be meaningfully understood (as gender-critical arguments about sex assert), or the world becomes an operationalization space (and challenge) downstream from the conceptualizing process, as implementation forms a later step in a conceptual engineering project.[15]

Second, conceptual engineering emerges as a rational and deliberate activity in which active subjects (mainly philosophers) observe concepts and reflect, with some detachment, on their choices for conceptual redesign. Once formed and validated, these reengineered cognitive objects can be described, transferred, and understood, independent of the comprehending subject's vantage point, since the concept's required networks get transferred with it. At moments, concepts available for reengineering resemble dilapidated (or otherwise outdated) objects in a "marketplace of ideas" (Queloz and Bieber 2022, 674), where those surveying select the ones deemed worthy of acquisition and renovation. In undertaking this selection, engineering's association with mechanics surfaces—of precision, careful adaption, retooling, and fixing.[16] Conceptual engineering pays little attention to irrational, affective, playful, sensory, experimental, and unreflexive modes of conceptual understanding and practice, or to more-than-linguistic conceptual practice. It also pays little attention to conceptual engineering undertaken by institutions, such as medicine, education, and law, particularly when this happens in nondeliberate ways—that is, as the cumulative effects of how institutions deploy concepts, such as law's deployment of sex in legislation, and the structural force such embedded concepts can have. Attending to this conceptual force requires approaching the forms that concepts assume apart from the figure of the tool (consciously and purposefully deployed), a figure that surfaces frequently within conceptual engineering. In chapter 2, I explore some of the concept's other shapes.

The location of concepts within cognition and as word-meaning pairs that are instrumentally deployed within communication comes from, and in turn reinforces, the split between meaning and materiality, something that this book counters. Concepts, I suggest, are not exclusively tied to reason, and they do not reside or get expressed in speech and texts alone. Rather, the definitional anchor of this book is of concepts as the relationship between the imagined and material organization of meaning, where this relationship is in flux and *intra-active* (Barad 2007)—that is, it does not preexist social life as an already established set of divisions. This recognizes that the conceptual division between imagining and materiality is made, changes, and is contested, and that imagining and materializing can form stopping points on a plane rather than polarities. This is a conceptually engineered way of understanding the concept, but it is also, importantly, one informed by social life and politics in that it attends to the many ways that the material expression and imagining of meaning continuously shape each other and *chooses to place this relationship within the concept rather than outside it*. It is important to see this as a conceptual choice; there are other ways of understanding what it is to be a concept—as conceptual engineering, among other fields, demonstrates. One reason to place the tension between imagining and materiality within rather than outside the concept of the concept is to avoid the separation and distancing that come when concepts are treated as ideational tools affecting or observing a separate physical realm. A second reason is to give concepts greater relevance and value since they are not ontologically restricted to the realm of thought but are always about different forms of materiality—even ghosts are known by the effects they have on their environment. In addition, and this is a methodological point, the counterintuitive character of approaching concepts as material entities gives concepts analytical traction. This is a point I develop practically through the book, as strange meanings and incongruous conceptual partnerships prompt modes of exploratory and experimental thinking that move away from established grooves.

Concepts are about the material and imagined organization of meaning, but what does this entail? The imaginary aspect of concepts is well established—that they are about ideas, beliefs, narratives, knowledges, values, understandings, and more. But what does it mean to say that concepts have a material dimension; and how does this dimension relate to meaning's imagining? Attention to the materiality of the concept runs through different veins of critical scholarship; however, all too often one kind of materiality gets prioritized over, or to the exclusion of, others. This book attends to six interconnected aspects of the relationship between conceptual materiality and imagining. Briefly sketched, they are the following:

- How material life structures and shapes conceptual imaginaries. This works through different registers and scales of materiality. It includes the social relations of power that naturalize, validate, and guide dominant conceptual imaginaries and that also affect and shape subordinate and oppositional ones, as critical work on ideology and discourse explores. It includes the effects of everyday material life on people's conceptual imaginaries—how experiences of violence, home life, politics, and work, for instance, shape the beliefs, affects, and meanings associated with concepts. And it includes the ways that materials guide and structure conceptual thought—how walls are imagined when built from wood or glass, how the concept of hair is imagined when depicted in oils or pencils, or in a performance piece.

- The material cuts and joins invoked in imaginaries of concepts, including when material changes lead to new cuts and joins in how concepts are imagined (for instance, where legal men giving birth changes how concepts of pregnancy and parenthood are understood). Also important are the material instances that are typically folded into conceptual thought as explicit or subconscious instantiations of what it is to be a state, owner, or masculine, for example, in ways that are far from neutral. These normative instances may be conceptually stabilizing, but they can also prompt and provoke change, including in the generation of new counterimaginaries.
- The imaginaries folded into concepts' enactment where the elements making up concepts include an element of reflexive ideational expression. This can be observed with institutional concepts, where imaginaries of the concept (such as of state, woman, or lawyer), held by practitioners and others, form part of the concept's material enactment. Again, these imaginaries are far from neutral. They may align with, and so support, conservative forms of realization: for instance, civil servants who express hierarchical and rigid understandings of what it means to be a state as part of how the concept of the state materializes. However, the potential to insert contradictory meanings is an important lever for conceptual activism.
- The diverse ways that meanings are materially expressed.[17] Conceptual engineering foregrounds meaning's expression in texts, language, and voice, but meanings are also expressed in art, dance, music, bodily gestures, war, care, economic exchanges, and public service—indeed in all areas of social activity. While the expression of counterhegemonic meanings—for instance in relation to concepts of governance, international relations, democracy, and freedom—may be undertaken for affective or experimental purposes, a frequent hope with prefigurative conceptual practice is that the premature or anticipatory enactment of counterhegemonic meanings will contribute to their material realization.[18]
- The materiality that simply comes from being a concept, since the organization of meaning is part of our social world. Karen Barad, in conversation with Daniela Gandorfer (2021, 26), describes concepts as "specific material doings or enactments"; they are "not just an idea,

let alone an idea of the mind, detached from the world . . . to describe the world, or capture something with it"; concepts, she declares, are "of the world."[19]

- The oscillating relationship between how concepts materialize and how they are imagined, especially evident when concepts change—think of marriage, freedom, security, or personhood, for example. These oscillations can be contested, blocked, and disrupted, but they remain in motion and are, typically, entered in the middle as imaginaries and material enactments, already in existence, press on each other (Cooper 2014). This interplay is discussed in different academic literatures, but often analysis focuses on practices either of imagining or of materialization in contexts where it becomes hard to keep the movement between them in view. Sociolegal scholar Bronwen Morgan, when interviewed, made a point along these lines, drawing an analogy between concepts and how light is constituted (and appears): "It's either a wave or a particle depending on your angle of observation. So, it's either an ideational concept or a material practice. It's actually both at the same time, but at any one point of observation you're gonna be able to only capture one aspect of that."

These different dimensions of conceptual materiality and imagining weave through the discussion of this book—starting with the Census conflict, which I turn to for the rest of this chapter. The struggle over the sex question and guidance for the 2021 Census for England and Wales shows conceptual engineering in action. However, I also draw on the conflict to demonstrate some of the limits to a framework that treats concepts as ideational blocks, held and communicated by protagonists, rather than an evolving, complex, contested material set of practices. Approaching concepts as conceptual engineering does obscures the dynamic and processual character of the conceptual struggle that took place. Conceptual engineering's tendency to treat communication and implementation as a downstream concern underestimates the importance of materiality to how meaning is expressed, realized, forged, and imagined. Materiality does not just carry meaning like a bowl carrying soup; it shapes, constitutes, and sometimes even realizes meaning in contexts where the division between how meaning is imagined and how it materializes is often unclear or suspended. The struggle over the meaning of sex and gender for Census purposes emerged and changed across a series of junctures as social action took place. To explore this action in ways that draw on conceptual engineering while also foregrounding materiality, social praxis, and an approach to conceptual meaning that does not rely on notions of orderly reason, I turn to conceptual activism. My focus is the struggle between advocates of sex realism and the ONS, self-described as the "UK's largest independent producer of official statistics" and responsible for the Census.[20]

Conceptual Activism over Sex in the Census

In the conflict over the sex and gender identity parts of the 2021 Census for England and Wales, the volatile social life of conceptual activism comes vividly to the fore. Conceptually reengineering sex and gender may not have mattered much to sex realists when this was restricted to the community practices of trans and genderqueer organizations, but when new accounts of sex and gender trickled (flooded?) into the Census—identified as the British gold standard for survey question design (e.g., see A. Sullivan 2021, 639)—the stakes rocketed. Sex realists' concerns were triggered by several factors: the role of Census data in shaping subsequent public policy and resource decisions, the legitimacy that Census use gave the categories deployed, and the perception that other surveys would adopt Census categories and wording.[21] Sex realists feared that ostensibly nonstandard uses of gender and sex concepts would become mainlined. Specifically, they feared that the Census would feed the growing conceptual logic of gender as plural and self-identified, trumping and displacing immutable binary sex, not least by importing ideologies of gender diversity *into* concepts of sex.[22] This importation would cause sex to naturalize and legitimize gender ideology; and this, it was feared, would lead to troubling and distorted assumptions (or inferences) when analyzing data about women and men, for instance in relation to sexual violence or income disparities.[23]

The conflict that ensued over how the sex and gender Census questions should be asked, and the guidance to be given, is conceptual activism in process. Should the categories of sex and gender be open or closed, flexible or inflexible, singular or plural, subjective or structural, exclusive or inclusive? Tracing the interplay of different practical concerns demonstrates the need for accounts of conceptual activism to go beyond the snapshot view, to follow instead the dynamic processes by which conceptual meanings develop, are countered, and reorganize. This is not a case of ex parte conceptual activism (or engineering), where one constituency confronts roadblocks, while developing and asserting new meanings, as Adam Gibbons (2024, 3355–56) describes: "Conceptual conflict occurs when an agent (or group of agents) deliberately attempts to block or otherwise impede the conceptual engineering efforts of others." Instead, it is a case of shifting entanglements as different conceptual meanings get materially advanced and enacted in conditions of mutual resistance.[24] Recognizing how meaning is relationally formed and manifested as context evolves also decenters proprietary tendencies in conceptual engineering that treat meanings as belonging to those who explicitly establish or believe in them—a scenario of forces communicating stable and coherent chunks of meaning that they own.[25] Instead, it approaches the meanings that materialize as formed out of, and so as belonging to, the agonistic networks through which they emerge, including as negative attachments for those whose actions help constitute meanings that they simultaneously oppose (see chapter 4).

The conflict that came to a head in the lead-up to the 2021 Census for England and Wales had been brewing for some time.[26] One initiating factor was transgender activists' and organizations' struggles over the compulsory sex question and how trans people should answer it.[27] In 2011, ONS official guidance was clear. It stated, "Please select either male or female for your sex. Transgender or transsexual: select the answer which you identify yourself as. You can select either 'male' or 'female,' whichever you believe is correct, irrespective of the details recorded on your birth certificate. You do not need to have a Gender Recognition Certificate."[28] In 2011, those unsure how to answer were invited to authentically self-report, to provide a personal assessment based on personally determined categorization criteria. Yet, with its bold font directive, only "transgender or transsexual" respondents were invited to "select the answer which you identify yourself as." Thus the ONS depicted sex as a commonsense category status that, only for a minority, would prove more complex. In 2011, this guidance was online for a Census predominantly completed on paper. This meant advice to trans respondents to self-identify remained somewhat contained, bracketed from a majority who would rely on prevailing understandings and classifications of sex, never feeling uncertain how to answer and so having no reason to consult the guidance. In the lead-up to the 2021 Census, sex-realist critics placed significance on this earlier discrepancy, between digital guidance and paper Census, to oppose a similar approach in 2021 when the Census would be "digital-first" with households encouraged to fill it out online. For 2011, critics subsequently claimed, only those specifically looking for the guidance would have found it. Yet it was not only sex realists who were concerned about the 2021 Census sex question. The 2011 Census had asked only about sex, and it only admitted two responses. For proponents of gender-(as)-diversity, this was inadequate.

Thus we enter a complicated tale of conceptual activism revolving around the ONS's development of the 2021 Census question on sex, the wording of the guidance on how to answer it, and the possibility of an additional question on gender, as established, new, and also nostalgic meanings materialized in reports, testing, research, legislation, debate, a court order, the final Census format and guidance, and respondents' survey answers.[29] From a gender-critical and sex-realist perspective, this was a tale of "policy capture," of an ONS unduly influenced by trans-positive organizations and developing the 2021 Census by cocreating policy with them (Jones 2020, 7; A. Sullivan 2021).[30] Jane Clare Jones and Lisa Mackenzie (Jones 2020, 8), for instance, describe "advocates of a sex-denialist transgender ideology [having] captured the process of policy-making in our institutions," with a parallel story told about the Scottish Census (e.g., Murray and Blackburn 2019). Evoking Gibbons's (2024, 3363) comment on conceptual engineering, that "the downstream effects of adopting a given ameliorative proposal are such that one group will benefit greatly while another bears some costs," gender-critical feminists and other sex realists argued that trans-positive approaches would negatively affect women (that is, nontrans women), and that this was something the ONS had disregarded. In focusing its consultations on how to ask about gender and sex with trans organizations, it had failed to consider what effects this might have for its data on women. Surveying ONS reports from 2016, Jones (2020, 15) describes issues that she claims had come to "bedevil" the Census process. These included "consulting *only* with government and trans stakeholders" based on "confidence that consulting only with trans stakeholders will enable a clarification, rather than an obfuscation, of 'concepts to be measured'" (Jones 2020, 15).

Meanwhile, for the ONS, in its concern to achieve buy-in and so elicit meaningful responses from trans communities, how to ask about sex and gender had become pressing. By the late 2010s, ONS reports depicted sex and gender as a changing realm where the traditional binary categories of male and female no longer afforded the best approach.[31] One report from 2017 stated, "Within today's society the traditional view of gender as a binary classification, male or female, is changing. There are now more varied conceptualisations and self-descriptions of gender and non-gendered identities."[32] ONS reports recognized that people could have genders that diverged from their birth sex, that these genders could be nonbinary, that people could assume nongendered identities, and that such genders might be "fixed or variable."[33] Oriented to the need to produce an effective Census along with subsequent data-user requirements, the ONS considered different approaches, including "sex assigned at birth, transitioned sex, reclaimed sex, acquired gender, gender or gender identity."[34]

In conceptual engineering terms, the ONS's approach foregrounded the function of the sex question—what it was and ought to be for—to consider the conceptual approach to sex that would best support this function (see generally Köhler and Veluwenkamp 2024, 411). Gender identity research, commissioned by the ONS, noted that a compulsory sex question that did not respond to a diversely identified population would cause problems:

> Decisions as to which question or questions might be mandatory and which voluntary must take into account several factors: acceptability to respondents, the potential impact forced response might have on data quality . . . and legal considerations. We would tentatively recommend that an unchanged 2011 Census question should not be mandatory, for the benefit of, particularly, intersex and non-binary people who cannot choose male or female as a reflection of their current sex or gender. We would also recommend that a question specifically about sex at birth, or one that forces an answer indicating a trans identity, should not be mandatory given the needs of trans people living with disclosure concerns.[35]

Similar concerns were raised by a two-step approach—of a sex question followed by a gender one—since it was feared this would "out" trans respondents or produce ambiguous data.[36] But by 2018, this appeared to be the preferred official approach—a mandatory binary sex question followed by a gender identity question—as more radical changes got withdrawn.[37] Sex categories proposed for the Census would be female and male exclusively (options for a third sex category having been rejected; see also UK Government 2018, para. 3.43). But disagreement continued over the guidance that respondents should be given when recording their sex. During the autumn months of 2019, a Census rehearsal was planned for four local authorities in England and Wales. The rehearsal guidance on the sex question stated, "What is your sex? Select either 'Female' or 'Male.' If you are one or more of non-binary, transgender, have variations of sex characteristics, sometimes also known as intersex, the answer you give can be different from what is on your birth certificate. If you're not sure how to answer, use the sex registered on your official documents, such as passport or driving licence, *or whichever answer best describes your sex*. A later question gives the option to tell us if your gender is different from your sex registered at birth, and, if different, to record your gender."[38]

Guidance for the rehearsal drew on earlier tested advice, revised thanks to feedback from respondents.[39] These revisions reveal the nuances of trans conceptual politics along with the ONS's readiness, at this stage, to recognize that different gender statuses might be held simultaneously, that a nonstigmatizing concept was needed for people previously identified as intersex, that the self-identified sex category of a transgender person was something real, and that sex categories might be better or worse descriptions rather than a binary code of right or wrong. Yet this proposed approach to the guidance was not to remain in place for long.

With a two-step question seemingly settled (as concepts of gender and sex got split and repackaged into two discrete questions), critics' attention turned to the ONS's approach to sex. For some while, critics had lobbied for a formal, binary, and clear definition of sex.[40] Writing on the Census conflict, Alice Sullivan (2021, 642) describes how "eighty quantitative social scientists" signed a letter to the UK Census authorities in December 2019, expressing their concern "about the proposed online guidance to accompany the sex question in the 2021 census, which advises respondents that they may respond in terms of their self-identified gender."[41] On June 24, 2020, a roundtable meeting, hosted by the ONS, to discuss guidance on the sex question was held, as described at the chapter's start (see also A. Sullivan 2021, 643). Several quantitative social scientists, along with other academics and a handful of representatives from NGOs and public bodies, were invited to attend. Different opinions were aired but a way forward remained elusive.

Then, in February 2021, the UK Statistics Authority published its methodology for decision-making on the 2021 Census sex question and guidance (Rosiecka 2021). It identified five ways of approaching the concept of sex: "registered at birth," "recorded on birth certificate" (which might differ from the sex registered at birth for people who acquired a Gender Recognition Certificate), "recorded on legal/official documents," "living/presenting," and "self-identified." The report suggested that the third approach—sex as recorded on legal/official documents—was "the target concept for the sex question within census 2021" since it "most closely reflect[ed] the census 2021 sex question response options, harmonise[d] better with other UK nations, and . . . aligned with future usage of administrative data" (Rosiecka 2021).

Yet despite this win for sex as a formal, settled, binary characteristic, many sex realists remained unhappy. In ways that reveal the contingent character of the split between sex and gender—that there is no natural distinction but one that needs to be continually made, and with effort—sex realists argued that anything other than sex registration at birth or on a birth certificate "confound[s] sex with gender identity" (A. Sullivan 2021, 647). In February 2021, sex on a birth certificate was a way of referring to legal sex since it included people who had obtained a Gender Recognition Certificate, allowing them retroactively to change the sex designation on their birth certificate. However, the Census guidance proposed, and then issued, was broader, permitting people to refer to the sex that was recorded on official documents, including passports, which could be altered without a Gender Recognition Certificate.[42] Opposing this framing of sex category membership, the gender-critical organization Fair Play for Women went to court seeking judicial review; their success would mean that the court recognized and enforced a concept of Census sex that corresponded with legal sex status (see also chapter 3).

Fair Play for Women won interim relief.[43] The judge stated, "So far as concerns the guidance as presently published, the words 'or passport' should be removed. My view is that an appropriate order is one that requires the [guidance] sentence to read, 'If you are considering how to answer, use the sex recorded on your birth certificate or gender recognition certificate'" (para. 19). In reaching this decision, the court rejected the notion that "'sex,' as used in the Schedule to the 1920 Act and Schedule 2 to the [Census (England and Wales)] 2020 Order, is to be read as referring to any of biological sex, sex recognised by law, a person's self-identified sex and indeed, any answer as to the person's sex recorded in any document issued by the State" (para. 10). And it rejected a reengineered concept of sex as a broad "umbrella term" (para. 10). The court also rejected the notion that the ONS could be "the arbiter of what the particulars [of Census sex] mean, rather the matter is one of construction of the Act and the Order and, ultimately, the responsibility of the court" (para. 16). Since a voluntary question on gender identity was included in the Census (England and Wales) Order 2020, Parliament's expectation, the court declared, was for data to be generated on two separate "particulars"—sex and gender identity (paras. 9, 26).[44] In this way, through the court's interpretation of statutory law and finding of legislative intent, sex and gender identity were produced as two discrete legal phenomena with distinct meanings. Despite this being only an interim order pending full judicial review, the ONS withdrew its defense. The case was settled, with Census guidance for England and Wales revised to direct respondents to only record the sex listed on their birth certificate or Gender Recognition Certificate (para. 19).[45]

The Census conflict, as I have described it, reveals a series of junctures where divergent conceptions of sex and gender confronted and shaped each other. Here the same term, sex, was used and wielded in contrasting ways as the publicly staged world-to-mind stance of sex realists met, if not quite a mind-to-world stance on the part of the ONS, then a pragmatic inclination, anchored in sex's vernacular and diverse usage. In the process, justifications based on acceptability, efficacy, data use, law, privacy, and common sense mixed. This is conceptual activism in motion. While the conceptual imaginaries of political activists, regulatory officials, and social movement organizations may not have changed significantly over this period, how they were expressed, used, and represented did. Letters, meetings, inquiries, reviews, research, draft papers, guidance, and the Census itself enacted an imaginary in flux.[46] Census sex skipped from embracing gender to being differentiated from gender, identified as plural, depicted as binary, conceptualized as a contested term, tied to formal identification, and, lastly, limited to birth registration and legal status as evolving networks of authority, power, and constraint came to the fore, to shape the meanings that materialized and what they could be used to do and accomplish.

And here, it would seem, we might stop, with the authority and power of the court defeating other bodies' ability to determine what sex in the Census could mean. Indeed, in an act of autonomic authority, the court declared that determining what such particulars mean was a matter "of construction of the Act and the Order and, ultimately, the responsibility of the court."[47] Yet, one striking outcome of this conflict was that neither the court nor law, more generally, could *realize* the declared meaning of sex (that is, as legal sex) within the Census process, in the sense of determining how respondents answered the question. The sex question could be mandatory, and the court could engineer sex to mean legal sex, but they could not control what respondents did when they completed the form.

In the aftermath of the court decision, one transgender organization advised, "Our advice to non-binary people . . . is to respond with whichever one feels closest to your understanding of your sex." More generally, it wrote, "The guidance around using any identity document as proof may have been withdrawn, but this does not mean you should feel obliged to put down incorrect information. . . . Give honest information which reflects the truth."[48] For some respondents, this "truth" may have been "lived sex" despite clear and contrary Census guidance. Some sex realists suggested that giving false answers knowingly was a criminal offense;[49] but the threat of a subsequent criminal charge could not preclude people from answering the sex question according to their own preferred conception of what sex meant. The ONS had long recognized this, that in answering the sex question, people would draw on different accounts of sex, and that imposing a concept of sex that lacked credibility with many trans communities would not diminish the use of different concepts of sex but simply make them harder to identify, muddying data and undermining analysis.

In a letter to the Office for Statistical Regulation on November 14, 2023, almost thirty-two months after the 2021 Census date, the gender-critical organization Sex Matters raised data-quality concerns over the sex and gender identity questions.[50] While critical of the ONS, the concerns they expressed expose a similar recognition of the difficulty (or impossibility) of eliminating Census respondents' own conceptual activism.[51] Claiming that the Census data "was driven by the adoption of concepts and questions promoted by lobby groups that seek to replace sex with gender identity," and that use of the terms trans woman and trans man by the ONS in national statistics "gives official status . . . to neologisms that have never been debated or defined," they concluded, "Data on gender identity (*including the sex of the people identified as transgender*) is not fit for purpose."[52] In its own post-Census analysis, the ONS described the gender identity question and the responses it had generated as an emerging category: "Gender identity estimates from Census 2021 are official statistics in development. This reflects their innovative nature and the evolving understanding of measuring gender identity, along with the uncertainty associated with these estimates." As a result, it declared, "the gender identity estimates from Census 2021 are no longer accredited official statistics."[53]

Concluding Remarks

In this chapter, I have begun to address two of the book's main threads: understanding conceptual activism as a material practice that reorganizes meaning sociopolitically; and the conceptual struggle over sex and gender in contemporary Britain. Conceptual activism is an integral aspect of many social movements and political projects; this chapter, however, has taken its relationship to conceptual engineering as a springboard, attending to discussions in analytic philosophy on the challenges and efforts of designing new conceptual meanings to advance social justice, the imperatives and pushback from other conceptual purposes, the material conditions that lead counterhegemonic meanings to appear nonsensical or that minimize take-up, and the difficulties in making new meanings stick and become operative. Conceptual engineering offers a helpful literature for thinking about conceptual activism, attuned to the value, work, and difficulties encountered in redesigning the meaning of concepts. However, it has limitations, as this chapter has explored. With some exceptions, its orientation toward instrumental functionality, rational determination, the ideational depiction of concepts within a world/mind divide, and the focus on linguistic acts and contexts limit its value. The conceptual activism explored in this book draws from conceptual engineering, but it also draws from, and pivots toward, other critical traditions and fields attuned to the materiality of the concept.

To explore the materiality of conceptual activism in relation to the struggle over sex and gender, the chapter's discussion focused on the conflict over the 2021 Census questions. Here divergent sex and gender imaginaries were expressed and constituted through rehearsal questions, reports, meetings, practice guidance, letters from critics, social movement engagement, judicial review, the final Census text, and, of course, respondents' responses. The conflict that burned through ONS reports, meetings, letters, litigation, and more demonstrates the evolving, relational, and coproduced content of conceptual activism, where positions publicly enacted were shaped by opponents' claims, professional logics, Census rationalities, and the materials at hand. Texts and speech, here, were more than neutral carriers of meaning. Through reports, letters, meetings, tests, and litigation, sex and gender were represented and performed. But they were also, partially, realized in conditions where the institutional depiction of sex and gender forms part of what makes these concepts up. This was one of the paradoxes of sex-realist activism. While it explicitly presented sex as a binary, immutable, *biological* concept, its actions contributed to the materialization of sex as something else.

The enactment of sex and gender in the Census dispute reveals the different conceptual ways that they entwined; how they shaped each other and also (in different ways) split apart. This exposes some of the problems with a foundational presumption of separation, and the work done by this presumption, particularly for sex realists who relied on it to differentiate and distance women's issues from trans ones. Given the data-collecting context of this episode, claims for communicative clarity and conceptual continuity over time had a particular salience,[54] and sex-realist forces drew on this to justify separate sex and gender questions, depicting sex as the original category and as intrinsically different from gender—being natural rather than social. For the ONS, on the other hand, the material purpose of creating a workable and acceptable Census, in conditions where people had to be relied on to provide accurate (or useful) responses, steered it toward trans-accepting conceptions of sex and gender, which blurred the distinction between the two and treated informal gender change as (sometimes) changing sex, even as the ONS's status as an official body, subject to judicial and legislative oversight, led it ultimately to revert to a more conservative stance.

This chapter has focused on conceptual meaning in relation to sex and gender and how the organization of such meanings shifts and changes, both materially and ideationally. But what can conceptual activism over institutional sex and gender categories teach us about the form of the concept; and how does this form and its affordances shape our understanding of conceptual activism? Framed by discussions on conceptual engineering, this chapter has focused on the concept as a tool or aid, purposefully crafted to advance and support specific philosophical or political projects. While this account of the concept dominates conceptual engineering work, the Census conflict also shows how concepts can work in other ways. Certainly, opposing forces deployed concepts of sex and gender as aids in their struggle over the meaning of sex and gender and how people should be categorized. Yet the Census conflict also shows how concepts of sex and gender assumed other shapes, including as worlds, cells, and currents, as different versions of the concepts became inhabited and tended, observed in their movement, and felt. These other conceptual forms and moves are central to conceptual activism's vitality and effects, and it is to them and the relationship between them that I now turn.

2

How Concepts Dance

As Sea Urchins, Mushrooms, and Little, Tiny Angels

SWETHAA BALLAKRISHNEN: Bland acknowledgement, I like that. . . . I think of these co-exist stickers in the US, I don't know if you've seen them . . . Or something like "intersectionality" which gets used all the time. But when it's so vast everyone's quick to jump to the bandwagon . . . but it's not because they've actually considered it, it's because they've just recognized that social cues require them to . . .

DAVINA COOPER: Yeah. Actually, I was saying "land acknowledgement" rather than "bland acknowledgement," but I take your point.

(A brief prelude on the conceptual generativity of online conversation.)

This book approaches conceptual activism as the reorganization of meaning in both imagined and material ways.[1] It argues that it is this relationship between imagining and materiality that gives conceptual activism much of its power and vitality. But how do these two dimensions relate in the case of concepts? And how does thinking about concepts help us to understand how imagining and materiality relate more generally—a relationship grappled with through many fields and terms, including ideology/materiality, discursive/extradiscursive, meaning/context, and mind/matter? Addressing their relationship through the concept, I want to avoid an account of materiality and imagining that reinforces their separateness and distinction, as if they were lands joined by the concept-as-bridge or two sides of a pincer. In considering a relationship that is intra-active and enmeshed, I also want to move away from the more common focus on specific concepts to consider, instead, the concept of the concept as it takes shape within conceptual activism. Concepts of sex and gender continue to surface in this discussion, but other concepts appear too as I explore the form of the concept, how it works and moves, and what this brings to conceptual activism.

Focusing on the concept of the concept may seem overly abstract, monolithic even, disregarding concepts' relational and plural character as they take shape through and in relation to others. I return to this more interactive and social form in the next chapter. However, this discussion is about what it is to be a concept that, while shaped by its environment and the elements that make it up, constitutes a particular kind of being (or beings). Typically, concepts are understood as slices of thought, abstract forms of classification, or pieces of word-meaning, as the last chapter's discussion of conceptual engineering explored. Foregrounding the materiality of concepts invokes other ways that concepts are organized and operate to express, depict, constrain, revise, and realize meaning. Conceptual materiality animates meaning, giving it life, force, and plasticity. But how do we access this animated form in ways that can complement discussion of specific concepts, including gender and sex, the focus of this book?

This chapter offers one approach. Building on the account of conceptual activism in chapter 1, it explores the form and affordances of the concept within conceptual activism, drawing on interviews with twenty-three interdisciplinary academics about their conceptual practice.[2] Conceptual activism is not exclusive to academics, and other chapters in this book address regulatory, governmental, and community organizations' engagement with concepts, and the material forms this engagement takes. However, academic conceptual activism has distinctive methods and approaches; exploring them offsets the reverse assumption as well—that conceptual activism is not something that academics routinely do. Between 2022 and 2024, I interviewed participants from diverse fields including law, geography, sociology, politics, critical race studies, gender studies, and social policy. To different degrees, these interviews bore disciplinary and subdisciplinary understandings—for instance, that concepts were academic creations, modes of thinking, parts of language and expression, social actants, or institutionalized frames of knowledge.[3] In their discussion of the concept, Martin Holbraad and Morten Axel Pedersen (2017, 5) suggest that anthropologists take up "ontological questions to solve epistemological problems." This chapter undertakes the reverse, drawing on academics' conceptual imaginaries, and understandings of the concept, to advance an ontology of the concept (what it is to be a concept) for conceptual activism, focusing on the concept's form and relationship to human subjects. My intention is not to pin down the concept—to say this is what concepts really are (or are like)—but rather to draw on the interviews to trace an account of the concept that is attentive to its different shapes, capabilities, and values.

Interview data are hybrid creations, with coproduced conversations shaped by the time, place, structure, and expectations of their happening. In this chapter, I do not try to "cleanse" the interview material of its conditions of production (see also chapter 3), because it was in (and through) this collaborative thinking, as ideas moved and developed within—but also between—interviews, that this account of the concept acquired shape (see also John Clarke 2019a). In talking with academics about their conceptual practice, asking questions about how they imagined or envisioned concepts, and sharing perspectives from other interviews, certain accounts rather than others surfaced.[4] And through the course of a single interview, different ways of imagining the concept and different relationships to the concept emerged. For instance, early in the interview with geographer Kath Browne, she referred to concepts as "stale and old and dusty." Yet, as discussion progressed, the value of concepts and conceptual innovation for her work became increasingly apparent, as did the work of forging and nourishing new concepts. Concepts don't just exist; they require energy and maintenance to emerge, develop, change, displace, endure, and sometimes to be kept from dying. The tending and repairs required by concepts in conditions of conceptual activism are an important part of this story. Conceptual engineering addresses maintenance and reparative work, but placing the concept within ideational and linguistic realms limits what this work entails. When we recognize the polymorphic materiality of the concept, as explored in chapter 1, the landscape of maintenance and repair becomes more complex but also more dynamic. This chapter adds a new layer to the story.

From In Here to Out There (and Back Again)

During interviews with academics, they described how they shared space with concepts. More than that, they described rubbing up against concepts; sometimes they feared losing themselves within concepts. Interviewees described how they adopted new concepts, knitted them to practices, used concepts to build connections, and whittled away or hybridized concepts for transformative political purposes. Interviewees described what concepts felt like and how they were experienced, how they made demands, pulled at subjects (both themselves and others), and underpinned and guided subjects toward a sense-making that was both semantic and physical. Performance scholar Erin Brannigan (2018, 366) talks about "feeling-thinking-doing," and this resonates with the conceptual movement explored here—with concepts, by concepts, through concepts, and against them.

One distinction to emerge early in the interview process was between concepts as "out there" and "in here" (see also Law 2004). This evokes the difference between "essentially contested concepts" (Gallie 1955–56) being observed and "conceptual engineering" being undertaken (see chapter 1), between studying manifested concepts with their overlapping, divergent meanings and designing or inhabiting new conceptual landscapes.[5] In interviews, "out there" concepts were observed and tracked; animate, molecular, and cell-like as they expanded, contracted, rushed around, split, joined, and stretched. Concepts "in here," on the other hand, were kin or at home—proximate, familiar, attached, and committed to. Legal scholar Mohammad Afshary described the close, almost comradely, relationship between a concept and its user: "As soon as you start thinking about the law . . . the state, the revolution, . . . in whatever movement and social phenomenon that you're looking at, it becomes like a companion in that journey. A companion that is in a way there to help you."[6] Repeatedly, and in different ways, academics moved between different subject positions—stepping back to observe the conceptual practice of others; coming in close to their own conceptual attachments and activities.[7]

Interviewees connected and switched between "in here" and "out there" as each turned into the other. Concepts characterized in familiar or personal registers became stretched, gifted, or externalized, turned into social things with their own independent life (see also chapter 3). Observed conceptual matter became incorporated into academics' own conceptual repertoire through developing affinity.[8] Legal scholar Sameer Ashar described, "You keep reading about an idea or a concept, or framework, and hope it becomes part of your vocabulary and the way in which you think about things and talk about things." Conceptual acculturation was not always a happy or positive process. Talking about the concepts of transparency, accountability, and procedural justice baked into "a particular version of legality," sociolegal scholar Bronwen Morgan said, "I often have this image that we were collectively thinking of these values, which are actually concepts, as little, tiny angels flying around. So, you've got all this messy stuff on the ground and then you've got these little glowing angels, which is what you're aspiring to advance. . . . And I hated that. I felt like it was divorced from that much more interwoven imbricated way that they actually relate."

And so, as research for this chapter developed, the limits of an "in here" and "out there" frame became increasingly apparent. Its binary ordering proved less good in attending to the complexity of conceptual relations, the negative attachments people can have to concepts (explored in more detail in the following chapters), and positions that are not straightforwardly "in here" or "out there."[9] It also proved less helpful in accessing a concept-centered perspective by too firmly foregrounding subjects' vantage points. I therefore moved toward a different framing, folding the conceptual movement of "in here" and "out there" into other figures: aids, worlds, currents, and cells. Approaching concepts as aids or worlds treads familiar academic ground—with concepts as tools that do stuff, as work on conceptual engineering addresses (e.g., Eklund 2024; see chapter 1), or as immersive spaces that can be entered, journeyed through, and developed. But concepts can also be felt like currents and, like biological cells, be observed in action as they protect, nourish, and sometimes destroy their ever-changing host environment. These figures help to make sense of the concept's form and affordances, while ties to other contexts stimulate and feed the conceptual imagination (see also Tilley 2002). As such, cells, currents, worlds, and aids can be seen as "active" metaphors for the concept (see also M. Black 1993, 25). But I don't want to read them in this way. A problem with metaphor is that it tends to assert epistemic norms of proper place—of the figure that moves from where it belongs (as the proper name of a thing) to where it does not.[10] If these figures are metaphors, then concepts are not *really* aids, cells, worlds, or currents; they are just imagined as such to give the concept's form and affordances recognizable substance. As Andreas Philippopoulos-Mihalopoulos (2021, 271) writes, "One vests the concept with a physicality in order to perceive it."

A primary aim of this chapter is to revitalize methods for undertaking transformative conceptual work, to *rehome* the figures of currents and cells, as well as aids and worlds. This account of conceptual practice, therefore, approaches these four figures as neither inevitably temporary borrowings nor fictive materializations. Instead, they offer loosely patterned forms that concepts assume, recognizing that the concept qua concept also bends what these figures mean, are, and do in the process.[11] This does not mean the incongruity of some of these figures (especially current and cell), in relation to concepts, is unimportant. On the contrary. Rather than enhancing our understanding of something unfamiliar by drawing on familiar metaphors, this discussion is intended to prompt less familiar ways of understanding concepts by bringing unexpected figures into play. Metaphoring rather than metaphors (see also Tsoukas 1993) may be a better way of identifying a method that brings something across and acts as if it fits, while relying on the incongruity of what is brought across to understand the targeted thing anew, where what is brought across is also not a single term or idea but an assemblage of associations.[12] Metaphoring describes a practice rather than a feature of the relationship between two concepts and so stays studiedly open to further innovation and change. In his historical analysis of the sociological metaphors used by scientists to explain and represent biological cells (which I turn to later), Andrew Reynolds (2018, 72) describes the metaphor "as a kind of 'experimental technology.'" This phrase resonates with the method adopted here, anchored in the relationship between two necessary and paradoxical elements—of incongruity and enacted congruity, where the incongruity of approaching concepts as cells, for instance, operates simultaneously with the equally important exercise of treating concepts as if the imagined and material organization of the cell identified what they are or could become.

But what does it mean for a concept to be or become a cell or a current? What does this tell us about a concept's operations or shape? At the end of the chapter, I suggest that the figures of aids, cells, worlds, and currents offer forms akin to dance moves, being steps that concepts assume. Dance may seem to pile metaphor on metaphor (or, rather, metaphoring on metaphoring). But it provides a way of characterizing a concept's changing form and affordances while drawing on an onto-epistemic network of embodied expressive movement. If we think of a concept taking up the dance move of a cell, metaphoring shifts from questions about what cells are *really* like to the form and movement that an animate cell invokes, and so attends to what conceptual figures do and make available. Discussing the evolution of social metaphors for the biological cell, Reynolds (2018, 71–72) describes how the metaphor of the factory was not simply an imagined or narrated reframing of little consequence but a way of understanding cells that supported their commercial exploitation. Approaching the four figures here as dance moves may seem to dematerialize the concept: What kind of materiality is present (or evident) when the concept of gender is taken to assume the dance move of the cell? Yet dance is quintessentially about physicality, and while traditionally this concerns the physicality of bodies, other material elements are also present, including objects, garments, spaces, and socio-affective networks, particularly when dance becomes a mode of patterned movement and ontological accomplishment beyond the expressive gestures or representations of club and stage. Diverse materialities are central to the way that concepts dance, as I explore in more detail in chapter 3.

Concepts in Conceptual Activism

Using Concepts as Aids

Concepts hit my work as a way of making sense of something very, very messy that I need to articulate but without wanting to over-articulate or over-generalize. So, concepts here are a very provisional, temporarily limited tool to understand a mess and share it with other people. —AMY COHEN, legal scholar, interview

The tool or aid is probably the most familiar way of approaching the concept, where what concepts are comes from what they do as instruments of use, "cognitive tools" in Michael Prinzing's (2018, 858) words.[13] For historical sociologist Gurminder Bhambra, concepts are (and work as) "shortcuts . . . fundamental to shaping our mental landscape . . . and how we then engage with the world" (interview). While much work on concepts, including in conceptual engineering, focuses on changing the meaning and members of a conceptual category, what I want to address here, in discussing the concept as aid, is the relationship of use to form. In interview, Afshary considered the plasticity of concepts—how their shape could change depending on need. Drawing on the figure of the hammer, he said, "A hammer is always gonna look that particular way. But I suppose when you start thinking about concepts . . . you can start thinking about, okay, well if I need a hammer to look this way for now, maybe I can change that concept and that tool in a way that would suit me." Afshary's account was prompted by his research on the concept of revolution, as developed and deployed in Egypt in 2011. He described how a "lofty idea of revolution" was deliberately used "to entice people to join," not because they "initially . . . thought what was actually happening was a revolution" (see also Afshary 2018).[14]

Concepts are used in an infinite variety of ways.[15] When it comes to academic conceptual activism, this includes acts of critique and repair, the imagining of radical alternatives, reframing and revaluing practice, inspiring and encouraging action, and analyzing the use of concepts by others. These uses are not necessarily separate. Critique can work through the conceptual reimagining of preferred alternatives—akin to the critical distance that utopianism offers, where objected-to, often overly familiar, understandings are troubled (or estranged) through accounts of more desirable possibilities rather than through direct attack. In her interview, sociolegal scholar Flora Renz described a similar conceptual move within disability politics to define

> everyone as potentially disabled, and technically we should be talking about everyone as disabled because everyone has the possibility of being disabled or sits on—oh, I hate this language of spectrums—a sliding scale of disability. . . . Normally, as a concept, disability is used to describe a minority community. . . . Even the people who say disability is something to be celebrated, and it's great, generally only apply that label to people who, in whatever way, aren't living up to mainstream society's expectations. Thinking about it in those broad terms is quite interesting because it's saying, "Actually, we're not describing a minority. We're describing everyone."

Critique is an essential dimension of academic conceptual activism. But as Renz describes, conceptual revision that generates a more expansive understanding of a traditionally stigmatized category not only provides a way of exposing and troubling existing understandings (and the assumptions they depend on). It also establishes new thoughtways, as here, where it reframes some people's relationship to their bodies as *temporarily not disabled*. The practical effects of this on how people relate to their and others' bodies, and on policy planning and services, depends on how reimagining disability is manifested—and what it is used to do. However, its take-up as a strategic or expressive practice prefigures disability (in what it means and how it applies) as a potential that we all carry, anticipating a future in which we will all lose capability. The importance of reinventing concepts, or taking up abandoned or neglected concepts, as aids to advance social and ecological justice was identified by several interviewees. Public policy scholar Janet Newman commented in interview, "You can't just mourn the things that you had before, you have to keep inventing new ones. Actually, I think it's a productive process. . . . People are radical, political movements are radical, and concepts are a tool that we have." Other interviewees agreed, describing the need for concepts that could support more progressive and collective ways of living. Legal scholar Sarah Blandy made this point, detailing the need to have property concepts that supported rather than undermined community: "What I want to do is change the narrative I suppose, so think about property much more as something that is shared, that should be shared, and that—because of the increase in flats and gated communities, etc.—you know, we've got to rethink it because people are living together whether they like it or not."

For Blandy, less familiar but already existing concepts, such as commonhold, merited greater attention, concepts that could facilitate people living interdependently thanks to shared and contiguous spaces (see also Blandy 2021).

Others suggested that concepts could help by reconfiguring how practices were framed. Geographer Miriam Williams took up this theme in relation to food bank activities when reconceptualized as care: "I think that there's power in calling it an infrastructure of care. There's something quite important about acknowledging the brokenness of existing food systems and poverty relief, and saying, well, here are all these people maintaining life in a particular way that is often hidden, so there's something important about that, I think." Newman similarly described a process of identifying concepts that could be useful from studying and reflecting on social life. "By exposing yourself to experience of whatever it is, you can draw things out of what's embedded in that experience. Shape it, wrap it, turn it, test it, challenge it, and come up with something." Revised concepts, cultivated by academics, could also be passed on as "a way of describing . . . that maybe could travel, that maybe could provoke, that maybe could have responses, that maybe capture some of what people are experiencing or feeling in a way that you can hand back to those people or to others" (Cohen, interview). At the same time, while interviewees stressed the value in developing useful concepts, including through relations of coproduction, many placed this within an extended temporal arc.[16] Here, an important aspect was letting go, refusing to hold crafted concepts so tightly that they atrophied in conditions where, in a looser form, they could have flourished. Politics scholar Shirin Rai said, "If you want your concepts to have purchase in other people's imaginations, . . . you just have to have that sense of confidence . . . to let go. . . . For me it means being incorporated in other narratives in different ways, right? . . . A concept finding different spaces and different places in different narratives, whether those narratives are words or posters or whatever."

Concepts are clearly used in a variety of ways within academic conceptual activist projects, including to critique, repair, build community, disrupt, desire, and transform. But what do these different uses tell us about the concept's form? What is the relationship between what concepts do as aids, when it comes to conceptual activism, and the shape they take? Critique, repair, community forming, disruption, desiring, and transformation might suggest concepts assume the shape (and function) of, say, knives, bandages, ties, flyswatters, ocean landscapes, and saucepans; yet among the conceptual shapes to emerge in interview discussions, two stood out. One was the container. For Williams, this was the bag filled with a range of conceptual tools. For other participants, individual concepts had a container-like function. Bhambra, for instance, described the concept of citizenship as a "container that's organized on the basis of the histories that are acknowledged, that gives it shape." Sociolegal scholar Amelia Thorpe similarly referred to concepts as being like "baskets": "a way of categorizing something or a group of things . . . putting things together in some sort of consistency, grouping ideas or grouping thoughts and practices in a way that makes sense to yourself and to other people, and in relation to other things." If concepts are baskets, conceptual activism leads the basket to change its shape so that it holds different things or holds them in a different way. And as the conflict over the sex and gender questions and guidance in the 2021 Census demonstrated (see chapter 1), what gets included within one concept rather than another can prove highly contentious. The question of where to locate the basket's sides and determine its contents was also at issue in the conflict over decertification, which I discuss in chapter 3, and in how policymakers treated sex and gender categories, discussed in chapter 4. Yet concepts can also assume other figures.

One figure identified by several interviewees was the concept as lens. For Rai, "a lens allows you to see both the concept and 'reality' in different, multiple, and layered ways, which is why I like the kaleidoscope . . . because it's the same pieces of glass, but actually, when you move it, it's got different layering of meaning." While the basket foregrounds what is inside or left outside, the lens focuses on how things constellate and the way that different conceptual devices configure these relations. As an optical tool, lenses can seem to maintain a distance and differentiation between what is viewed and the tool doing the viewing, a relation of boundedness that other sensory devices attuned to the touch, taste, or heightened sound of concepts may disturb. Yet viewing devices, as Rai's account highlights, are also entangled with what is observed (see also Barad 2007).

Geographer Peter Kraftl described how "notions like embodiments, emotion, affects and materiality . . . sometimes are just about observing what children do, . . . or how they interact with the world or how they make meaning or how things matter to them." For Kraftl, these "notions," or what I describe here as concepts, are both aids for undertaking analysis and observed practices—that is, they are in here and out there. While these positions are related and coconstituted, what I want to emphasize here is the movement between them when it comes to the concept's form: how concepts can assume the figure of the academic aid—used to make sense of what is there—and then (or simultaneously) assume the figure of the observed social practice in terms of what materializes and how practitioners understand it (even if they use different terms). While these conceptual vantage points are sometimes assumed to converge or blend (or concepts are assumed to bridge the gulf between the academic imagination and social practice), academic conceptual activism often lies in the tension and movement between them, something that acquires an additional layer of entanglement when what is observed is academic practice itself.

I return to this entanglement shortly in relation to academics' conceptual worlds, but one thing done by approaching concepts as tools is to bring their condition, maintenance, and repair to the fore. Robustness and staying in good condition was something on which several interviewees commented. Law scholar Amanda Perry-Kessaris suggested a concept should "be formed with enough coherence and strength that you can actually do something with it. . . . Just being able to get inside it or grab onto it is not going to be enough if there's nothing there in it, if it sort of explodes in a puff once you get your hands on it." For Thorpe, conceptual robustness came from usage as new conceptual imaginaries acquired the "hinterland" status of common sense (see Law 2004; also chapter 4). Browne similarly emphasized the importance of usage by others to a concept's robustness: "You can start a concept, but you can't maintain it by yourself."

In other cases, however, excessive usage was thought to undermine conceptual activism. Geographer Craig Jeffrey described concepts becoming "worn thin through overuse." Legal scholar Ruth Fletcher related this problem to routinization, witnessed with concepts such as apology and land acknowledgment. She described the need to build in variation to keep helpful concepts alive: "It's about when it . . . starts to become empty or stand in for a commitment, and that commitment, in whatever way, seems absent. . . . It's important to pay respect to the material change that that repetition is trying to achieve."[17] When concepts are approached as linguistic tools, their capacity and limits align with the capacity and limits of language. Thus, in this context, the repetitively uttered verbal apology has limited remedial value thanks to the combination of rote and token use, and lack of practical follow-up.[18] But if we think of the apology or land acknowledgment as a conceptual tool with material dimensions that can be enacted in different ways, the distinction between statements and actions (such as reparations) is not a distinction between the symbolic (or ideational) and the material but a distinction between different modes of material enactment. Black studies scholar Marquis Bey took up this point: "We're wanting for things to be done in relation to the land, in relation to other populations, rather than simply stating what we understand as a fact." Describing the need for other things to accompany the conceptual, they clarified that these "are also conceptual things. I don't want to make this clear distinction between the conceptual as this abstract, philosophical thing and the material or the practical. . . . *Those other things are also conceptual.*"[19]

Concepts as Inhabited Worlds

I've always been interested in the world-making practices of particular concepts and ideas. . . . In my work in urban thinking in particular, it's been about looking at some of those dominant narratives of injustice and . . . not necessarily wanting to have those

hopeless narratives be the main or the only stories that are shared, whilst recognizing the importance of highlighting and making visible injustice, and exposing inequality.
—MIRIAM WILLIAMS, geographer, interview

Concepts contribute to social worlds through the knowledges they help to create. But concepts can also be inhabited *as worlds*. While the figure of the aid attends to how concepts are used, the onto-epistemic world of the concept identifies how they are inhabited—as formations that are entered, experienced, moved through, tended, and built. This world may center on a single concept, pulled away from others and amplified, to form the starlit subject of its own staging. Alternatively, a single concept may offer a guide or portal into a wider conceptual network, as sociolegal scholar Morag McDermont described: "If for us the concept of social justice is a driving concept in what we do, then that very much shapes how we encounter the world, how we try to engage with the world." Concepts (and different conceptions of concepts) also coexist as multiple overlapping worlds.[20] Morgan remarked, "I think it's interesting that there are a lot of instances where you see people pluralizing a concept that they feel has become too reductive. So, economies plural rather than economy. And you know, people often insist, 'remember we are talking about economies or we're talking about laws, plural, rather than the law.' So, there's a political way of emphasizing that there isn't just one."

This plurality may relate to dissimilar members of a category (what counts as an economy or law?) or to different overlapping conceptual imaginaries (what does it mean to be an economy or law?). Yet, in both cases, approaching conceptual activism through the figure of the world can seem to fall victim to the critique that the figure of world, in its normativity and holism, fails to attend sufficiently to those historically unable to engage in world-making practices (see also Dekeyser 2023). In interview, sociolegal scholar Swethaa Ballakrishnen suggested "dreamscapes" might be better as a substitute for concepts, "because the world feels like it has limits, right, and it's bounded, and there's stuff at the core and stuff at the surface." Ballakrishnen's notion of dreamscapes can be read as prefiguring the concept: "I think concepts are dreamscapes because they're imagined and there are parts that are real. There are parts that expand, and they can blend into other dreamscapes more effortlessly than worlds. . . . Worlds seem to me self-contained; and part of a utopic re-imagination of concepts is to think of them as truly capable of being interconnected, right?" Ballakrishnen's dreamscape offers a rich utopian reimagining of concepts but, for now, I will stay with the figure of the world to foreground the material aspects of concept formation and maintenance, something that seems harder to identify with the dreamscape.

The figure of the world also productively identifies some of the problematic ways that concepts extend their reach.[21]

While the figure of aid focuses on what reengineered concepts *do*, a worlding approach to conceptual activism focuses—beyond the entry and immersion of participants—on how new or revised conceptual worlds are constructed.[22] Paralleling Bhambra's mobile invocation of the "shortcut," refugee studies scholar Tom Kemp posited the figure of the path when asked about concepts' shape: "When people walk across a field in a particular way, and they all walk in the same direction, they create their own map of a space . . . and then you might want to walk a different way. . . . And that might annoy people, or something, because you're not going the way you should be. But, you know, the first path was just the way people wanted to go over an actual land." By redesigning and developing concepts, including through occupancy, conceptual activism can be seen to cross conceptual terrain in unexpected fashion, giving rise through repetition to new geological features, connections, and paths as Kemp describes.[23] But conceptual world-building can also take other forms. It can involve deliberately stretching the borders of an existing concept to take in other terrain, which might include terrain not intended to be entered. It can involve accessing conceptual worlds (which are also materially configured worlds) without invitation. This may be an appropriative, even colonial, act and, as such, spark political criticism—for instance, where powerful outsiders seek to inhabit and tend to Indigenous concepts as if they were their own. In other contexts, inhabitancy or occupation can operate subversively and radically, countering prevailing relations of power by claiming entitlement to take up and revise hegemonic concepts, in the process making them habitable for others, at least for a while. An example of leftist occupation (or reclaiming) can be observed with the concept of the state as Newman described in the following interview extract:

> NEWMAN: I use reimagining as a way of claiming the territory as well.
>
> COOPER: Okay, I want to ask about that . . . . Reclaiming territory. Explain a bit more.
>
> NEWMAN: Well, reimagining what a public world might be . . . claiming a state, staking a claim on that word or those material things as being important. Reimagining the state is about saying the state is important and engaging with what it is—or could be—it's a political act.

Reimagining leftward what it could mean to be a state, as a worlding project, approaches the concept of the state as a complex landscape, with education, health, democracy, the arts, and justice among its defining features. In this reimagined conceptual landscape, care and welfare assume new places and forms—open, expansive, and central, rather than bordered, conditional, and peripheral. Instead, it is penal structures that are now the state's fragile features—serially forgotten or neglected (see also John Clarke 2019b), while militarism and war are things of archives and critical memorializing.[24]

The example of the state usefully demonstrates the tending that conceptual activism involves as it seeks to refit a reimagined conceptual world (see also J. Newman 2019).[25] While the maintenance of tools, aids, and other devices foregrounds mechanical processes, tending to conceptual worlds evokes a more ecological imaginary. Like plants or other forms of life, concepts evolve and grow, including through expressive and ontological practices. Cultivation and gardening emphasize the continuity of life—things change form, seeds grow, plants die, but things rarely, if ever, erupt from nothing.[26] The concepts explored in this book, of gender, sex, property, economy, decertification, activism, and play, are also not approached from scratch. They are not empty terms that come to be filled with new, initially unintelligible meanings but terms with competing and overlapping meanings that are subject to change through ideational and material reorganization. Instead of engineering, then, we might think of conceptual gardening. Gardening is not a "clean" concept; its racialized, colonial, and perfectionist associations, and targeting of foreign "invaders," have been well discussed.[27] Yet gardening or tending, as a mode of ecological care, can be done in less oppressive or disciplinary ways and can support new dissident forms to counter hegemonic structures.

One concept that can be "engineered" to describe this process is guerrilla gardening (Adams and Hardman 2014). Guerrilla gardening is an example of the kind of "heteronymous" conceptual engineering (by means of a prefix) that David Chalmers (2025) describes (see chapter 1). It characterizes illegal or uninvited gardening, typically in public or common spaces (or spaces that it is felt should be common) that have been used in ways that those intervening perceive as neglectful or improper.[28] Conceptual guerrilla gardening builds on this prior conceptual praxis to denote a worlding project that fosters new meanings. We might think here of concepts such as agender or families of choice—concepts that seize and recultivate traditional terrain of gender and family. For what conceptual guerrilla gardening underscores is a refusal to vacate or abandon hegemonic concepts. In contrast to forms of conceptual activism that reject specific conceptual worlds because they seem too tightly aligned with, and contaminated by, dominant forces and structures, guerrilla gardening practices involve their deliberate entry, inhabiting, and tending (see also chapters 4 and 5). In this way, conceptual guerrilla gardening could refuse to relinquish the concept of the state to capitalist imperialist forces or relinquish gender to patriarchy. Instead, it acts to establish a different imaginary of the concept's world. This holds on to selected aspects and, importantly, acts in relation to the concept's history so that more than simply semantic continuity is at stake.[29] Conceptual guerrilla gardening seeks to prefigure a desired conceptual landscape, capabilities, and habitat by acting as if it has the right to bring the changes sought after into being.

Concepts as Felt Currents

My third figure of the current foregrounds the energy and vitality of concepts through the forcefields that concepts help to generate and sustain. This figure and the cell that follows are important in showing how concepts act, interact, and intra-act, including with their environment. While the concept as world creates its own somewhat bounded environment, and the concept as aid is brought into the environment of its users, concepts as currents and cells signal the work that concepts do in maintaining, changing, or undermining the social environment of which they are part.[30] Thinking about currents brings images of electricity but also waves to mind. Tim Ingold evokes a similar idea, describing how we "swim in an ocean of materials" as the "coagulation and dispersal" of materials in a constant flux of combining and separating bear us along (2007, 7).[31]

Conceptual currents affect people, things, systems, and more. Being pushed in a specific direction can feel oppressive and unsettling; it can also feel secure, thrilling, or emancipatory. While currents foreground what is felt, approaching the figure of the current through conceptual activism brings the work involved in changing a current, and what changing it does, to the fore. Kemp, for instance, when interviewed, described the current force of British citizenship, a concept that had become increasingly "an object of defense or exclusion and policing." Proposing a reengineering in how citizenship is obtained, Kemp commented, "If there was a much more decentralized understanding of who could be in it, if I could choose to be a British citizen or not be, . . . then British citizenship would become less of an issue." Kemp proposed weakening the citizenship current by making it elective, for when it comes to dominant concepts—property, defense, incarceration, even citizenship—the involuntary force they exert on those subjected to them is immediately evident.[32] Also evident is the difficulty in reducing or redirecting the currents that these concepts, as institutional concepts, embody. But conceptual countercurrents exist. They exist in mainstream spaces and, often more securely, in minor-stream ones, where alternative concepts or conceptions of concepts, such as law, property, democracy, and freedom, are institutionalized to maintain the space and its identity.[33] In discussing the force of concepts, however, interviewees largely focused on the former—of conceptual countercurrents within mainstream spaces, both those present and those that could be present (see also chapter 5). Yet while such conceptual currents might be sought after, advocates were not seen as immune from their force. McDermont described how embodying progressive conceptual currents, trying to harness and mobilize them—as a form of "sensuous reasoning" in Nicholas Shapiro's (2015, 381) words—could be affectively powerful to the point of jeopardizing one's own well-being: "[When] it's a driving concept in what we do, then that very much shapes how we encounter the world, how we try to engage with the world and so those driving-concepts can change us quite dramatically." She added, "When I was doing work with a rights agency, I worked with an advisor who was really passionate about the work that he did. And I remember him saying to me something about social justice, he said that social justice was so important to him, but he said, 'And it's nearly killed me,' and what he meant was that he'd been so passionate about some of the work that he'd just . . . you know, it had taken over his life."

We might read this instance as a case where an "out there" concept became deeply internalized in ways that proved overwhelming. In other cases, interviewees described moves in the reverse direction, where "in here" turned into "out there," as they traced the reactive, sometimes intricate, dance their own conceptual activism took as they moved away from concepts perceived as politically tarnished. Newman described how "there was a period where, on the left . . . people started talking about governance rather than government to imply softer, more relational, more networked, more emergent ways in which the state worked. And then we realized that that was profoundly awful because as the state dispersed its functions, everything became fragmented and that fragmentation was profoundly damaging. So, we had to step back from that and rethink it. It's temporal, things get appropriated and distorted and reworked in ways that you hadn't imagined."

Such experiences reveal the relational, plastic, intricate moves that conceptual currents generate. We can interpret such moves as a reorganization of the conceptual toolkit, where the take-up and refashioning of concepts by powerful forces, or their deployment in unexpected ways, lead others to jettison specific concepts as damaged or sullied aids. Reading this conceptual aversion through the figure of currents, however, foregrounds how a concept's altered course can be experienced as a force that alters what people do, like deciding not to swim in the ocean, finding a different beach to swim from, or changing direction once in the water, thanks to a current's strength or direction. McDermont described this pivot in her own research, how she "had to move away from . . . the idea of regulation," because the pervasive idea of regulation within housing policy concerned "the role of the regulator, and of being audited." She continued, describing her subsequent attempt as a researcher to redirect regulation, to conceptually reengineer its currents:

> I was particularly trying to switch round an idea of the regulation *of* engagement to regulating *for* engagement, . . . so that regulation became something that was enabling . . . to try and see how people felt their spaces of everyday life were regulated, controlled, shaped, and then to try and turn that round and think about, well, how would it be possible for it to be other . . . to change those inequalities of power, to change the inequalities of resources so that it's more equal, that it is more possible for people to have some control over those things in their everyday life that they feel they are constrained by at this stage. (See also McDermont et al. 2020)

Conceptual currents are important. The power and effects of conceptual meanings are things that conceptual activism both targets and tries to deploy. Yet conceptual currents are often elusive in the sense that conceptual force works through different material forms and so is often hard to grapple with directly. This means that a critical conceptual activism often ends up responding to conceptual currents' effects or forms rather than being able to harness the currents themselves. Interviews such as McDermont's exposed some of the difficulties in changing currents or introducing new ones (such as regulating *for* engagement rather than the regulation *of* it) in ways that echo some of the difficulties that conceptual engineers identified for bedding in new concepts (see chapter 1). Proposing new concepts or tweaking and tinkering with old ones is relatively straightforward, as the proliferation of conceptual creativity in texts and speech reveals. The challenge comes in attempts to give conceptual revisions social force, particularly when they lack institutional power.

Concepts as Observed Cells

And yet conceptual revisions may be observed, moving—cell-like—through their host environment. This final figure of the cell draws on a long-standing history of travel between sociopolitical and biological thought, witnessed in the case of concepts such as immunity, resistance, social control, and disease, as well as contagion, viruses, and invasion.[34] My turn to the cell, however, is not intended to restitch biosocial relations together but to consider how concepts assume the figure of the cell in relation to conceptual activism.[35] The cell shares with the aid a sense of purposive directed action and, with worlds, a spatiotemporal interior replete with life and change. Like currents, the cell also relies on a wider environment of which the concept is an integral part (Conklin 1939;

Nicholson 2010). At the same time, while the current describes the force that the movement of water (or something similar) generates thanks to the elements that act on it, the cell is a figure of substance. Nineteenth-century protoplasm theory depicted cells as "naked blobs of a homogeneous, jelly-like 'life-stuff'" (Strick 2019, 346), and something of this understanding can be seen in some interviewee comments on concepts. Perry-Kessaris said, "I would go so far as to say the ones that aren't useful . . . are like a blob and they just sit there in the world. . . . An inanimate object, right? Whereas the useful concepts are . . . a bit floaty, . . . that's when there's energy inside them and they have the potential to do something and to respond to something, to push back." Ballakrishnen made a similar point, emphasizing the capacity of concepts to expand: "If I was to imagine it as a physical object . . . I keep thinking of the amoeba, right, . . . something that expands and doesn't have a shape, it's a blob and it keeps expanding."

Concepts and cells are shapeshifting. Yet, in taking up the figure of the cell, I want to retain the place of boundaries and definition. Both are important, if often contested, aspects of conceptual form. But saying boundaries and definition are important does not mean that concepts clearly have them, simply that attention toward them is part of what makes concepts up (see also chapters 4 and 6). Without some pressure around closure, the significance of conceptual activism abates. Fletcher made a similar point in her interview. While she described concepts as "porous, allowing exchange across the boundaries," she also said, "There's a kind of skin-like quality to them. . . . It's like not wanting to represent them as completely open-ended. . . . I do think of them as having a shape." As the struggles over sex and gender exemplify, tension over meaning constitutes, in part, the skin that concepts bear.

Conceptual activism works with the bounded yet plastic figure of the cell in several ways. One is by making the concept's genetic makeup visible, including by exposing the harmful or oppressive inheritances that contemporary, seemingly benign concepts carry. This was something that Bhambra stressed, discussing the concept of citizenship and its relationship to nation and colonialism: "I would argue that the problem isn't the problem of the concept. The problem is the histories that we acknowledge in the construction of that concept." Bhambra described a process of critical exposure, of identifying those conceptual parts and histories that have tended to remain submerged (see also Bhambra 2015; Somers 1995). In the conflict over sex and gender, for instance, concepts' genetic legacies were important to understanding contemporary anxieties on different sides—for instance, in relation to femininity, masculinity, sexual violence, and motherhood (fatherhood received very little attention). In other instances, conceptual activism operates by switching on specific conceptual networks. Here, earlier activations may make some network elements easier to switch on than others. For instance, arguably one reason why sex realists were able to effectively deploy the concepts of protection and vulnerability in their utterances and sociopolitical actions was these concepts' prior activation. Women's vulnerability and need for protection were both ideationally and materially resonant, concepts around which other things were still organized that could facilitate their return to common sense (see also chapter 4). Muted (if not fully dormant) in Britain in recent years, claims of women's vulnerability and need for protection were not strange or outlandish despite long-standing feminist critiques of their racialized, classist, patriarchal, and patronizing histories. Reactivated, these concepts validated a distinct sex-based concept of "women and girls," one that would be materially secured through single-sex services, data collection, law, and policy talk; and they validated a concern with, and framing of, specific forms of harm—namely, to those registered female at birth.[36]

Once turned on, protection and vulnerability acted as weapons and shields, arming the concept of woman to both attack and defend against competing rights claims by other gender politics (indeed, to constitute and define them as competing rights claims).[37] In this way, protection and vulnerability got mobilized to ward off attempts by others to enter and claim membership of the category of woman, where these others were deemed not to belong (see chapters 1 and 4). Like the figure of the white blood cell, sex-nativist conceptions of woman-whose-vulnerability-requires-protection surged to identify and track "invasive" or "fraudulent" claimants, and to stop concepts of woman from being improperly inhabited and replicated. Materializing as signs, utterances, hostile bodies, litigation, judgments, and more, sex-nativist concepts clustered at sites identified as places where entry and harm were taking place—including women's toilets, prisons, sports, refuges, and changing rooms.

The figure of the cell can suggest combat and destruction, but cells of course do not only operate in this way. Cells perform an array of tasks associated with bodily maintenance, development, life, and death; so too do concepts. For mainstream concepts and sites, this may operate in ways too normalized to be noticed apart from when change or conflict draws attention to what concepts are doing. In the case of minor-stream spaces, the work of concepts is often both more unexpected and more marked. Conceptual activism may bring established concepts, like equality, care, freedom, and law, into spaces where they are not conventionally seen to fit, but where their presence helps to sustain and enrich new organized practices, even as the concepts are changed in the process. This is something I have explored elsewhere, including the conceptual work done by property at a democratic, self-governing school and by care at a women's sexual bathhouse.[38] The ideational and material presence of transplanted and revised concepts is crucial to maintaining alternative social processes within intentional communities and everyday utopias. While the figure of the current foregrounds the force that concepts have, the cell identifies the business and movement of organized meanings as they feed, validate, and help to integrate countercultural environments (see also chapter 5).

Concluding Remarks

Conceptual activism works the relationship between how meaning is imagined and how it materializes, but identifying the concept as the material and imagined organization of meaning does not tell us what concepts are like when it comes to their form. This chapter has offered four figures through which to explore how the conceptual organization of imagining and materiality takes shape. It can seem tempting to identify one figure or another as the right or best one to depict what concepts are and do, and in much academic work, including in conceptual engineering, the figure of the aid (or tool) comes routinely to the fore. Here, the concept extends and facilitates scholarly intent—as McDermont remarked, a concept is "never detached from those who are playing with it or working with it or resisting. . . . They are always going to be shaped by who or what is working with them." Perry-Kessaris made a similar point: "For me with concepts there's always a human there wanting to understand something, share something, investigate something, capture something, find a relationship between something, and that's what gives it the energy." The aid is clearly a recurring and tenacious form for concepts, especially in subject-centered accounts. But in manifesting and expressing meaning—as social phenomena that help to make up the world and act—concepts also inhabit other figures. Or to put it another way, people have relationships to the concept other than as something that can be used. This includes relations of observing, feeling, and inhabiting.

Different contexts and research methods produce these relations in ways that can lead aids, worlds, currents, and cells to appear as distinct conceptual forms. But the boundedness and stability that this suggests is misleading.[39] Take the concept of sex, perceived as a demographic tool to generate data through two exhaustive categories—female and male. In designing the questions and guidance for the 2021 Census for England and Wales, the Office for National Statistics recognized that this binary and static account of sex was losing support given the growing visibility and presence of transgender people and trans-positive understandings. Thus, revising Census categories necessitated immersion in the concept of sex—and its different iterations—to provisionally and temporarily traverse a multiplicity of worlds (a pluriverse, perhaps) variously organized around sex as biological, legal, birth registered, transitioned, and lived (see chapter 1). For objectors, however, institutionalizing most of these conceptions of sex risked validating new policy currents organized around self-identification—a process aggravated by the gold-standard status of Census categories, and their influence on other data-gathering and public service activities. As a result, gender-critical activists mobilized and litigated, hoping to harness law's powerful conceptual currents to support a narrower sex concept. In 2021, this would not be biological sex as registered at birth, but it could be the next-best thing of legal sex (as certified at birth or amended through a Gender Recognition Certificate). Activists' success meant Census sex became "legal sex."

The figure of the cell identifies how legal sex, discussed in chapter 1, evolved; how it traveled through different sites, surfacing authoritatively in court; how it fought off opponents, metabolizing support and criticism; and how it came to rest in the Census guidance. Yet while we can trace how legal sex assumed the figures of cell, world, aid, and current, this does not mean legal sex took up these figures easily or completely. As a conceptual current, for instance, the force of legal sex remained uncertain, defied by those Census respondents who recorded their sex using other definitions (see chapter 1).

In the previous chapter, I traced the conceptual activisms over Census sex to show the movement and evolution in how concepts are engineered and re-engineered, that there is not simply a before and after, since conceptual change and redesign is not an atemporal, flat act without duration. Approaching the Census conflict over sex as something relational and interactive—intra-active also, since elements are brought into being and differentiated through conflict—we can view the figures discussed in this chapter as patterned (and improvised) moves, where the *concept is relationally constituted in and through such moves*. In other words, the concept does not preexist the moves through which it forms but acquires shape in the dancelike pattern of cells becoming aids, becoming worlds, becoming currents, and so on.[40] These are not the only steps possible; but they are ones evoked by the discussion of concepts and conceptual activism within my interviews. Describing these moves as dance moves brings the dynamic, agentic, expressive qualities of conceptual action to the fore, even as the dance itself may form background tissue (see chapter 3).[41] It also explains why the cell, world, aid, and current are not metaphors but rather ways of describing conceptual movement, where what concepts do and how they appear arises from the sequences they form—sequences that overlap, connect, and compose each other in messy, asynchronous ways. The dance that concepts engage in because they are concepts is historical and emergent; it may not be predictable, but it is not unconstrained, being shaped by apparatuses of power and affect, and by the networks that concepts are part of. This shaping matters. It conditions the steps that happen (and don't happen) and is an important feature of conceptual activism even when it is also what conceptual activism resists.

This chapter has focused on the academic vantage point—a vantage point from which concepts are observed as they move, grow, die, are used by others, and have (or don't have) impact. Yet academic practice, as this and the previous chapter explored, is not limited to studying the conceptual praxis of others. Academic engagement in conceptual activism also means revising and whittling concepts in new critical ways and in ways that identify and support new practices. In the process of building and fine-tuning conceptual aids, academics immerse themselves in the conceptual terrain that this demands and, as McDermont narrated from her experience with regulation, they become subject to the conceptual currents that other bodies forge (including institutional bodies), which they, in turn, may seek to redirect, thwart, or avoid.

Inhabiting new conceptual currents, even when they are desirable ones, is not trouble-free. McDermont described the adviser who felt as if social justice had almost ended him. In the chapter that follows, I remain with the challenge of academic conceptual activism in a context where new concepts, intended to aid gender's critical reimagining, became subject to sharp countercurrents. My terrain for this discussion is "decertification"—a concept academically coined to describe the dismantling of sex and gender as assigned and legally guaranteed statuses. The chapter explores the conflict that circulated through decertification over what gender and, specifically, legal gender should mean and become, including in relation to sex. In conditions where both critics and advocates adopted nonnegotiable accounts of category membership and centered these accounts in their conflict over sex and gender, I also draw in an institutional account of gender formation, to attend to the part certification played (and continues to play) in how gender and sex get made, acquired, held, and used. Studying these processes takes us to the concept of economy, but this is economy reimagined to decenter capitalist market processes in *what economy can mean*. Thus, while the present chapter focused on the dance moves taken up by the concept qua concept, in the next chapter I explore a more complex dance, in which economy, reimagined, provides the dance moves for gender, sex, and their decertification, reregulation, and future.

3

Speculative Imaginaries

Decertification as Economy

It has become commonplace to talk about economies of pleasure and desire, yet what the concept of economy brings to these discussions varies. Sometimes economy operates as a synonym for value-accruing modes of circulation and exchange; sometimes economy points to relations of consumption, production, and labor, or to the take-up of specific terms—spending, investment, and such, as in David Bennett's (2010, 2016) analyses of post-Enlightenment erotic discourse. In this chapter, I take up the concept of economy to do something different—namely, to consider how law allocates and helps to create gender categories, as well as the transformative possibilities available to change how these categories work and, ultimately, to change gender itself. But I also take up economy to think economy otherwise. Foregrounding economy's conceptual presence in the connected relations of making, accessing, holding, and using, this discussion contributes to currents of progressive work intent on exploring more-than-capitalist relations in economic imaginaries. In so doing, it also displaces current divisions established between matters of economy and matters of social policy.

As in the last chapter, I pursue these aims by focusing on academic conceptual activism before turning, in chapter 4, to the conceptual activism of public bodies engaged in policy practice. However, unlike chapter 2, which used a conversational approach to explore the affordances and form of the concept through interviews with other academics, this chapter examines academic conceptual activism via a speculative law reform proposal. From 2018 to 2022, I was part of a research group exploring the speculative meaning and effects of decertifying sex and gender in Britain.[1] Decertification is a term we borrowed and reengineered from its more familiar application to describe the withdrawal of formal authorization or accreditation from agencies, officials, and elections, usually for reasons (often politically contested) of wrongdoing. Instead, we took it up to denote state law's withdrawal from confirming and formalizing sex and gender as legal status categories.[2] Decertification would not ban state law from using gender's terms (including sex), but in conditions of decertification, the sex and gender of persons would no longer be state assigned or legally held in place. This would bring sex and gender into line with sexuality and ethnicity (or, in the language of UK equality law, "sexual orientation" and "race")—social characteristics that are self-identified and alegally acquired.

Decertification can be advanced for different reasons. As a critical and feminist proposal, its most compelling rationale is to help upend the informal social hierarchies, divisions, disciplinary effects, and exclusions that formal status distinctions carry and contribute to. Decertification challenges the fixity and significance of sex-based distinctions; it disturbs normalized processes of gender socialization and organizational treatment; and it frees people to live outside formally imposed categories. Yet decertification's effects on the current gender order are uncertain; they are also disputed. One site of disagreement is whether deformalization would weaken the regulatory responses developed to contain and counter men's superordinate status and greater likelihood for violence. Critics repeatedly made arguments along these lines, slating decertification's adequacy as a policy tool. One commentator compared it to a toddler sticking their head under a blanket to become invisible, under the mistaken impression that if the toddler could not see out, others could not see in.[3] Another compared it to taking a license plate off a car and saying the car was no longer a car and so no longer polluting.[4] Such certainty, however, about the division between forms of reclassification or declassification and the nature of the thing may overstate the ontological stability and fixity of what exists (see chapter 1). A car without a license plate is still (it seems) a car (at least for certain purposes), and a toddler under a blanket is still a toddler under a blanket. But withdrawing certainty from sex and gender as aspects of legal personhood—taking away the guarantee that state law accords category belonging—changes how the categories are accessed and, as a result, changes what the categories mean. This also facilitates life in categories currently unrecognized legally, such as agender, which no longer remains outside a tightly walled and validated structure of gender authorization.

Conceptual activism is something that academics study; they can also undertake it. One way of undertaking conceptual activism, as an academic, is by making something; allowing imagined meanings to materialize in ways that respond to and act within a wider sociopolitical environment. Decertification demonstrates this interplay. In the discussion that follows, I track it through three ontological forms: as an idea for legal change expressed through evolving speculative law; as the withdrawal of a regulatory device (certification) for managing membership of sex and gender categories; and as ambitions for gender, more generally, in what it might come to mean and do.[5] Through these three forms, decertification's different imagined and material networks come to the fore. But to understand the networks that decertification relies on, creates, and changes, this discussion also introduces another concept, reimagined for critical and analytical purposes: economy. Approaching speculative law, regulatory categories, and gender's revised future ontologies through economy is something of a counterintuitive move. Why bring economy in to understand the deregulation—or more accurately, the reregulation—of gender and sex, something seemingly better approached as a matter of political administration?

Despite divergent views on the benefits and risks of decertification and allied reforms to deformalize sex and gender categories, advocates and critics of reform occupied common ground in their shared governmental and juridical frame of reference. This is unsurprising since governmental and legal rationalities saturated debates about gender reform: as social justice rationales for retaining the current system—of standardization, formalization, identification, and consistency—met counterdiscourses of equality and freedom from state control.[6] One activist interviewed for the research described the presence of sex on birth certificates as a "shackle"—a state attempt to impose order by pinning down category membership. If legal categories of sex and gender are disciplinary controls or shackles imposed by the state, approaching decertification through governmental concepts makes sense since decertification is, at heart, a political measure to reform the state's use of categories to govern. Indeed, while decertification in Britain remained legally very far from accomplished during this period, its de facto governmental presence was striking. Between 2018 and 2025, many public bodies acted as if decertification were underway—that is, they acted (at times and in places) *as if* "sex-gender" were self-accounted for, with *legal* status as women or men no longer being determinative when it came to inclusion within sex- and gender-specific provision (see also chapters 1 and 4).[7]

This chapter does not jettison a juridical and state policy perspective. However, it suggests that this perspective can be augmented by attending to the relations of making, allocating, and using at play, and by understanding these relations as economic relations. Approaching gender decertification in this way may seem unexpected; legal and governmental processes are not typically considered economic stuff in the way that things more obviously produced for monetary exchange are. Certainly, gender scholars and activists have long recognized the impact of gender relations on economy and, in turn, how economy contributes to the making and maintenance of gender in racialized, class-stratified ways. From here, we might speculate about decertification's impact on gender-based forms of exploitation, work, and consumption, for instance. But this is not what the chapter addresses. Rather, its focus is how decertification itself can be rendered intelligible through the concept of economy, a move that extends the analyses that feminists and others have long undertaken in bringing the concept of economy to contemporary nonmonetized relations, such as unpaid care work. Policymaking and laws, however, are rarely included within this broader economic discussion as things produced (as opposed to things that govern what is produced).

I take up the challenge to reimagine the concept of economy so that it treats law, policymaking, and gender categories as economic stuff—and not simply as regulating or mixed in with economic stuff—for two main reasons. First, it is part of a wider shared project to decenter capitalist and competitive market relations within progressive economic imaginaries. This project does not ignore capitalist relations and logics (which would be foolish) but treats them as one kind of economic mode of ordering among others that capitalism meshes with, coconstitutes, and operates in relation to (while also recognizing that capitalism is a sprawling heterogeneous formation that is very far from monolithic). Without question, capitalism is hugely powerful and dominant, with heavily destructive consequences for people, other forms of life, and the planet. However, recognizing economic plurality—provincializing capitalism—constitutes a prefigurative move to nurture more hopeful economic imaginaries (Gibson-Graham 1996). How this is done matters. Some ways of enacting new economic imaginaries are more powerful than others. However, for my discussion here, new ways of organizing economic relations are not so much being imagined and depicted, as existing cuts and joins are being rerecognized as economic. Attending to relations of making, holding, and use that are not exploitative or extractive (or, at least, don't center these qualities) responds to the injunction to change what we think from so as to think differently (see John Clarke 2020, 26) and to build confidence in other possibilities. This expands the concept of economy in ways that foreground its contingent and socially constituted character (see also Rittich 2023), while avoiding the trap that John Clarke (2020, 18) and others have signaled in which the figure of economy "commands the stage," imperially converting life's manifold qualities—from future weather, water quality, and ecological crisis to gay pride—into neoliberal sites of commodification, market exchange, financialization, and profit-making.[8] Second, reimagining economy foregrounds decertification and certification, as well as gender categories, and gender more generally, *as things that are made, allocated, held, and used*, albeit in ways that evolve and fluctuate over time, and that can be harmful or valuable. As such, economy offers a societal counterframe to those currently prevailing conceptual accounts in which a biological understanding of sex meets a personalized, individualized, or communitarian account of gender. But before exploring decertification any further, let me introduce some key aspects of economy's reimagining.

Reimagining Economy

If the concept of economy is to effectively reach away from capitalism, in a conceptual activist project intent on prefiguring what economy could come to mean, key elements need revising. How to reinvent the concept of economy has been subject to different developments; in this chapter, the main move is away from the specifically marketized concepts of production, exchange, and consumption to a broader set of meanings based on making, allocation/having, and using, where value (and nonvalue) is qualitative and noncalculable as well as subject to comparative forms.

- Making raises questions about what is made and how. It includes tangible and intangible things, services, and activities, but also policies, histories, identities, future statuses, and more. Making encompasses exploitative relations of capitalist production, colonial extraction, and patriarchal care work. But it also extends to relations of making that are collective, voluntary, pleasurable, and egalitarian (even as these may not take shape at a distance from hostile and exploitative economic practices). In this chapter, prefigurative law reform proposals, certified sex, reregulated categories, and future gender ontologies are made.[9] While "making" may seem an overly mechanical description, suggesting something rigid and routinized—where making gender or legal policy, for instance, is analogous to making cars or chocolates—making can happen in other ways, including in ways that are more idiosyncratic and evolving, where what is made is constantly re-formed rather than taking shape as a discrete one-time act (see also Appadurai 1988).

- Acquiring and having can involve commercial exchanges, but they can also involve modes of distribution (including by state bodies) that are obligatory, elective, or shared, such as for nonscarce identities and things held in common. Reclassification, self-authorship, sharing, and gifting, like claiming and seizing, offer nontransactional modes of acquisition that, in turn, foreground different ways of having (or holding) a thing and passing it on.[10] These can be understood in property terms, as I explore, but doing so requires a conception of property that encompasses relations of access, use, revision, and circulation that does not depend on a sovereign owner.
- Use is a deliberately broader term than consumption.[11] It recognizes wants, desires, and needs but also recognizes disagreement and contingency surrounding them—for instance, in relation to how gender identity is used. Use does not assume depletion, that things used are used up or wasted, or that a clear division exists between making and use (although it includes these possibilities). For gender and other regulatory categories, use does not consume or sit apart (down the line) from production but contributes to it.[12] Use also attends to nonuse and disuse—features that make use helpful for thinking about the deproduction of sex-gender, including through decertification.

Making, allocating, holding, and use surface here as key features of a prefigurative conception of economy, one that does not assume economy is solidaristic, just, and ecological but makes room for this as one possibility among others. What economy as a concept also, importantly, foregrounds are the loops and connections between different processes. The systemic or circulatory character of economy, and the value that accrues from this, is a signature quality of much economic thinking—from critical work on capitalist economies to optimistic analysis of ecologically sustainable or moral economies. In this discussion, the many (contingent) connections and loops between making, allocating, holding, and using when it comes to speculative law, regulatory categories, and gender are central to their economic character. Approaching decertification through a governmental imaginary can cause these processes to appear as a linear tripartite staging in which a proposal (designing a new law) leads to regulatory reform (revising how gender is allocated) and finally societal change (how gender is used).[13] Attending to the multidirectional loops that form disrupts this ordering as complex nonsequential relations arise between decertification's proposition, regulatory reform, and new gender ontologies.

What also emerges is a concept of economy that reaches beyond markets, capitalism, money, trade, exchange, debt, and investment. As suggested, competitive, extractive, exploitative forms are not necessarily excluded or marginalized within a prefigurative economic imaginary (in terms of what counts as economic; they may be marginalized and excluded as acceptable material processes), but they are also neither determinative (as neoliberal logics imply) nor exhaustive.[14] This builds on accounts of diverse, progressive, and alternative economies by J. K. Gibson-Graham (1996, 2008) and others who argue for the need to attend to noncapitalist features of contemporary neoliberal economies, such as household labor, commoning, sharing, neighboring, and public welfare provision.[15] Making these economic relations more visible makes them "more credible" and "viable as objects of policy and activism" (Gibson-Graham 2008, 618). This recentered attention rebuts accounts of capitalism as an all-consuming system on the basis that such totalizing accounts marginalize other economic logics—whether present or in formation—especially cooperative ones, withdrawing the oxygen they require to grow.

Critical and progressive conceptual activist work has broadened what comes within economy's auspices. However, such work perpetuates the tendency to align economy with labor, things that are quantifiable and ownable, and goods and services conventionally identified as economic, that perpetuate capitalism, or that are necessary for sustaining life.[16] Analyses practically revise how labor, ownership, production, and consumption can and should happen—widening and remaking the boundaries of what counts as economic in the process (see also Chatterton and Pusey 2020). Nevertheless, the things that get attended to as economic things assume a certain notion of what economy is about.[17] While they have been extended through feminism's focus on domestic labor and a shared concern with the goods and services that support life and well-being, administrative and policy practice has tended to remain outside this discussion. Speculative legislative proposals, regulatory categories, and gender ontology are not typically regarded as economic stuff; yet they are as much made, allocated, held, and used as the more conventional commodity-things associated with economy—such as cars, money, and food.[18] Bringing them into economy extends and deepens the capitalist market decentering that Gibson-Graham and others propose, foregrounding the nonmarketized, heterogeneous ways in which the material and immaterial stuff of the world can be (and is) crafted, acquired, held, and used.

Decertification, then, can prompt a more expansive account of economic things and processes. But as an application of conceptual activism, how should we imagine the conceptual relationship between its active terms? Building on chapter 2, I return to the figure of the dance—to orient our attention to the evolving, patterned, conceptual relationship taking place between making, allocating, holding, and using in relation to speculative law, regulatory categories, and gender's future; and the connected moves and countermoves of proponents and critics of decertification as these took shape in relation to gender, decertification, and economy.[19] Chapter 2 focused on the solo dance of the concept. Here, the dance involves conceptual partners taking choreographed and improvised steps in a dance that is both imagined and found. In other words, this is a dance that materializes (in texts, dialogue, policy decisions, community practice, and angry words), but this is a materialization that needs to be folded back into the imagination to be consciously approached as an economic dance.

Dance may seem a contentious figure to mobilize given the harmful social practices and power relations at stake when gender is at stake, particularly when dance suggests sensuality, desire, agility, and audience. But dance has other meanings and contexts, from the dance performed by bees to its critical everyday use when a merry dance leads someone astray and into a series of difficulties. What dance is and means has also been thoroughly interrogated, challenged, and reimagined, as debates over conceptual dance exemplify.[20] Questioning what counts as dance and what dance does, as conceptual dance scholarship undertakes, supports the analysis here, where the bodies are concepts engaged in a virtual dance (albeit with material steps), where there is movement but also stillness, and where boundaries (and distinctions) between partners, and between dances, come and go.[21] Dance takes the bodies of concepts to show what (else) they can do.[22] And yet we might also think of this dance as one of disruption. Decertification—the conceptual newcomer on the scene—appears, threatening to destabilize how gender is made, allocated, held, and used. Decertification's arrival gives rise to a new, turbulent dance, full of passion and presence, as it both diffracts and challenges stable naturalized assumptions—namely, that state law should properly mirror the binary reality of sex.

A Tale of Three Dances

The Speculative Proposal Dance

Societal experiments have a long and checkered history. From state policies to transnational projects like Esperanto, to small-scale initiatives, social experiments redesign and re-create the spaces, practices, and things that social life entails. In recent years, experimental practices have enjoyed a new surge of energy and interest, from the digital and technologically oriented "maker movement"—"part workshop, part art studio, and part laboratory" (T. Smith 2017, 131)—and the textile politics of craftivism (Vachhani et al. 2025), to critical mimetic replays of institutional structures and events (councils, panels, inquiries, and more) that act on behalf of life's subordinated and vulnerable (see also chapter 5).[23] Many of these smaller-scale experimental practices are forged with an open-ended, democratic, participatory ethos. But while shaped by feminist, anarchist, socialist, and prefigurative grassroots politics, their making also sometimes involves governmental bodies, through funding, partnerships, and at times incorporation (see also Perry-Kessaris 2026).

In recent years, feminist legal scholarship has developed its own experimental practice, most notably in projects to rewrite significant (historic) court judgments in more progressive ways. Originating in Canada and then the UK, twenty-first-century feminist judgment projects crossed quickly into other jurisdictions and into other agendas, including queer and wild law judgment writing.[24] These legal simulations-with-revisions combine "guerrilla gardening" techniques (see chapter 2) with "realist" agendas to demonstrate law's (or legal form's) capacity to develop feasible, more just decisions and sometimes processes.[25] In the case of decertification, the pursuit of more-than-legal ends—namely, gender's transformation and deproduction—combined with a pragmatic utopianism to demonstrate how law-as-it-is can accept and make sense of a reform to dismantle sex and gender status.[26] In other words, decertification is a technically plausible reform within the existing edifice of English law. It is also a research product of the neoliberal university and, as such, subject to its marketized modes and relations of production, including the evaluative rankings and temporary employment that externally funded research projects, and the academic outputs they generate, are compelled to operate within.[27] Recognizing this neoliberal terrain is important to avoid romanticizing politically progressive academic scholarship. However, given the volume of writing on neoliberal higher education, and given the book's focus on prefigurative forms of conceptual activism, I take neoliberalism as the unfortunate given in considering how a legal academic simulation can support economy's reimagining, and how this conceptual reimagining can illuminate what is happening when a speculative law reform proposal is made.

As a legal proposal, forging decertification drew on established law reform techniques of consultation, prototyping, and backcasting.[28] It also drew on over two hundred interviews conducted between 2018 and 2022, a survey to assess attitudes toward gender-related law reform, and, in its final eighteen months, several stakeholder workshops and focus groups to critically consider the legislative principles emerging.[29] Designing a new law in this area required a comprehensive inventory of where and how sex and gender status was legislatively encoded (a harder task than might be imagined since no such list of laws appeared to exist); it required projecting reform forward to attend to the potential consequences of different regulatory options and provisions (see also Mische 2009), and to cast back from hypothetical future scenarios to tweak the legal principles emerging.[30] In some legal areas, sex and gender categories could be straightforwardly replaced with more precise terms—recognizing, for instance, that (legal) men can become pregnant and give birth.[31] But for other areas, writing a decertification law generated policy dilemmas and difficult choices: Should community and religious organizations be able to formalize their own conceptions of sex and gender in the absence of state-imposed category membership?[32] Should male primogeniture be prohibited while retaining the system of titles (with their archaic powers and privileges), or should the entire infrastructure of aristocratic status be abolished instead? What about immigration, welfare, and imprisonment? Many legal areas seemed inadequately addressed when decertification was approached as nothing more than a technical repair of existing law to remove the binary application of sex and gender categories while ignoring the other social justice issues that these laws raised.

In addressing the choices surrounding the making of decertification as a speculative proposal, questions of use come to the fore. Here, one key intended use was to stimulate discussion about the current system of legal sex and gender status. While cast as a legislative proposal (and so a putative framework for action to come), decertification was not intended to be straightforwardly used either as an anticipatory blueprint of a future statute or as a viable contemporary proposition to stand behind and uncritically promote. As a regulatory idea (rather than an ideal), decertification's task was to prompt law reform questions, to create a space for discussion and reflection, and to stimulate more utopian imaginaries of gender's future. A staff member from one organization, when interviewed, described academic designs as "a way of normalizing" radical ideas and bringing them into public fora. "It's very easy to think, just because it is like this at the moment, it's the way it's always going to be. . . . I think there is a lot to be said [for] thinking about how we could start moving towards [decertification] because I think, overall, it would be better for people," although they added, "but it needs to be done in a thought-out way, because there are ways it could be done really badly."

Prototyping decertification as a speculative law had to contend with sharply divergent opinions as it moved, over the course of its making, between a pragmatically viable legislative framework and more adventurous, politically ambitious law-writing. Schisms among feminists and other gender activists over sex and gender categories, aggravated by the use of law as a speculative "public thing," in Bonnie Honig's (2017) words, made it impossible to imagine a legislative design that could capture a common will.[33] At the same time, designing a decertification law, in Britain at this time, could not attend only to those in favor of it. Objections came from different quarters, including from some trans activists. However, the main wave of objections came from gender-critical feminists (see also chapters 1 and 4). Gender-critical concerns about the implications of decertification for women-only services, data collection, and affirmative action were expressed vociferously and sustainedly.[34]

Persistently framed in sex-realist terms, these objections shaped decertification's conditions of production, pushing the proposal to attend more precisely to the conceptual cuts and ties between gender and sex, and to address gender-critical concerns about how women's services could operate without formal identification of women. Objectors' concerns and agenda also contributed to the production of decertification's shadow: a speculative law that was crudely and naively designed to remove rights and protections in ways that would heighten women's and girls' vulnerability. In some ways, I am hesitant to call this formulation a shadow since it had a material existence, acted, and presented itself as the original proposal correctly interpreted. Arguably, there were simply multiple, iterative versions of the legislative idea, materializing on different stages, and created through different (but intersecting) networks and relations of production. At the same time, for us, as the researchers designing decertification, objectors' reframing appeared a skewed derivation—albeit one that often trailed in front. This shadow law turned decertification from an exploratory proposal (anchored in the retention of gender equality provisions) into a declaratory project that would strip out legal reparative measures for women. On social media and in public debate, critics tethered this shadow version of decertification to sex-based rights, reconstituting it as an undesired object that would take away women's and girls' rights (see also Peel 2025).[35] But why conceptualize decertification in this way?

Critics used decertification to amplify the threat posed by liberalizing gender categories—here, decertification stood as the "real" agenda underlying more moderate-sounding, trans-positive reform proposals. In a context where UK governments were consulting on easing the procedures for formal gender transitioning, decertification could be deployed to show what was fundamentally at stake and to spur opponents of change.[36] Critics' actions reveal the co-imbricated character of using and making, how an imaginary law that was not desired by critics can, nevertheless, be made to work against its own interests by being reconfigured in ways that enhance its utility as an effective but undesired object. What such actions also reveal is the presence of a diffuse and fractured property structure. When it comes to a speculative proposal, those authoring and designing it have limited ownership. Powers to access, revise, share, and represent are also held by critics, even as they may claim their moral, political, and epistemic distance from a proposal that, they argue, does not belong to them.[37] The diffusion of rights and capacities to access, use, and share decertification suggests that a distributed property model may offer a better way of explaining how such a speculative legal proposal is held than the legal imaginary of a sovereign owner wielding absolute control.[38] In this distributed model, relations of access and use form part of the property assemblage. They are not simply consequential rights held by the sovereign owner, or powers given to others, who are defined by their very use of such powers as nonowners. A distributed model of ownership shows how property powers can be shared more collectively, equally, and contextually. At the same time, when things are subject to different cuts, and to contestations over what the thing is, there is no single entity subject to property relations. If decertification is imagined in multiple, diverging, and overlapping ways, each will carry and create its own property networks, including in the modes of transmission and acquisition it supports, as the capacity and entitlement to pass on a proposal (or share it) form part of overlapping property bundles.

In decertification's design, we can observe an economy of prototyping and speculative legislative development with relatively open property relations. These qualities were also present in the relations of transmission established in decertification's development, echoing modalities associated with open-source software, commoning, and "maker" economies (see also Morgan 2024). Severed from monetary relations and private ownership, publicizing and sharing a legal proposal is like extending an "offer" or invitation. This is not a contractual offer, requiring acceptance and financial consideration to become legally animate, but a way of making something available in the anticipatory hope that others will find it of use (see also chapter 2), even as the wishful (if not willed) hope is that such uses will align, at least loosely, with the designers' intentions: here, for decertification to contribute to deproducing gender (as we know it).[39]

In this economic dance, designers, supporters, and critics of decertification moved through different step sequences as they contributed to the proposal's making, sought to exercise propertied power within an open and loose regime of rights and restrictions, and used the proposal for different purposes. Decertification appeared as an idea, set of legislative principles, and sequence of prototypes. But it was, as I have said, a thing with a shadow as critics constructed and circulated their own version—a process that was enabled by the virtual character of decertification as speculative law. Thus what got made remained in flux, in conditions where representation and thing—copy and original—could not be easily pulled apart or even ascertained. As a publicly available nonscarce entity, speculative legislative proposals demonstrate modes of access and sharing akin to commoning economies, where transmission takes the form less of a gift than of a standing invitation to use and remake. But such a standing invitation, as here, proved subject to complicated accounts of ownership. Critics treated us, the researchers, as "owning" the proposal in the sense of being responsible for it (for its creation as well as for its consequences). But they simultaneously deployed property powers of access, use, redepiction, transmission, and attempted destruction to "manage" their negative attachment. In a sense, in re-creating what decertification meant, they enacted a form of guerrilla gardening, occupying and reinventing decertification as a terrain that was not empty or abandoned so much as dangerously designed and mismanaged (see chapter 2).

A Regulatory Dance

Decertification can appear a movement of withdrawal, as a much relied on (legal) ground in the economy of sex-gender categories is dismantled, removing in the process a communicative link between the production process and the uses to which sex-gender is put. As an act of withdrawal, decertification depletes the value of recognized and supported categories—something gender-critical feminists argued would happen to the category of woman. In other contexts, powerful corporations and professional bodies use certification to manage and restrict entry by newcomers and so limit potential competition. From this perspective, decertification appears a subversive strategy to remove funnel necks and gatekeepers, and to open restrictive categories. Yet, like other deformalization moves, paying excessive attention to the grip that dominant players (or forces) exert, and seeking to undo it by removing certificatory statuses or privileges, underestimates informal power. It also underestimates how certification can support some less powerful constituencies or newly valued practices through recognized and targeted benefits. For instance, if decertification makes positive action initiatives for women harder to accomplish, this may benefit men. Yet a problem with certification, from a social justice perspective, is that protection is limited to already recognized groups; certification may enable affirmative action for women, but not for other subordinated gender constituencies, just as ecological labels can work against producers who avoid pesticides and farm responsibly but do not comply with the specific suite of requirements to gain recognition from an ecological label.

Decertification is also not just about the withdrawal of a selective form of recognition. Removing sex-gender certification changes—but does not eliminate—the categories of female and male, woman and man. In the context of contemporary Britain, what decertification does is to respond to the increasingly convoluted dilemmas that beset regulatory frameworks seeking to manage changes in category membership. As first-generation formal gender transitioning procedures came under review in Britain in the late 2010s, UK and Scottish governments turned to reconsider: At what age can a person transition; how many times; with what requirements and commitments; through what procedures; at what cost; into what categories; and for what uses? Amid the flurry of questions and dilemmas raised by amending the current classificatory structure, decertification offers a different approach.[40] In this discussion of sex-gender's regulatory economy, I want to focus on two main questions: How would category membership be acquired post-decertification; and what is wrong with the current certification system in terms of how it supports the making, allocation, and use of sex-gender categories?

At first glance, decertification unsettles a system in which people acquire a gender from birth thanks to social and embodied accretions that begin with genital observation and registration of a baby's sex. As an NGO staffer we interviewed commented, "It basically just comes down to: what do your external genitals look like? That is what actually sex on the birth certificate means. It doesn't mean your chromosomes. It doesn't mean secondary sex characteristics. It just means that." Removing sex from birth certificates, however, does not, by itself, stop people from gaining a legal sex and gender. While it removes the current mode of formal allocation and acquisition, what it leaves in place, or establishes, depends on how decertification is done. Decertification could cause sex and gender to re-form as matters of legal fact that law ascertains when required. This could reinstall biological sex in conventional binary terms on the basis that, when deemed necessary, people account for their sex and gender according to conventional views about what these categories mean and how they are to be known.

Decertification could also lead to alternative ways of designating sex or gender for regulatory purposes. For instance, self-identification could become in Britain a legally accepted way of determining or even making gender and sex identities. Alternatively, self-identification might function as a practical way of communicating information about sex and gender without any claim that these concepts are made through it (since the building blocks for sex and gender reside elsewhere). This latter position has been informally operative in Britain for some while as organizations rely on self-reporting, being unwilling or unable to ask for "evidence," such as a birth certificate or the display of "correct" exhibited body parts (see also Renz 2023), even as they generally refrain from treating self-identification as what sex or gender actually is or is made from.[41] A different mode of acquisition (that might also be a way of making gendered subjects) involves specific social practices. Post-decertification, one might socially *become* a woman, man, or other gender-sex through inhabitancy over time, prompting questions as to what social acquisition of a gender would require and when (if ever) it would have legal force. "Living" as a woman or man is an element of current legislative tests (although, by itself, it is not enough to gain legal category membership in Britain).[42] The Gender Recognition Act 2004, section 2(1)(b), for example, requires people to live in their "acquired" gender for at least two years before their application. Evidence of doing so includes having a name, title, and gender marker on a spread of different documents that, prospective applicants are told, should "match[] up with your affirmed gender."[43]

In the late 2010s and early 2020s, despite the persistence of legal sex status, gender and sex categories typically operated as presumed (or background) social facts whose determination, when required, relied on individual identification, self-presentation, and lived experience.[44] Decertification, then, as a regulatory reform, should be seen not as introducing new acquisition methods so much as letting previous methods function without the threat of certificatory override. But what follows from "acquiring" gender (or sex) category membership more freely post-decertification? If we draw on concepts of property, we might ask whether such acquisitions can be meaningfully owned, and whether they can be shared, cultivated, destroyed, or given away. Do these possibilities make sense; and what would sex and gender be like for these possibilities to make sense? In my final discussion, I turn to consider more speculative possibilities of what gender could become. But first I want to consider these questions from a different angle. Decertification draws people's attention to the current regulatory system, whose taken-for-granted status is fractured by the proposal that it could (or should) be dismantled or withdrawn.[45] But what, if anything, is wrong with certification in helping to make, allocate, and use sex and gender categories?

For sex-realist critics, certification protects and helps those subjugated by male power rather than those privileged by it.[46] While a critical history of sex registration can be told, attentive to the place of sex-gender categorization within patriarchal propertied relations,[47] gender-critical activists, in particular, have come to tell a different story about what legal certification is for in their drive to legitimize, and so retain, its production and dominance. Emphasizing protective and facilitative uses, their arguments resonate with claims made about commercial certificatory processes where certification operates as a communicative device that tells users about the standards and quality of the identified product (or process).[48] In food contexts, for instance, certificates confirm that products meet required standards for health and safety, fair trade, religious acceptability, and organic status. In other contexts, certificatory processes confirm educational attainment, professional registration, the standard of residential care (a nursing home, for instance), geopolitical mining conditions, electoral integrity, and more. Certificates authorize authority; they denote the good standing of an official or professional, such as a nurse or police officer, at least in the view of the state. More generally, certification confirms or guarantees a standard, process, or substance, or that specific properties are present (the rituals required for kosher food, a strong undergraduate performance, a well-run school)—typically, when these qualities do not seem easily determined by users or consumers (see also Mutersbaugh 2005a, 2005b). This inability may be because nonspecialists cannot assess quality—where quality depends on a complex mix of factors, including professional judgment, or arises from a process that is not easily observable, such as the correct ritual blessing, use of non–genetically modified seeds, or decent labor conditions. By guaranteeing what something is or what it has been through, certificates encourage (even as they depend on) users' reliance and trust while often reinforcing and legitimizing the black-boxing of the process or assemblage that becomes certified.

In this way, certification processes avoid users' need to get up close. For critics of decertification, having a reliable birth record that confirms whether someone is (or is not) a woman means more intimate modes of scrutiny can be avoided, even as some critics contentiously claimed that women were very capable of determining a person's biological sex by looking and so didn't need to rely on certification: "As a non-medical person, it's pretty obvious to me who is a man and who is a woman. I don't see it as up for question, really. I know who I don't feel safe around and who I do feel safe around" (women's NGO manager, interview). Yet despite claims like this one, opponents of reform identified certification as essential for sex-specific activities, provision, data collection, and rights. Certification provided an agreed-on, authoritative classification that confirmed what someone was and so was able to trump counterclaims.[49] "Almost everything we now fight about—women's voice in politics and decision-making, . . . violence against women and girls, . . . the labor market, the care economy . . . rely on us having a definition of sex which is generally agreed, and which is based on a broad consensus. If we are not able to measure those things in that way, then all the things that we know about those indicators that I've just listed would be rendered invisible" (women's rights expert, interview). The importance of having a stable definition was also stressed by a senior member of a women's service organization who was concerned about how to draw the borders of category membership in conditions of decertification: "It's hard to see how . . . we could legally continue to offer women-only spaces, because anybody presumably could then say that they are entitled to access that space."

Yet despite frequently expressed concerns that decertification would lead to opportunistic entry and the unraveling of women's services, use of certification in practice remained unclear. Women-only spaces, such as domestic violence shelters, during the period researched did not standardly ask for birth certificates or for people to disclose their legal sex (Renz 2023). British data collection also relied, in practice, on self-identification, including in contexts where the sex asked for was ostensibly biological or legal (see chapter 1). Yet limited use of legal sex evidence did not discourage advocates of certification, who argued that it provided a much-needed normative background, confirming biological reality and making it available for public policy. A manager at a women's NGO remarked, "Sex is a biological material reality. I don't hold with the language that it's assigned at birth. I think it's *observed* at birth." Sex and gender did not exist *because of* certification; still, certification gave these categories certainty, clarity, and authority. Formalization through certification secured sex and gender, protecting them from becoming sites of repeated interrogation and uncertainty (see also Jessica Clarke 2015). As with forms of commercial certification, critics of reform argued that change would cause problems as well-defined, stable differences became muddied or overridden.

In researching decertification, we responded to these concerns, outlining how affirmative action and gender-specific services could work without assigned legal status.[50] Yet, in assessing whether certification is needed, a foundational issue concerns the relationship that certification has to acquiring category features and not just to communicating those features. Disagreement over whether sex is observed and recorded or, as sex-gender, constituted (and set in motion) through birth registration echoes similar tensions within commercial certification over the impact of certification on what is made. At first blush, commercial certification would seem to concern entities that exist independently of the labeling process. Yet research in different sectors has demonstrated that certification is intricately connected—more than that, *formatively* connected—with what is made, held, and used.[51] Certification processes establish and define value; they rearrange and consolidate hierarchies, including of access; and they affect demand by making certain goods more (or less) attractive.[52] Beyond this, certification processes also define and materially affect what things are, specifying and arranging the material cuts and joins required to become organic, fair trade, or kosher, for example, identifying certain qualities as essential and others as less so. But certification can also go a step further to form an integral part of what is made: Certification of a third-class British university degree is not simply information about a thing; it is an important and integral part of the thing.[53]

Critics of decertification, of course, recognize certificatory effects—indeed their argument for the continuation of certification depends on a positive reading of such effects to maintain the utility of sex categories while keeping opportunistic, fraudulent, and threatening male incursions into the category of woman at bay. However, they refuse to accept that this demonstrates certification's ontological contribution to making up sex-gender, that criteria for sex categories are contingent, or that there is a confluence or intra-active shaping of sex and gender categories from birth onward. For these critics, sex is quintessentially a world-to-mind relationship, where material forms should drive and determine representational categories (see chapter 1). Yet to suggest the relationship between certification and sex-gender is better described as a mind-to-world one instead—in which arbitrary certification *determines* the sex-gender category (sometimes implied by the claim that sex-gender is "assigned")—seems overly idealist. As work on certification and institutional categories suggests, the relationship between certification and what is certified is more evolving and entangled. Certifying sex is part of a lifelong process of making gender (as well as sex). This is about the gender-sex that individuals accrue over time and what it means to have a gender or sex thanks to how subjects, gender, and sex are regulated, guided, and disciplined, where regulation both gives rise to meanings and expresses them (Holzer 2019). Decertification, then, not only changes the method of sex-gender acquisition, it also fundamentally changes what is acquired, since the removal of legal status (or the shift from state designations to community ones as certification becomes decentralized) alters what sex-gender is, removing previously core qualities such as being inherently stable, naturally directed, and binary. More than this, decertification confronts the gender that society itself acquires within this economic dance. For in considering what the withdrawal of sex-gender certification does, we need to broaden our focus from matters of individual identity to matters of the social—not because society is allocated to a sex or gender category but because sex and gender certification are part of the productive conditions within which societies form.

In the next section, I turn to the question of gender's future and the speculative economic dances that take shape when gender's emancipation from state-assigned classifications is imagined. In conditions of state deregulation, different ways of acquiring gender and sex emerge, giving rise to different ways of *producing* sex and gender, since the meaning of what is produced—and so how it is produced—is guided (even driven) by modes of acquisition. (If gender category membership, for example, comes from *living* in a category, this tells us something significant about what gender entails.) State deregulation, as I have said, does not mean an absence of rules and norms. As discussions of certificatory processes attest, certification can be done by different bodies, and the withdrawal of state machinery from guaranteeing what someone (or something) is does not mean other bodies will refrain from (or be forbidden from) occupying this space.

Decertification may mean that multiple normative structures determine and regulate sex-gender category membership. In such conditions, sex-gender (or, more precisely, gender/sex or gender-sex-gender) starts to resemble other sectors where state withdrawal destandardizes what is produced, outputs become subject to localized manufacturing norms and processes, and labels become specific to their context. For instance, people may acquire different gender classifications in their temple, football club, school, and friendship circle. Here, not only do the categories to which people are assigned vary, but what the categories mean and how they are determined may vary as well. What the concept of economy highlights are the connections between these different localized processes. This may be because state (or transnational) law becomes compelled to recognize the category memberships created (or at least some of them); because the sectors giving rise to sex-gender categorizations are not easy to disentangle; or because divergent categorizations come into conflict. Yet what an economy of sex-gender also highlights are the dilemmas of responsibility that follow from, and track, how categories are made and acquired within different normative spaces. For instance, what responsibility does a conservative religious, lesbian feminist, nonbinary, or sports community have for how it creates gender category membership and the effects of such membership on other spaces? Questions of extended responsibility emerge within mainstream policy discussion when dangerous things are made and sold. Could the decentered regulation of gender-sex-gender and gender/sex in conditions of decertification contribute to such discussions—in terms of what responsibility means and entails for the things of life (including identities) that different bodies create and support?

Dancing Gender's Future

What might gender's future be in conditions of decertification? How will gender be made, acquired, held, and used, and what economic loops and relations do these processes suggest? While, of course, in one sense, future presents and what they will bring (or make) are unknowable, in another sense these questions speak to imagined speculations taking place now, as anticipated or hoped-for futures shape current politics. In this final discussion, two imaginaries of gender's economy postdecertification are sketched—one involving proliferation, the other termination—to explore three questions: What kinds of gender subjects and societies might be made? What is the place of use in this making? And can gender's production and use cease?

Identifying gender's hoped-for future, postdecertification, as one of proliferation locates decertification within a constellation of moves that seek to free gender identity and expression from the institutional grid of female and male, feminine and masculine (see also Cull 2024, 2). This is an economy where use shapes the genders made as, emancipated from law and other formal institutional constraints, gender names qualities of self-expression, pleasure, personal development, and social relatedness. Here, selves-in-community (and both self and community are crucial) develop gender as they work with, and through, the subjectivities available, replenishing and augmenting what exists. Imagined as a hoped-for future, this could be a form of gender commoning, where participants draw freely on openly available resources.[54] At the same time, moves to encourage proliferation may continue to lean toward gender as property, albeit now anchored in labor invested and what is necessary for subjects' well-being rather than formal assignment. Here, individuals hold property in and over their gender to determine, revise, share, and abandon it—in conditions where others are ethically obliged to recognize and support self-property's changing course.

An interviewee from a gender and sexuality NGO described this vision of gender diversity: "I think that, overall, people don't want a world where gender doesn't exist, but a world where gender maybe has less meaning . . . that there can be as many genders as there are people on this earth, and that each individual person's relation to that is individual but doesn't then come with any kind of negative things. Rather than removing [gender], just freeing it, and allowing it to be whatever it is without any major consequence." For this respondent, deinstitutionalizing gender's conditions of production, through measures like decertification, remakes what gender is. They continued, "Whether we would then interpret that as gender is a completely other thing." Gender is a name, but it also remains something more, something that exceeds the terms in which it is established, such that gender can outlast gender, or, perhaps more accurately, gender streams into (and becomes) something no longer recognizable as gender.[55] But what is this more or else? What does it mean to say, "There can be as many genders as there are people on this earth"? Does it suggest a kaleidoscope of gender colors—to take up the analogy used by Sandra Bem (1995, 334)? Here, gender might name an infinitely varying mix of colors or qualities, but what are these qualities when they are gendered qualities? Central to many feminists' concerns about celebrating gender's proliferation is the reliance placed on masculinity and femininity as meaningful terms, despite being pluralized and remixed. Anca Gheaus (2023, 34), for instance, writes, "We should hope that all talk about 'femininity' and 'masculinity,' whether 'toxic' or reformed, will cease, and be replaced by genderfree discussions about which behaviors and dispositions are likely to promote morally and prudentially good lives."

From the vantage point of proliferation, decertification constitutes a progressive form of denationalization in which the state divests itself of its role in determining sex-gender classifications and in holding sex-gender as an allocatable property.[56] With sex radically reorganized to signal multiple bodily forms based on contingent and severable features, or to simply indicate gender, gender (with or without sex) reverts to a cottage industry subject to local norms.[57] This does not mean the state withdraws, completely, from gender's production and use. Law and public bodies can support gender's proliferation (for instance, through arts-sector support), oversee or otherwise regulate how civil society organizations engage with gender and sex categories, and continue to address the harms (including violence, shame, discrimination, and exploitation) that gender inequality generates.

By contrast, gender's abolition involves state and legal power terminating or winding down gender's production as if it were a toxic or harmful sector akin to nuclear power or tobacco.[58] Shutting down gender is a difficult and ambitious project, with decertification, at most, one small contributing aspect. In part because gender is forged through multiple inter- and intraconnected processes, with different degrees of accessibility, cost, and complexity, it cannot be easily terminated. Abolitionist approaches—particularly those influenced by analytic philosophy—sometimes seem to imply that the key challenge is the compelling rational justification, with "implementation" taking place after successful arguments have been made and reasons given (see chapter 1; also discussion in Weltman 2024). Often, implementation seems little more than a mundane operational challenge. But the demotion and compartmentalization of implementation do a disservice to the material dimensions of gender. What it means to abolish (or eliminate) gender depends on what gender means, and this is materially structured and evolving. In addition to the multitude of sites and processes that contribute to gender's making, abolitionist projects need to also attend to how gender is used.

Gender seems forged through being used, unlike consumables, which get depleted or used up. Therefore, addressing gender's uses in care work, militarism, violence, sex, and more is paramount.[59] But if uses contribute to gender's making, this suggests that uses can also counter or thwart gender's production. In other words, from an abolitionist perspective, rather than focus on how gender is made, as if it were anterior to how gender is used, might a focus on gender's uses provide another, less attended-to entry point? One possibility here is reuse or diverted use, as witnessed in lesbian feminist communities where women's care work got directed toward other women rather than toward men. Another is the nonuse of refusal, epitomized in gender boycotts or strikes (typically through the withdrawal of women's domestic and sexual labor as women remove gendered services from men rather than by men boycotting women's gendered work or undertaking it themselves). A further application involves gender's depletion and wastage.[60] Here, decertification might align with gender uses that are "excremental (giving, spending, dispersing) rather than incremental (cumulating, accumulating and collecting)" (Linstead and Pullen 2006, 1303). In other words, there may be mileage from an abolitionist perspective in gender's overuse—or at least proliferation of non-institutional uses.[61] Zoe Belinsky (2019) suggests that gender might be expanded "to the limits of its mythological sphere of possibilities to the point at which gender ceases to be an operative term in the distribution of resources and labor, and instead becomes a merely aesthetic or 'personal' vector of identification." Gender's overuse, then, might give rise to overproduction—producing a proliferation of diverse identities that, in turn, could disrupt or "hack" existing relations of gender production (e.g., see Wang 2023).

Back in 1995, Bem wrote, "I propose that we let a thousand categories of sex/gender/desire begin to bloom in any and all fluid and permeable configurations and, through that very proliferation, that we thereby undo (or, if you prefer, that we de-privilege or de-center or de-stabilize) the privileged status of the two-and-only-two that are currently treated as normal and natural" (330).[62] Matthew Cull (2024, 169–70) explores a related point. Drawing on Belinsky, Cull considers whether gender might be overcome but not eradicated. Overcoming gender confronts its harmful contributions to land use, design, domestic and governmental life, militarism, work, and more; its unequal resourcing of social subjects; and its androcentrism, while avoiding the temptation to root out every gender expression and use, such as those anchored in dissident histories.

Approaching gender's future as an economic dance attends to gender's capacity to be used and made differently postdecertification. Leaving state control behind for more decentered forms of gender regulation invokes both utopic and dystopic imaginaries of what gender could become, where gender finds happy uses or, conversely, is freed up for harmful ones. This is an economic dance in which expressive pleasure and oppressive forms of injury and exploitation meet, and the tensions between them are palpable. Deproduction and proliferation in economic terms appear as competing moves—of winding down and winding up a sector. Yet what recent writings on gender pose is the possibility of winding down a sector by winding it up—or, at least, that the sector is radically changed through how it is wound up.

Concluding Remarks

Academic work routinely attends to the conceptual activism of others, both critically and positively. It also engages in conceptual activism, making new meanings and sometimes, reflexively, attending to what does or doesn't follow from them (see also chapters 1 and 2). Decertification of sex-gender is an example of the latter. Designing a speculative law to abolish legal sex provided a vantage point from which to explore the struggles between sex-realist and gender-(as)-diversity forces. It also offered a further arena for this struggle and—as a proposal that some observers feared might be introduced into law—proved an intervention in the conflict. As an abolitionist proposition, decertification provided material that sex realists could feed on and metabolize, further evidence (as they saw it) of the dangers and nonsense of gender-(as)-diversity (see introduction). Yet decertification was not just a hazardous legal proposition for present-day gender relations. Signaling a future beyond the narrow technicalities of amended legal status, decertification tied wider debates about gender-sex's proliferation and abolition to the question of what to do with its regulatory categories: how they should be made, used, acquired, allocated, and held. For some, this prompted new thoughtways directed to the expendability of legal sex and gender, while for others, allegiances to established legal category structures surfaced. Fundamentally, reengineering the concept of decertification brought the uses of certification to the fore, prompting questions, in turn, about legal status's importance to gender's production, distribution, acquisition, and use.

This chapter has focused on the imagined dimensions of conceptual activism—where the reorganization of meaning works through new speculative cuts and joins. But this reorganization also has a material dimension. Reimagining gender through an economy of decertification brings three different cases of conceptual materiality to the fore. In the first, decertification is an idea that gets materially manifested within a loosely mimetic legislative form—to provide an artifact for discussion and engagement. In the second case, decertification functions as an imagined mode of withdrawal from the material regulatory relations of sex registration that currently exist. In the third, existing social and legal practices of gender's diversification, diminution, and equalization are imaginatively stretched and extended. But what is going on when we speculate about how contested concepts could materialize? Within academic writing, the tendency to treat contestations as ideational means language, narrative, and discourse are often the terms through which disagreement is explored. However, the material, embodied, and affective character of the colliding, coforming projections discussed in this chapter makes dance more apt. In this discussion, I have kept dance *behind* the analysis to avoid the suspicious or skeptical search for recognizable dances—whether accomplished or imagined. And yet some dances slipped into the limelight, offering intricate and reactive steps as critics and advocates of decertification moved with and against each other (see also chapter 1). In the first dance, developing decertification as a speculative law reform proposal, attempts to prompt gender's regulatory rethinking were taken up in revised form by sex-realist critics to create a hostile object, sutured to wider moves to oppose governmental reforms to gender transitioning. In the second dance, of decertification as a regulatory move to withdraw status guarantees, critics countered the notion that it would liberate life choices, practices, and self-expression from legal classifications. Instead, they claimed, it was a regressive distributive move that would withdraw emancipatory and protective resources from women and impede the capacity of governmental and other agencies to allocate protective benefits and goods by sex. In the third dance, of gender diversity and flourishing in an imagined postdecertification landscape, critics objected to the notion that a revised form of gender would support personal well-being by individuals-in-community. Instead, they approached gender as a toxic output whose rightful elimination (as an illusory form or social inculcation) was being persistently undermined by an affirmative-oriented gender-scape.

In tracking these dances, it is important to attend to the dances and moves that did not happen, that happened without attention, or that were constantly eclipsed. Decertification did not come out of a structuralist mold, but it was academically crafted to foreground institutional and systemic gender processes (a form of craftivism, perhaps).[63] Yet in conditions where narratives of individual and class-based formation dominated wider discussion, this more structural orientation had little traction. Sex-realist and gender-(as)-diversity forces disagreed on how gender and sex were made, held, and used, and they disagreed, specifically, on the role certification played, and should play, in sex's and gender's becoming. But where they did agree was on the notion that gender or, for sex realists, sex was a quality belonging to subjects, whether as individuals, groups, or classes. When gender and sex were made or applied, it was people that this productive process centered, and when gender was refused, it was individuals who undertook this refusal in relation to their own lives (see also Cull 2024); as one interviewee remarked, "Gender doesn't exist for me. I don't see myself as anything. I don't really like those terms being used *about me*."[64]

Approaching gender and decertification through a trio of interconnected economic dances, I have sought to trouble this subject-centered presumption. While the making, allocation, and use of gender can address social subjects, economy's emphasis on process and circulation decenters the subject to foreground the movement of (and in) value, systems, procedures, and things. In the case of gender, this draws attention to the relationship between gender's social use and formation, forcing an interrogation of how gender is made, and how gender could and should be made if gender's uses radically changed. Economy also pays attention to different scales—to what multiple small-scale practices establish as well as the larger-scale practices and structures that give rise to them. In this way, it supports a more socially constellated conception of gender, recognizing that gender contributes to ongoing processes of societal formation and change, in capillary as well as larger-scale forms.

Extracting an economic conceptual imaginary, albeit for a reengineered concept of economy, from the experience of crafting decertification brings academic work on commercial practice, progressive and diverse economies, and economic change to gender's discussion. One economic feature to stand out here is acquisition—for it is this that decertification most directly targets. For critics, gender's acquisition was the wrong political focus given the exploitative and violent ways that sex is used (and gender is made). They argued that these uses and makings needed to change before the borders on who counts as a woman could be eased or abandoned. But processes of acquisition are not ulterior to how sex and gender are used and made, and they cannot be kept apart from them. Like other economic media whose production and use are fundamentally shaped by relations of acquisition, such as money, what sex-gender is takes shape from how its categories are allocated, gained, and held. Taking decertification for an economic dance brings these processes to the fore.

Economic imaginaries help to make sense of decertification, but what this chapter has also attended to is the way that this relationship can be reversed. Treating the making of speculative law reform, regulatory categories, and gender's future as matters of economy denaturalizes economy. It reminds us that the boundaries of what counts as economic are socially made, contingent, evolving, and subject to political projects and choices (see also Mitchell 2008).

In questioning taken-for-granted boundaries between economy and social politics or economy and administrative regulation, decertification shows how economy and its grammar can be reimagined.[65] Here, processes and practices of making, allocating, holding, and using gender, and the recursive links between them, come to the fore, as having and making gender categories fuse, separate, and spin together, and as use drives and shapes making. In this conceptual expansion of economy, the centrality of neoliberal market capitalism contracts, to become one economic logic within a conceptual world (or pluriverse) of others.

Capitalism is powerful and deeply harmful, but it cannot wipe out other logics and arrangements. These others have been extensively studied in recent years; however, the exploration of alternatives has largely revolved around things already commodified—even if they shouldn't be and aren't always—or around forms of labor that prop up capitalism directly or indirectly. If, however, commodification and capitalist labor support are no longer the basis for identifying and counting as economy, its terms can be used to explore other processes. For economy, here, is not about some goods rather than others, or centrally about work or wealth. Susana Narotzky and Niko Besnier (2014, S6) extend economy to encompass "sustaining life across generations"; similarly, care, solidarity, and affective labor are important features of economy within feminist and diverse economies writing. Extracting an imaginary of economy from decertification extends this conceptual trajectory to take in experimental academic processes and artifacts, regulatory categories, and social identities, to consider how they are made, acquired, held, used, and wasted—recognizing that this is as applicable to speculative law writing, gender, and its regulatory categories as it is to houses, financial instruments, and tobacco. In the process, a conceptual interplay takes shape between governmental and commercial processes that are typically held apart even when they draw on similar devices, such as certification. This interplay supports conceptual activism when it comes to the regulation of sex and gender. It also supports conceptual activism around other economic relations, not least because of the different economic rationalities that decertification brings to the fore as a speculative proposal, regulatory reform, and new gender (or degendered) future. These rationalities include plural, collaborative, and accountable relations of making, commoning and gifting, dispersed ownership rights, and responsible and creative uses (and disuses). But at their heart, they are about *what* is made, acquired, held, and used—a normative and political issue that can sometimes get lost in discussions about whether economies should grow or shrink or in the attention paid (and rightly paid) to how economic goods are made and acquired.

In the chapter that follows, I leave the conceptual activism of academics and turn to that of policy actors engaged in reparative gender work. This shifts the materiality of conceptual activism from the depiction of a speculative legal idea and proposal, aimed at undoing an existing hegemonic regime and supporting (and extending) counterhegemonic tendencies, to practical efforts to recognize and bed in newly emerging gender norms through the policies and service provision of public bodies. In exploring what such bodies bring to the realization of conceptual activism, I also attend to the concept of activism, something that has remained pending in the discussion so far. What does it mean to say that policy bodies are doing activism? And can this public register of engagement, with its care-full attention toward competing and antagonistic interests, help us to reimagine what it could mean to do activism more generally?

4

Common Sense and Facing Both Ways

When Public Bodies Do Activism

When you're trying to do something which is not being done elsewhere, there's a risk. . . . If there's a risk of even having a conversation, the risk of then doing something is like ten times more. And, yeah, and then the legislation . . . the caselaw . . . it's evolving a lot and going into spaces that it hasn't gone into before, so it's really easy to misstep, and it's really hard to know what the right thing is to do. . . . And nobody wants to be that caselaw example; even if you win, nobody wants to do it. —CITY OFFICIAL, interview

We always know that we're doing the right thing if we're seen as a bit mad and bad. —CITY OFFICIAL, interview

On May 9, 1986, my first year as an undergraduate law student was almost over when I turned up for the morning's administrative law lecture, tired from a late night at the municipal count. By a handful of votes, I had been elected to Haringey Council, a municipal authority in North London, and home to about

200,000 people. I was part of an intake of new councillors prepared to develop and implement a governing program at odds with the deeply controversial Conservative agenda of Prime Minister Margaret Thatcher's government. Having abolished the metropolitan authorities and Greater London Council shortly before the 1986 council elections, central government faced municipal districts like Haringey without any midlevel authorities to moderate the conflict between them.[1] Thus, the mid-1980s saw a loose network of urban councils in a state of intergovernmental combat as they resisted central government's authoritarian, financially stringent privatization agenda, while simultaneously developing progressive initiatives to advance equality, diversity, alternative economics, participatory democracy, environmentalism, and internationalism.[2] But as Haringey and other councils developed leftist agendas, they found themselves increasingly under siege. Rightist local and national forces constellated, mobilizing against what they characterized as "the loony left." In Haringey's case, antiracist, antisexist, and pro-gay policies became primary targets. Opponents and tabloid newspapers declared that the council had banned the words "manhole covers" and "black binbags" on equality grounds and was promoting lesbian and gay "positive images" to schools, children, and parents. Before long, and with Haringey one of its main targets, section 28 of the Local Government Act 1988 was born, a legislative provision introduced by central government to prohibit local authorities from "intentionally" "promoting homosexuality" or promoting in schools its "acceptability" as a "pretended family relationship."

I wrote about the experience and precarity of left municipal government in *Sexing the City* (Cooper 1994). Inspired by the possibility that municipal state apparatuses could be temporarily captured by counterhegemonic forces, I wanted to consider what short-lived, progressive municipal states might do. For councils, like Haringey, this was an activist state in direct conflict with superordinate central government apparatuses, willing to consider breaking the law (or at least certain laws), and equivocal about staying within the bounds of hegemonic common sense.[3] Despite being part of a formal state infrastructure, Haringey, like other left councils of this time, conformed to an image of heroic activism—defiant, brave, and ready to fight; its target, in the 1980s, being another state activist project, one that was neoconservative and neoliberal (e.g., see Durham 1991). Today, forty years later, rightist state activism is again at the fore globally (in some places, it never went away), as authoritarian governments use their powers to advance conservative agendas hostile to social and ecological justice in the face of local, regional, and sometimes legislative and judicial objections.

This chapter, however, addresses a different kind of institutional activism, in place in Britain between 2018 and 2025. Progressive but also low-key, this variant is less easily or readily recognized as defiant or brave. Some may argue that this style of activism is part of a wider cultural shift in how public bodies do progressive politics—from oppositional to more accommodationist forms. This discussion remains open on this point. My aim, rather, is to identify the presence and importance of quieter forms of activism, able to operate under the radar thanks to the governance techniques they deployed: of common sense and facing in different directions (which, in this discussion, boils down to facing in two opposing directions). While reliance on common sense foregrounds the rationalizations used to establish new norms and understandings, facing in different ways comes into play when the development of a sense that can be held in common fails. This bifocal (or multifocal) attention is not something that always happens, but it is a technique of governance that I want to consider as a way of doing activism. Against assumptions that activism necessarily attends to one set of concerns exclusively, I want to consider an account of activism with a wider gaze. This does not mean being neutral or not taking a position. But it does involve a complicated relationship with the competing positions that public bodies confront. In considering how taking a position can combine with a stewardly attention toward others, I draw on the concept of "care-fullness," used by scholars to identify an attentive responsibility to the well-being of others (which here includes organizational members, communities, and other forms of life).[4]

What can we learn about activism from how public bodies take up common sense and care-fullness? I use "public bodies" here to include local government, trade unions, regulatory bodies, and umbrella nongovernmental organizations (NGOs). Legally, and in terms of their remit and role, these are very different kinds of entities. However, they are grouped together here because of what they share. In general terms, what is common to the different bodies discussed is their noncommercial accountability and responsibility to a constituency that is too large to personally know. More specifically, for contemporary gender politics during this period, what they also shared was an orientation toward gender realism: in supporting trans minorities, accepting self-identification, in separating gender from sexed embodiment, and in the governance techniques these bodies used to develop such policies in the face of resistance from sex-realist opponents. These governmental ways of imagining and enacting gender can be read as soft decertification (see chapter 3). But it is important to state from the outset that soft decertification was not ubiquitous among British public bodies. Many remained disengaged from gender-(as)-diversity politics, retaining hitherto unquestioned understandings of gender as binary, sexed, and presumptively stable. Even among organizations actively developing a different approach, considerable unevenness existed, while the balance in conceptual leaning (toward gender or sex realism) often fluctuated over time. Nevertheless, between 2018 and 2025, a new gender agenda found a home among a selection of public bodies.[5]

This new agenda involved material forms of policy practice: access to single-sex services, funding decisions, which local publics to explicitly hail in job ads, pregnancy initiatives, and more.[6] These policy choices were not the result of laws or directives from superordinate bodies—central government, for instance, directing local councils on how to act—but developed as public bodies responded to the interests, agendas, and anxieties of members, whether as trade unionists, local electorates, or funding recipients.[7] During this period, public bodies sought to remain, at least ostensibly, within their legal powers and responsibilities. However, as central government moved rightward, as sex-based rights gained legal and popular salience, and as what was deemed legal changed, this was not always possible.[8]

This chapter explores how public bodies responded to the gender-critical challenge in the years before the Supreme Court decision in *For Women Scotland Ltd*, which defined sex for equality law purposes as biological sex—or "the sex of a person at birth."[9] During this period, public policy practice was an important arena where conflict over concepts of sex and gender took place. It was also an arena in which uncomfortable attachments to the objected-to conceptual activism of others surfaced.[10] It is tempting to think of conceptual activism as hopeful and positive—advancing meanings that prefigure sought-after ways of living. But as my earlier discussion details, conceptual activism can also involve other kinds of relationships to the meanings being developed. This may involve exposing the damaging meanings associated with benign concepts. It may involve using opposed meanings to advance a political agenda, as critics did with decertification (see chapter 3). And it may involve assuming or being compelled to take responsibility for the (objected-to) conceptual activism of others, as this chapter discusses. During this period, gender-critical workers brought a series of employment law cases, claiming that organizational employers were in breach of their duties by harassing and discriminating against staff who manifested gender-critical beliefs—for instance in their statements at meetings, research, employee networks, social media posts, letters, and signed petitions.[11] Engaging "responsibly" as an employer or organization with objected-to concepts that hang around, and that expose themselves in undesirable forms of display, is a form of conceptual activism that reorganizes how meanings materialize. Yet understanding responsibility in these terms also brings the concept of activism into relief. So far, this book has focused on the conceptual, with activism left hanging. This chapter rescues activism from such dangling. At the same time, approaching activism from the vantage point of public bodies engaged in quieter, slower, more care-full forms of activism through their policy practice takes the concept in less familiar contentious directions.

Reimagining Activism

In recent years there has been growing interest in conceptually reengineering activism, to take it beyond the adversarial, attention-grabbing initiatives to embrace intimate, everyday quiet-seeming action.[12] Manuel Tironi (2018, 439) describes intimate activisms as lying "at the intersections of passiveness and action, coping and contesting, reclusion and mobilization and feeling and knowing[,] . . . a mode of acting and thinking that brings into relief mundane yet purposeful doings," which Tironi describes as "hypo-interventions." Yet whether activism seems loud or quiet, its association with ambitious change *pursued by forces who lack the capacity to accomplish their goals* has led activism (at least within everyday understandings) to appear antithetical to what public bodies do.[13] Communities do activism; public bodies do law and policy—modes of governing that can confidently realize (or at least advance) what they seek.[14] Yet, depending on what public bodies want to accomplish, successful achievement through policies, service provision, and even laws may falter. This is especially evident, as the 1980s municipal left moment showed, when public bodies reach beyond their conventional remit and brief, as happened then, to advance socioeconomic equality, sustainable environments, fair trading, animal justice, peace, antiracism, and more. The calculated resistance shown in response by others—including national politicians, ministerial departments, regulatory agencies, firms, lobbying groups, and religious organizations—is one kind of impediment. But resistance can also be more subtle or indirect, taking effect through obstructive laws, insufficient funds, or an inability to leverage or compel other bodies to act (see chapter 1).[15]

Ineffectiveness in pursuing left agendas is often used to demonstrate why public bodies aren't activist but are instead watering-down machines.[16] This skepticism and critical attention is important (e.g., Phipps 2025; Swain 2025). But there are also good reasons to conceptually reengineer activism so that it is not defined by the bodies that undertake it or the style of its undertaking. Activism is often equated with resistance—both are seen as attempts to oppose dominant exercises of power and to institute change. However, this book approaches activism as deliberate or purposeful sociopolitical action *in the face of resistance*. With resistance integral to defining action as activism, public bodies can be understood to engage in activism when, faced with processes and forces that rein in, slow down, or divert what is happening, they participate in projects for change or, conversely, seek to maintain current arrangements against change.[17] Public bodies' activism may be left- or right-facing, but in both cases what activism reveals is a readiness to confront and counter emerging, declining, or stable sociopolitical projects—whether the project be democratic welfare-statehood, sex realism, liberal diversity, conservative authoritarianism, or something else.

I have deliberately adopted a broad definition of activism to counter two divisions endemic to activism's framing; their countering is important for the discussion that follows. The first is the premise that the state is subject to a clear material and imagined boundary that distinguishes it from nonstate entities.[18] While this chapter is not only about state activism, attending to it, alongside activism by other public bodies, blurs the definitional and empirical boundaries between state and nonstate.[19] It also makes room for state formations to radically vary, be internally heterogeneous, and share policy frames and modes of operating with other kinds of bodies (as in how they approach equality or gender). Activist agendas are often undertaken by elements within a state apparatus who are officially or informally networked with other bodies, including grassroots civil society actors. In such conditions, one state part may support an agenda against or in disregard of other state parts. Such activism may involve the national executive, for instance, promoting international and extranational policies, but examples closer to my discussion include municipal initiatives to advance sanctuary city projects, lesbian and gay equality, nuclear-free zones, and boycotts of Israel. These initiatives are often complicated by divisions and disagreement within the local government bodies themselves.[20] However, what they reveal is that when it comes to public bodies' activism, divisions between state and nonstate entities may not be the primary cleavage at stake.

The second assumption I want to counter, common also to conventional accounts of activism, splits activism from nonactivism in ways that equate activism with a certain ethos or style of being. Reimagining activism as something that public bodies also do prompts questions about how activism can and should be done, countering the prevailing aesthetic and normative imaginary of what an activist is and is like (see also Bobel 2007). Bringing contemporary public bodies into a discussion of activism tugs against a heroic, individualized, combative ideal, which, in a British context, is too often conjured around an independent, purposeful, confident figure that is also implicitly male, young, and able-bodied. By exposing, all too clearly, the limits, flaws, and compromises that run through political projects, public bodies' activism brings into relief and also, importantly, troubles an impossible standard of unwavering heroic ideals. Instead, it orients activism toward something cloudy and impure that can be, as I go on to discuss, hesitant, equivocal, and care-full—even intimate—given the vulnerability and hurt that staff doing activism, including gender activism, experience (see also S. Hunter 2015).

Approaching activism from the vantage point of public bodies engaged in policy practice reorients what activism entails. It recognizes activism as something done across very different contexts by very different kinds of bodies working with diverse cultures, powers, technologies, constraints, and relations of accountability. Public bodies, for instance, have access to a kit of resources and political techniques typically unavailable to grassroots social movements.[21] This allows them to operationalize new imaginaries, and so do conceptual activism, including gender-based conceptual activism, in ways that other kinds of bodies cannot. One city official interviewed described practice as "the best way that you bring about change. . . . You have to *show* people what the alternative way of doing something is." In relation to gender, public bodies did not mainly *advocate* for new meanings to emerge—claiming, for instance, that life would be better if we were all nonbinary or genderless. Rather, what public bodies did was work with, and select from, conceptual categories and meanings that had already emerged. In tacitly exercising choice over which categories and meanings to recognize and respond to (while presenting the situation as one driven by policy, law, or community demographics, and so lacking choice), and in the finely tuned ways that new gender identity categories were discursively represented and materially acknowledged, public bodies presented the present as already different.

At the same time, public bodies faced distinct challenges in undertaking activism thanks to their representational status. As one city official observed, "As a public organization, yes, we have more power, we have material power to do certain things." At the same time, describing the difficulty of operationalizing transpositive approaches to violence, she continued, "But we have to . . . it's almost that we have to be led there by our community stakeholders because if we're suddenly putting out a position that they don't agree with, it's really hard for us to get them on board." Rather than approach activism as a stock register of action done by a specific kind of actor or actors in relation to a subject and target, activism here becomes something that moves between actors, changing as it flows, as political rationalities and resources circulate between differently situated bodies.

In the rest of this chapter, I explore how public bodies undertook gender-based conceptual activism, drawing on two sets of research interviews with staff carrying an equality brief based in NGOs, trade unions, regulatory bodies, and local governments in England and Wales. One set of about seventy interviews was conducted as part of the Future of Legal Gender Project between 2018 and 2021 (see chapter 3); a further twelve interviews (including a few repeat interviews with earlier participants) took place in 2023 and 2024.[22] To explore conceptual activism over sex and gender, my discussion starts with common sense as something to both develop and rely on. I then consider how, when common sense fails to establish common thinking, conceptual activism by public bodies may require the advancement of preferred meanings to be accompanied by techniques to manage division and dissent. This management role necessitates care-full attention toward divergent agendas, including hostile ones. The chapter explores how care-full attention, attuned to values of care, responsibility, and enablement, involves practices of balancing and mediating, as governance techniques are sometimes used to explicitly recognize disagreement, and sometimes to defuse or circumvent it. But care-fullness can also include other kinds of policy practice, including critical forms of attachment, where objected-to meanings and their manifestation are treated as belonging to the public body concerned and not just to those advocating for them. In closing, I turn to slow activism as a register of activism that more easily and fully incorporates public bodies' practical and care-full work.

Advancing a New Common Sense

We are looking at our systems, in terms of payroll, our recruitment system, and we are looking at gender-neutralizing those. We have introduced an Mx option on the recruitment portal. . . . We have got obviously a toilet for those who are disabled, but we are just thinking, could we do signage to make it gender neutral. How can we balance the reaction of our organization as well because there might be some people who . . . really, really, want to hold on to . . . their gender. . . . We are also looking at redrafting our family leave policies and making sure we avoid gender language. We are trying—well we haven't done this yet, but we are in the process, I am in the process . . . looking at using things like "main carer" and "partner parent" instead of mother, father, and things like that. —LOCAL GOVERNMENT HR OFFICIAL, interview

Conceptual activism by public bodies involves reparative policy practice. Central to the rationale for reimagining what gender and its categories entail is the hope that these reimagined meanings will create new remedial currents in public services, data collection, and the arts that, in turn, will positively change the experiences of users, staff, and others (see chapter 2). But policy practice does not simply reside downstream from new conceptual imaginaries; it also prompts, guides, and shapes how reparative categories are imagined. Approaching this relationship as dynamic and recursive, I want to begin with the specific place of common sense. This is not something that simply and flatly exists. Common sense is better understood as a sedimentary mix of connected (but also unconnected) elements—made, allocated, acquired, held, and used in an economy of common sense (akin to the gender economies discussed in chapter 3). Establishing a new common sense is central to many radical projects because commonsense status naturalizes and legitimizes what has been brought into being.

Consequently, public bodies tend to act as if the commonsense qualities of their policies were already in place—adopting a form of conceptual prefiguration (see introduction) as they develop measures that treat the sought-after meanings as already valid. For instance, interviewees described how new meanings could be baked into services and policy initiatives for sex and gender, by amending the categories used in job advertisements or signage on toilets and changing rooms—a city official remarked, "not making assumptions about people's gender and using gender-neutral language when their gender's unknown to you."

Deliberately remaking common sense, however, is challenging.[23] Academic conceptual engineers have grappled with the philosophical challenges in revising meaning (see chapter 1). When the task is undertaken by public bodies, other difficulties arise as one common sense is set up against another, and as institutional powers are used to withhold or pull back on new meanings acquiring common- or good-sense status. Common sense is contested terrain. But in tracing the struggle to develop and shape it, commonsense rationalities—tied to legitimate and proper public policymaking—come to the fore, as they get mobilized to build a new substantive common sense. For gender realism, one rationality here was the demographic concept of "what exists." This proved central to the approach taken by equality governance staff toward nonbinary subjects, gender diversity, self-identity, and the separation of sex from gender—where what *was* constituted an empirical reality that, correctly defined, it would be wrong to ignore.[24] Simplicity and practicality, rather than abstraction and complexity, here formed key aspects, echoing Clifford Geertz's (2000, 89) claim that with common sense, "the really important facts of life lie scattered openly along its surface, not cunningly secreted in its depths." A trade union official described her union's commonsense approach to the category "woman" as follows: "So, we don't have . . . a complicated theoretical exposition what a man is, what their issues are, what a woman is, what their issues are. . . . Because they self-define, they are women. And we deal with all the issues related to them being a woman in the workplace and in wider society. . . . Does that make sense?" Common sense, here, does not start with how a category is defined as an abstract political challenge, but with the interests of members anchored in the categories they deploy. For a union, common sense means attending to the harms that members self-identify as having encountered.

Need and experience were also identified by staff as commonsense rationalities in reshaping policy practice. One city official described the importance of being "responsive to [community] needs"; another described the importance of experience, particularly for effective communication: "Across diversity and inclusion, where I've seen to have the most engagement, . . . it's where I'm bringing a story and I'm showing where people can identify with that person." A striking feature of interviews was the unstated assumption that, when it came to shaping policy, needs and experience were superior to opinion. Viewpoints could be protected in terms of freedom of expression; however, the belief that society would be better off without gender, for example, did not carry the same legitimacy in bankrolling policy practice (or being taken up in narrative) as experiences of hardship, say, from having a nonconforming gender identity. While some beliefs about another person's gender (or sex) have become legally recognized and protected under the heading of "philosophical belief" in British equality law,[25] public officials I talked with did not treat such beliefs as carrying the same moral weight as people's beliefs about their own gender (see also Renz and Cooper 2022). An ex–council officer made this point, criticizing local and national government for saying how people should live: "Commonsense surely is about live and let live, you know."

Commonsense status protected the conceptual activism of public bodies and their staff as they developed policies, initiatives, and service provision according to the principles and values of gender diversity. Here, the productive relations and processes that made someone into a woman, man, or other identity category were resolutely black-boxed—deemed not only irrelevant but also intrusive (and sometimes illegal) when they entailed inquiry about individuals' sexed trajectories. Yet while commonsense techniques were used to forge new commonsense understandings of gender, the edges of this formation proved vulnerable. Agender (or genderlessness) largely remained an unacknowledged category in early twenty-first-century Britain. It was nonbinary that occupied the outer edge of a—then emerging—common sense. It was also nonbinary that proved vulnerable, during this period, to dismissal from a counter–common sense anchored in binary, immutable sex. As a result, those who wanted to keep nonbinary as a recognized gender category remained vigilant about its importance and relevance. One city official commented, "If we didn't say nonbinary, there would be a whole load of people in [our city] that don't exist. Literally don't exist."[26] Similar vulnerabilities were described for other aspects of gender-(as)-diversity's emerging common sense. A senior manager in an equality charity described the response her organization had faced from focusing on gender rather than sex, and from treating gender as a spectrum rather than a binary category:

> The backlash was: this program is now meaningless because you're not thinking about females anymore and you've made it all nonsensical. And I suppose our first reaction was just to ignore that. And then the challenge became more legal, and how were we using data. . . . And so, we still have a

principle of recognizing gender as a spectrum, but the reality of implementing that has become messy and clunky and I think confusing for our members, and at times confusing for us in terms of, like, "What is the law?" So yeah, I mean we're not legal experts and it got quite legalistic quite quickly.

As this interviewee describes, the depiction of gender as a spectrum got attacked as nonsense (nonsense as rubbish rather than unintelligible, but perhaps that also), and as making a pro-woman brief meaningless since, if gender were a spectrum, categories like woman and man would become matters of degree (like dusk or dawn) rather than bounded and determinate.[27] What it also shows, though, is how attacks on a new, emerging common sense may sometimes be disregarded by policy designers or elicit relaxed bemusement until coercive forms of authority, such as law, are called on. In this conflict over gender categories, the status of law as a taken-for-granted determinant of policy practice became increasingly visible and authoritative (see also Emerton 2023). One city official said, "We're very much led by whatever is the law and legislation around gender, to be perfectly honest." Another remarked, "We've always got in the back of our minds legal challenge." If gender-as-spectrum identifies an imaginary that some staff attempted to bake into policy practice to generate new conceptual currents, the reassertion of legal sex formed, in the terms introduced in chapter 2, obstructive fighter cells whose successful growth and institutionalization might protect gender-critical countercurrents. She went on, "Who wants to invite that sort of tidal wave?"

In such volatile and precarious conditions, convergence with other bodies around norms of "best practice" proved an important security tactic. Following best practice, being attentive to what other public bodies do, has long been a commonsense principle of safe and active governance, including in conditions where "best practice" is taken to reflect and, also, secure new commonsense norms (see also Beckert 2010).[28] But "best practice" can impose brakes. An officer in a third sector organization described how their organization "couldn't reinvent the wheel. We have to go with what's best practice, and what's out there, and what's understood as far as it is understood." Common sense is about learning from other organizations rather than going out on a limb. But it is also about not abdicating one's judgment, particularly when the body giving advice becomes framed as contentious, and so no longer a consensual figure of "best practice" authority. In such conditions, common sense may involve defensive retrenchment or a wary refusal to act, as a city official described:

I think we do take a real commonsense perspective on [external advice organization]. . . . We treat them as . . . an external information source, the same way that we do anyone else. We don't rely on them. We consult a range of people, but . . . we make our own judgement as to whether we feel their advice is valid or not, and whether they're a stakeholder we want to engage with. . . . We're not changing our relationship with them based on public scrutiny and pressure. . . . I do think we take a commonsense approach of what is best for us and what is best for our citizens when we're challenged on these things, and what's our view on whether [the external advice organization has] acted appropriately or whether their advice is worth seeking, or are we over-relying on them, you know, that kind of thing.

As this response illustrates, common sense is a far from strainless governance technique given counterclaims about what common sense entails. I also do not want to romanticize it. Common sense inhibits as well as inhabits progressive conceptual activist practices, hierarchizing, dichotomizing, stigmatizing, and devaluing what gets deposited (or left) outside its realm. As an onto-epistemic quality that works, like everydayness, by masking itself, while banishing much of what isn't itself, common sense establishes a narrow realm of possibilities as intelligible and viable. Like claims to be "self-evident" (which treat appearance as its own evidence), common sense generates, as Geertz (2000, 85) describes, "an air of 'of-courseness,' a sense of 'it figures' . . . as inherent in the situation, intrinsic aspects of reality, the way things go." Geertz (75) writes, "It is an inherent characteristic of common-sense thought . . . to affirm that its tenets are immediate deliverances of experience, not deliberated reflections upon it." Common sense suggests sense has been determined by sensing, while foreclosing the extent to which sensing depends on the contingent production of sense (see also Bey 2022, 95). The dilemmas this produces were identified by a union official in relation to trans policies, where commonsense expectations of inclusion, based on experience and social justice, were upended by the presence of a proliferating sex-realist countersense: "I've just issued last week the actual trans inclusion statement, and I was expecting an influx in my inbox. . . . It's been febrile to be honest. *And so, then you, sort of, think 'Is this commonsense?' It feels like people are saying it isn't, and it feels to me like it absolutely should be*, and that's what the union policy should be as well" (emphasis added).

The capacity of public bodies to materialize new meanings in ways that help them to become commonsense is an important quality that public bodies bring to conceptual activism. Here, new controversial meanings are normalized as the (intended-to-be) unstated assumptions guiding and inhabiting what is practically and governmentally done. Developing a new or alternative common sense—producing a sense that is held in common—is central to hegemonizing social justice norms and practices, institutionally prefiguring them as already present. Yet for those actors engaged in developing a new or revised gender common sense, its edges proved only too apparent—whether as edges they were moving toward (as I have described) or edges that were moving toward them as critics recoded emerging gender norms as foolish and controversial ambitions. In such contexts, protecting and resourcing new gender meanings' materialization depended (or was seen to depend) on effective commonsense techniques that could hold opposition at bay, including by deploying normative rationalities of experience, harm, presence, need, and best practice. Yet while these techniques may have seemed uncontentious when framed as rationales to secure a new emerging gender common sense, they were not as resilient and protective as users had hoped (or assumed). As a result, new meanings were vulnerable to exposure as well as to ridicule and attack, thanks to opponents' powerfully resourced counterclaims. Critics of gender-(as)-diversity drew heavily on their own posited common sense, as a sword to attack and demean initiatives that validated trans and other gender-nonconforming subjects, and as a shield to protect their own sex realism. In such conditions, public bodies faced a major challenge: how to enact gender-(as)-diversity while attending to its opposition, as I now explore.

Paying Care-full Attention

Common sense relies on (produced) agreement—whether conscious or otherwise—to shared understandings and ways of sensing the world. It is common sense that putting a finger in a flame will hurt. But when it comes to public bodies advancing new understandings, agreement is often absent. Then, other expectations come to the fore, including the expectation that public bodies, because they are public bodies, act fairly. But what does this mean? Fairness is often equated with being impartial, not favoring a side.[29] Yet this can be in tension with public bodies' role in developing policy, especially when policy development involves manifesting meanings that are controversial or resisted.[30] How can public bodies engage in conceptual activism, manifesting new meanings, while remaining impartial or fair?[31] Public bodies, as the term is used here, have different formal obligations in relation to impartiality; however, this discussion focuses on what they broadly share to explore how they approached care-fullness and looking both ways, while also advancing gender-(as)-diversity policies. At the heart of my discussion is the claim that the responsibility to face in different directions can contribute something distinctive to activism.[32]

Staff interviewed in public bodies repeatedly referred to their obligation to attend to competing concerns and interests. One local government official told me, "It is difficult because we have got a community where we have everything from the most socially conservative . . . [religious] communities, who impose very strict segregation on the basis of sex, right through to very socially liberal communities, a very large LGBTQ+, very large trans, nonbinary communities as well. So, *as a local authority, we are duty bound to provide services to everybody and meet everybody's needs*" (emphasis added). For some interviewees, as for this one, regard for their organization's distinct public role, here as a local authority, justified their vigilance toward different perspectives. A senior manager in an NGO similarly described how public funding required the organization to be "balanced . . . understanding both sides of the argument," meaning that they couldn't "be seen to be condoning or condemning either way." A local government officer explained how they could not degender their public restrooms since their governmental remit tied them to the "whole community" as an imagined formation to steward. "Some people will say to us, well, there is a theatre called . . . , they've got gender-neutral toilets, why don't we have? We are not a theatre; we have to cater for the whole community. We are a council . . . . We do have to strike a balance. We don't want to just sort of pander to the most conservative . . . but at the same time, we are serving the whole community."

Does "serving the whole community," in conditions of conflict, necessitate a level terrain where opposing positions receive equal attention and care? This interpretation was explicitly rejected by some interviewees, who stressed how evenhandedness could combine with an asymmetrical approach in conditions of inequality. One city official commented, "I would say we're neutral but we have an equity focus, so we're not . . . just talking about equality and people having access to the same things, there's a recognition where there's a power imbalance, there's a recognition where there's more discrimination, there's a recognition where there's structural inequality in society, and then we do try and rebalance that by having more of a focus on particular populations, individual demographics, communities, groups, etc. But that still doesn't mean that we're not being neutral." What neutral means in this extract is a little unclear, but what I think the interviewee is indicating is a refusal to exercise preference, to be partisan, as if one side were a favored team. Interviewees described the obligation on them to listen to different constituencies, including in ways that recognized flux and contestations around who was disadvantaged and which disadvantages to recognize. In the discussion that follows, I explore how public bodies managed these complicated moves as a responsibility to be care-full, and how this got mobilized in gender-based conceptual activism.

I approach being care-full as a "heteronymous" form of conceptual engineering that refashions careful in ways that rebalance it, drawing out meanings associated with responsible and ethical caring, and attention toward other needs, rather than the cautious conduct that the term careful conveys.[33] The city official just quoted went on, "[It's] being honest and transparent about the choices you're making and being as balanced as you can be." In the context of gender politics, justice can be understood as carrying an obligation of care toward those articulating views that the public body does not support. A union official commented, "We tread a careful line between protecting the right of people to self-identify and the right of people to have their personal beliefs respected. And we're also very clear that nobody should be harassed, nobody should be treated unkindly for what they have to say."[34] A city official described their ongoing efforts to find a "balance" when faced with staff complaints "asking for women to specifically be referenced" at a "menopause training" that used "very inclusive language . . . so I think we're always finding that balance."

Phrases such as "balance," "careful line," or "at the expense of" can imply a zero-sum account of gender interests, agendas, and "institutional logics" (Reay and Hinings 2009), placing binary sex-first advocates in a standoff with proponents of gender-(as)-diversity—where more resources and recognition for one "side" means less for the other. One city official observed, "People are very ready to say that [trans people] don't exist and that they don't have any rights and that any rights for them—it's a zero-sum game—is a removal of rights for women." This account of the threat posed to women echoes the sex nativism running through strains of gender-critical politics (see also introduction). But while some equality staff echoed a competing-interests formulation, others rejected it. The city official describing the menopause training remarked, "We're trying to put in both sets of terminology as much as we can. I think we've learnt that lesson that there's an expectation that everyone wants to see themselves in [the terminology], which is fine." A staff member from a Welsh NGO similarly commented in interview, "Having options that are beyond male and female does not dilute the option of being a woman or female identity, which is one of the arguments we keep getting from people that, by adding others, we are overlooking the systemic oppression against women. But woman is still an option. We have pushed back on that with the: no, it is entirely still there. It's just we've added others."

I want to turn shortly to some of the practical methods that public bodies used to avoid a zero-sum formulation and the attendant anxiety that this way of framing sex and gender concepts generates. Yet, whether presented as zero-sum or not, a striking refrain during interviews was a felt public responsibility to be attentive, to act as "civic mediators," and to build bridges. One equality officer remarked, "I think it's just being sensitive that you can meet your legal duties and promote all the values that I have mentioned in a way that tries to bring people along with you and not alienate certain aspects of communities unnecessarily." Seeking to balance competing claims can seem the death knell for activism, compelled to accommodate and bridge too many competing political positions for a coherent perspective and direction to emerge. I want to suggest, instead, that the care-full approach that public officials described invoked a distinctive form of activism. While it included "looking both ways," it married this bicentric attention to governance techniques of vagueness, compartmentalization, upstream reframing, and inductive reasoning to dampen conflict and enable new meanings to be taken up and adopted in governing and public provisioning.

Keeping categories vaguely defined gives public bodies ways of doing conceptual activism that bracket the assumption that such activism necessarily requires clarity and precision—whether in developing new meanings, enacting them, or recategorizing what is "out there." While terminology guides and definitions, including for terms deemed unfamiliar like transgender, cis, and nonbinary, proliferated in public bodies' gender work, staff also described the value in not pinning terms down. Vagueness was identified as conceptually necessary and practically helpful when core terms held incompatible meanings, had indistinct edges, referenced categories with contested membership criteria, and changed over time.[35] A trade union official described how "being very vague in our policy specification" might lead to accusations of "dodging" but was helpful in "navigat[ing] tricky waters by being as broad as we can and as inclusive as we can." A city official said, "In my day-to-day work I actively will tell my team not to fixate on terms, for me not only because terms are contested, they change. . . . What I've seen in my work over the years, particularly on inequalities, is it tends to be more alienating than it is effective."[36]

Contextual specificity and organizational divisions also helped public bodies undertake conceptual activism in ways that avoided situations where one constituency (or "side") was perceived as favored because their conceptual meaning had come to dominate in conditions where competing meanings were placed in direct collision. A union official commented on the "tension between articulating a view about women's oppression . . . and at the same time, saying you can choose whatever gender you want to be," and described how people managed to avoid the argument by "merrily plod[ding] along in our own little silos." During this period, organizational structures in public bodies often kept sex-realist and gender-(as)-diversity meanings apart from each other, with women's initiatives housed in a departmental apparatus that was separate and distinct from the one spearheading LGBTQ+ work. Keeping contrasting meanings from colliding also ran through, and structured, decisions about which terms to use. A local government officer described how their council "will use 'sex' when it is specifically about the protected characteristics. But at all other times, we would prefer to use 'gender' when we are talking more generally. . . . The legal definition is male and female. It is biological, but we would prefer to see it more in a societal way. Obviously, recognizing nonbinary, and fluidity, and so on." Other interviewees described similar strategies.

Displacement was a third technique described by interviewees—decentering a divisive concept, such as gender or sex, and replacing it with a seemingly less contentious one, like access, needs, or discrimination. While these concepts are controversial in other contexts, here their conceptual underspecification and decentering of specific groups (and group memberships) allowed for targeted and more flexible responses. Users hoped that this would reduce the political controversy and divisiveness associated with women's and trans rights. A union official described how "access needs" provided a concept that could move across different social inequalities to prompt responsive provision: "A fundamental part of work on accessibilities is that not everyone has the same access needs. And it is okay that people don't have the same access needs. If someone's access need is that they need a gendered facility, then the simple thing to do is to have some gender-neutral and some not. I think that works." The dilemmas of gender plurality could be managed in this way, bracketing the complexity posed by proliferation to adopt a person-centered approach instead, as this extract from an interview with a city official also reveals:

> I was told there were 72 genders, and then I was saying that to somebody, and they said, "Oh, no, I've heard there's 101," and I'm just like . . . I try not to get bogged down in that because I think that's a lot. . . . As a commissioner, I don't know how you'd commission for 101 different types. . . . It's very difficult, so you just have to do the best you can. . . . Look at the whole person in front of you and see what their need is. And then, on the basis of what you see in front of you, think about where best they fit or how best to support them.

Foregrounding a person-centered approach in ways that bracket or defer identity categories can be viewed, critically, as depoliticizing the construction of, and relation between, categories. However, it also allows for more flexibility in identifying the targeted group so that it flows from the data (and so may vary by context), rather than being presumed. This helps emerging groups whose legitimacy as targeted recipients of public provision depends on new evidence (see chapter 3). A staff member from an NGO described how they were adopting this approach to "monitor the number of people that come through who . . . say they are nonbinary . . . and work out if we at any point need to have a separate program. . . . It might be that there are sufficient numbers. But we don't yet know."

Vagueness, separation, reframing, and inductive categorizing demonstrate techniques of both care-full and careful activism—tending to divergent perspectives, groups, and subjects, while protecting the public body from political or legal attack. In other instances, care-full and careful pulled against each other, causing stress for those tasked with managing and developing gender policies. One interviewee described "walking on eggshells"; she said, "It is so polarizing. I've never known anything where people feel so strongly one way or another and there doesn't seem to be anything in the middle"; another described getting "splinters in her backside" from having to engage with a highly charged conflict where she could "see both sides" (see also Emerton 2023, 106). For some interviewees, the difficulty lay in the level of conflict they were obliged to negotiate in acting on behalf of a public body committed to embedding new gender meanings. For others, the challenge lay in how to enact new gender imaginaries that they were personally deeply committed to.

In interviews, staff described the difficulties that legal, financial, managerial, and media pressures generated in approaching gender as a plural and flexible set of categories, and in supporting trans and nonbinary constituents, along with members of other nonconventional gender categories. One local government officer described the

> nervousness amongst politicians and officers to actually take steps because they're worried that there's just going to be a flurry of FOIs [Freedom of Information requests] and people, you know, worry about their own personal safety. I mean, I've worried about my own personal safety. We had focus groups with transgender people . . . and we couldn't advertise as openly. . . . We just had to go to . . . closed groups, venues that we knew, to get people to sign up. And that probably meant that we missed people that we would otherwise have got but we couldn't advertise as publicly because we were so concerned that people would turn up, they'd be transphobic and so on. So, those are kinds of constraint, really.

Another council official commented,

> It's made me wary of having my name attached to things that go out in the public sphere. I am genuinely quite frightened of being doxed, of having letter writing campaigns, trying to get me fired. I've experienced

transphobia within work from colleagues who don't necessarily even know that it's transphobia, who think they're just having a conversation, or others that kind of, probably, did [know]. . . . And yeah, you do wonder sometimes how long can I do this for? And you can have all the support you like internally from your colleagues and your managers, but that's going to have an effect on your mental health and well-being. So, then, it comes back to when we're doing the equality work, and we have to explain why we're doing the work before we can do the work. You end up doing that in an environment when you are experiencing the . . . same minority stress that the people who you are trying to prevent experiencing [*laughs*] . . . , and sometimes I wonder if that affects . . . I try very hard to make that not affect my—what's the word? Not impartiality because I don't think you should be impartial in local authority. I think you must care. I think you must care about inequality of outcomes, and you must look at the evidence and understand the evidence and use that. So, I don't think impartial is quite the right word. But I do sometimes question myself about this and sometimes I'm—is this changing too fast for people?

I return to the question of policy speed shortly. However, I have included these two longer interview extracts because they highlight how the sensate and affective experiences of those engaged in conceptual activism in state governance contexts are affected by opponents' sense-making (see also S. Hunter 2012, 2015). Here, the forceful conceptual thrust of sex as binary, immutable, and real affected the working lives of equality officials committed to developing an enabling municipal environment for trans and gender-nonconforming residents. The interview extracts show how, in the process, care for the self can get nibbled away or trumped by an outward-facing care for others; how being careful to avoid exposing others to harm can limit a care-fullness that depends on a less security-conscious, more outward-facing approach; and how carefulness can mean justifying equality work before embarking on it in ways that mark the work as needing to be justified (and so feeding a narrative of special attention to minority interests, which can feel far from care-full).

What also comes to the fore in these, and other, interviews is the presence of equivocal and troubled attachments. Looking both ways and being care-full invoke responsibility for views that a staff member or organization may not support. This internal dissensus underlay a spate of litigation, in Britain in the late 2010s and early 2020s, in which gender-critical litigants claimed that employing organizations had adopted pro-trans and gender-(as)-diversity perspectives at the expense of litigants' own gender-critical beliefs.[37] In Ben Anderson's (2023) words, we might think of these legal dramas as "scenes of attachment"—between workers and their beliefs, between employers and workers (or organizations and members), and between organizations and the beliefs they failed to adequately attend to, or so litigants argued. Yet in court, protected beliefs were treated as belonging to the staff member alone. The question was whether they could be manifested or expressed at work—for instance, through speaker invitations, utterances at meetings, pronoun use, and funding decisions—without pushback or penalty.

Framing the question in terms of what people can do with the things that are theirs discloses a proprietary approach to belief—underpinned by human rights and antidiscrimination law, and by the assumption that beliefs belong exclusively to those who *positively* hold them (see also Cooper 2019a). This seems commonsense; central to beliefs is a position of belief. Yet there are ways in which people or organizations "hold" beliefs that they do not avow, in the sense that they know and attend to them. And this kind of holding becomes important when it comes to questions of care-full responsibility, such as the responsibility that organizations and staff have and exercise toward, and because of, the beliefs that other members enact.[38] The critical move, which treats the enactment of objected-to meanings—such as the sex-nativist belief that sex is inalienable and unchangeable and that trans women threaten (other) women's territorial property in their sex—as things to dismantle and void, misses a key step when it disregards the organization's relationship to (and responsibility for) the enacted beliefs in question. Because the manifested beliefs take place in a public body's space, are tied to their members, affect other members, and are relationally constituted thanks to the things that public bodies do, care-full and careful governance obliges public bodies to confront how to treat the negative things *that are also theirs.*

Hostile attachments to the artifacts and expressions of others' conceptual activism surface across this book. In chapter 3, I considered gender critics' attachment to decertification as an objected-to legal idea that could augment their political agenda. And in the chapter following this one, I turn to play as a register for managing and containing the pleasures that seemingly oppressive conceptual attachments may hold. What runs through these different uses is the way that objected-to conceptual meanings, such as what gender means, or sex—meanings that may arise from the conceptual activism of others—are not things of no concern to those who do not advocate or believe in them. Rather, they are ideationally and materially organized meanings that are present within critics' social lives and networks, and so legitimately matters to address. This address may be motivated or framed as one of responsibility, containment, or exploitation; it may be a progressive form of address or a reactionary one; but the liberal claim that quickly dismisses the concerns of others as being without "skin in the game" is the counterpart to the liberal claim that beliefs only belong (and are relevant) to those who believe in them. Conceptual activism, as this book discusses, brings attention to more complex forms of relatedness, including where nonbelievers know and take responsibility (or, it is felt, should take responsibility) for social beliefs they "hold" but do not positively share.

Bringing in Slow Activism

But how should this be done; and at what speed? Discussing care-full and careful policy practice, the presence, effects, and temporality of hesitation surface. Hesitation is present when policy actors face in different directions, bridge and mediate competing viewpoints, and try to manage conflicts of meaning or the objected-to meanings of colleagues. Hesitancy certainly has its drawbacks and can be damaging when swift action is called for. Yet in talking with equality governance staff, what kept emerging was an activism that didn't simply trudge through uncertainty and doubt or use its vacillations to legitimize inaction but carried it as something of value or, at least, as an inescapable presence. In this final discussion, I want to consider conceptual activism around gender policy practice as a slow form of activism.

Activism can approach slowness as a desirable sociocultural achievement, often to counter the unsustainable speed and intensity of capitalist life and waste (e.g., see Fuad-Luke 2016). Like slow cities or slow food, slow activism foregrounds process and the value of process (see also Liboiron et al. 2018). Yet, as well as functioning as a processual norm, slowness can also signal other features of activism. Max Liboiron and colleagues (2018, 341–43) describe slow activism as engaging low-key actions with less calculable results, in ways that avoid or, at least, decenter the spectacular, heroic, and climactic—the precedent-setting court decision, for instance, that overshadows the struggles and sociopolitical movements that gave birth to the litigation and continue after the case has been won or lost (see also FitzGerald 2023). Revising gender categories in a council job ad or for entry to a training scheme aligns with this conception of slow activism.[39] While the introduction of these changes may seem fast given their provocation to others, slowness can be found in their modest development as meanings form and solidify through unremarkable, repetitive forms of practice (see also Garforth 2025). Small adjustments and alterations may not explicitly hail an oppositional vision, but they can provide a footing for it, even as such changes face backward, anchored in an existing common sense.

Slow activism is not inherently better than fast (it depends on the context), but it is also, importantly, not any less ambitious. This last point is worth stressing given the assumed elision between slowness and incremental or minimal change—of one small step at a time. On the contrary, because it takes its time, slow activism may develop in unexpected directions and give rise to sudden lines of growth. It also provides a register for radical proposals that appear nonviable in the immediate present, such as decertifying sex and gender (see chapter 3). Slow activism takes on projects that cannot be accomplished quickly and so risk being discarded as nonviable.[40] By making room for a passage of longer duration, slow activism steps in to hold the momentum and keep development in play when realization is not presently possible, deferral is necessary or desired, or when activism is something to sustain rather than resolve.[41] With its focus on less showy or spectacular actions, slow activism can (sometimes) sidestep the polarizations and competing punches of its faster counterpart. It may engage with resistance in ways that dismantle its conditions of production rather than smacking up against its outputs. And yet slowness may seem inapposite given the focus of this book. Both gender-(as)-diversity and sex-realist projects may seem more plausible as instances of fast activism. Indeed, the pushback that gender-(as)-diversity has encountered in Britain (and elsewhere) since the late 2010s can seem part of a story about the limits and drawbacks of fast activism, particularly when the subject is a controversial one. This is not the narrative I want to tell here, a finger-wagging narrative that criticizes gender-(as)-diversity for moving too swiftly. Rather, I want to suggest, fast activism is not the only tempo present.

Discussing early twenty-first-century alter-globalization and occupy movements, Marianne Maeckelbergh (2022, 206) addresses the difference and relationship between "process" time (the time of "everyday organizing practices," which can be lengthy and unbounded) and "event" time ("moments of action and public mobilization" that are more clearly compartmentalized). The presence of these different tempos also applies here. Despite the visibility of fast event time, with its conflicts and calculable wins and losses, as concepts of gender became concepts of sex in public bodies' policy utterances, slower process-time rhythms can also be observed, akin to John Horton and Peter Kraftl's (2009) "implicit activism," oriented to the substrata rather than the surface of action.[42] Slow conceptual activism is an ethic or orientation that works with and through setbacks and uncertainty.[43] Public bodies may revert to a concept of biological sex as registered at birth under legal pressure, but recognition of this pressure points to the momentum in everyday policy practice toward a different conceptual approach. This different approach veers toward a social concept of gender and an emerging common sense of plurality, self-identification, and flexibility, where the relationship of gender to bodies and to inequality is more complicated and evolving than a simple, fixed, binary sex framework allows for. But along with the substantive common sense developing through fast and slow threads, what slow activism also points to is the need to assess and keep under review the technologies and rationalities of good sense as well as common sense that are deployed to legitimize and support change. Attending to these techniques is important because they structure and limit the meanings around gender—as well as around other social inequalities—that public governance develops. Attending also poses important questions about what other good sense techniques of governing might entail—including those currently perceived as improper, trivial, or irrational, such as kindness, the utopian, play, or hopeful futures.

Concluding Remarks

While the previous chapter reimagined gender through a speculative law reform proposal, this chapter examines how new gender meanings materialized—flowing into the policy practice of local government, trade unions, and other regulatory bodies as a form of conceptual activism. In doing so, my aim has been to develop three aspects of the book: how gender meanings got practically reorganized as new meanings were enacted; the concept of activism; and the management of conceptual conflict.[44] These three aspects are closely entwined, as public bodies' attention to objected-to meanings reveals.

For many of the equality governance staff I spoke with, gender identified a nonscarce plurality of subject identities and categories—for which individuals and groups rightfully exercised autonomy and self-determination when it came to where they belonged. Yet exploring public bodies' policy practice also prompts a different account of gender, oriented to gender as an institutional formation. This account recognizes gender (and sex) as structuring subjectivity—tracking the move from discrete and stable categories to gender as a looser grammar that individuals-in-community arrange and rearrange as subjectivities evolve and are rendered intelligible—but it also treats policy practice as shaping other aspects of social life. Gender's ontology includes ways of being, relating, identifying, expressing, feeling, and appearing, but it is about other things as well. Rules, norms, expectations, values, treatment, fears, and resourcing structures are part of gender also, and this gives public bodies considerable power as gender-makers, something implicitly acknowledged in the heightened opposition that their attempts to make up gender differently occasioned. Understanding gender as an institution (rather than as, foremost, an identity or category of subjectivity) is a specific way of giving gender meaning, of determining what gender is when gender is at play. And it follows that when public bodies reengineer gender in their policy practice, they are not simply representing gender differently or simply responding to gender identities in different ways. By operating on gender's ontological plane, they are also changing what gender is.

Exploring how revised conceptions of gender materialized in policy practice, this discussion has also attended to the concept of activism, to pull it away from spectacular action, the heroic subject, and the fight. Public bodies can adopt an adversarial activist stance, as 1980s British municipal radicalism illustrates, but activism, importantly, can also operate through other styles and registers. Or to put it another way, it is helpful to expand the concept of activism to include these other modalities. Policy practice does not have to be understood as a form of activism. However, one aim of this discussion has been to make the case for this approach. I have done so for several reasons. First, to unsettle the taken-for-granted division between public/state and grassroots bodies, a division that is reinforced when activism is treated as something that only the latter can do. Second, to expand the range of resources and techniques that activism can draw on when public bodies' policy practices are included. Third, to showcase other activist styles. This includes slow activism as a way of doing politics that responds to complexity; deploys open, less defined categories; accepts responsibility for objected-to attachments; and refuses the friend/enemy polarities that activism is typically bound up with. This slow style is a form of activism that public bodies have extensive experience in adopting. Certainly, it is a register that can be overly bureaucratized, hierarchically constrained, unexciting, and incremental in how it gives policy expression to social change. But while this may steady attempts to hail public bodies as activism's new godform, it is also not a reason to discount them. Both the strengths and weaknesses of slow, progressive governance activism come to the fore in the two techniques discussed in this chapter: forging a new common sense and facing in different ways.

For some years, public bodies have constituted key sites in the building of a new gender common sense. Yet the revision of gender common sense slides around. One moment it is an unremarked-on background condition, the next it has become contentious as its claims get contested by another commonsense project anchored in biological binaries and positivist social science (see chapter 1). Between 2018 and 2025, across different sectors, many public bodies struggled—attending to gender-critical perspectives as they simultaneously sought to operationalize gender-(as)-diversity. On the left, this practice of looking both ways has encountered suspicion, thanks to a well-evidenced fear that progressive politics weaken on entering public organizations due to competing commitments, agendas, and interests.[45] Care-full activism can be viewed as one response to this familiar predicament—in its efforts to advance new meanings while attending to the resistance that they encounter. In interviews, those I spoke with described their attempts to bridge and mediate between different gender politics. They also described the governance mechanisms deployed to avoid confrontations, including their reliance on conceptual vagueness, organizational separation, upstream reframings, and inductive categories. And yet, in a highly fraught conflict, these strategies struggled as organizations found themselves legally pressured to attend to sex rather than gender, and to respond to the experiences and litigation of gender-critical staff who publicly recounted the ostracism, harassment, and discrimination they experienced in manifesting unpopular beliefs.

Complaints from gender-critical activists about their organizational experiences highlight an important aspect of public bodies' conceptual activism—the relationship of organizations and members to objected-to things, policies, and events taking shape within the organization's (or community's) body. Typically, manifested beliefs that diverge from the formal commitments of the body concerned are presented as belonging to the faithful who author and commit to them—a framing given added heft by equality law. This chapter has suggested a reframing. If we think of the promotion of these beliefs as a form of conceptual activism, it is a conceptual activism that does not simply seek to promote these meanings within wider society, or even simply to change the organizational space that these engineered meanings and their advocates inhabit; it also demands that the organization and staff attach to the beliefs, despite their potential opposition to them. But what does such an attachment look like? Officials I spoke with described their difficulty and ambivalence in attaching to sex as a binary immutable quality, ventriloquizing the speech acts of others as if they were their own.[46] Such an act can be profoundly uncomfortable, even distressing. It is not one that I want to suggest should be necessarily facilitated, or that beliefs and concerns should be treated as valid simply because they are shared by some staff or members of an organization. Instead, what I have suggested is that the notion of collective attachment is here revised to identify responsibility. This responsibility for objected-to beliefs is important for thinking about public bodies' activism and is too quickly passed over when meanings get coded as the exclusive property of those who believe in them. If we approach objected-to things, policies, and events as belonging to the public body and its communities, this avoids the siloing effect of the privatized property frame in which believers alone are responsible for the negative consequences of what their beliefs accomplish. Instead, we might think of the social stuff of organizational life, including here the conceptual meanings of gender and sex, as collectively held. This is a way of thinking about how conceptual meanings are made, acquired, held, and used, by means of a property frame that is more contingent and public. It takes us to an economy of the concept, here of gender, that simultaneously disperses, collectivizes, and downgrades ownership, while posing questions about what shared responsibility for conceptual enactments that perpetuate social and ecological injustices entails.

So far, this book has focused on the fraught conflict over sex and gender concepts. In the chapter that follows, I consider property and gender from a different angle as discussion turns from responsible governance to play. Drawing on property as an institutional analogue, I explore how playing with property, including as an objected-to concept, can help us think about playing with gender as a mode of conceptual activism. In other words, I approach gender orthogonally to consider what we can learn about it as a concept, that is both contested and objected to, by studying property in play. Gender and property have many differences. However, this book approaches both as institutional concepts, and as concepts about which progressives disagree when it comes to whether conceptual activism should aim for reform, reimagining, transformation, or abolition.

5

Playing with Hazardous Concepts

The opposite of play is one-dimensionality or literal-mindedness. —STEPHEN NACHMANOVITCH, "This Is Play"

Humour is a way to become aware of the ethical ambiguities and paradoxes that we live with, without being paralyzed by them; to recognize and negotiate our own complicit involvement in wider economic and political processes and exploitative relations; to simultaneously express charm and haunting, delight and unsettledness, and to be critical, yet also hopeful. —IAN COOK AND TARA WOODYER, "Lives of Things"

This book has considered two gender projects that could converge but mostly have not. In one, gender appears as a social inequality to disassemble; in the other, gender constellates ways of identifying, appearing, and living that should flourish. In early twenty-first-century Britain, these gender projects have been in dispute even as they seem to invoke different understandings of gender: GENDER1 and GENDER2 in conceptual engineering terms—or gender as structure of inequality and gender as lived identity. Can the first be abolished or dismantled while the second thrives, or are they invariably connected and mutually sustaining in ways that are hard or impossible to disentangle? This chapter takes up the dilemma of what to do with gender when gender is approached conceptually, through a register of sociopolitical action that has had little traction in this dispute: play. This is a register disregarded by both gender-critical and gender-(as)-diversity forces—at least in public—and they are not the only ones to dismiss play. Within conceptual engineering discussions, play receives little, if any, attention. The focus on logic and cognitive rationality leaves little room for conceptual modes of action that prioritize pleasure, contradiction, slipperiness, and wit. But play is an important register through which meaning gets reorganized, if often fleetingly. This chapter investigates play's value for gender-based conceptual activism.

Play's value is, of course, recognized in other quarters. As well as children's recreational activity and adult leisure, play surfaces as serious play in commercial and policy arenas, as a tactical and satirical way of doing politics, and as a mode of containment for harmful concepts. Here, we might think of play spaces, such as the den or basement rec room (to take an American heterofamilial idiom), defusing the guilty appeal of concepts that have been banished from the ethical aboveground. Yet, as this chapter discusses, the capacity of play to contain dangerous things, including dangerous conceptual things, is limited. Leakages occur, and the relationship between play and other domains is part of what gives play its appeal and force. Play's contribution to conceptual activism is largely premised on play's capacity to permeate other spaces and generate effects beyond itself, transgressing and reaching beyond boundaries—whether these are spatial, normative, temporal, or affective.

Play is a register for conceptual activism, but if this is understood simply to mean that play provides a style or key change for conceptual activism, this misses much of what play can do. In chapter 2, I explored the different shapes that concepts assume, and how they combine in conceptual activist dances, focusing on the shapes of the aid, world, cell, and current. Play can certainly act as an aid within conceptual activism; it can also operate as a world, current, and cell as participants' relationship to play changes, moving between use, inhabitancy, experience, and observation. Recognizing these different modalities brings the polymorphic character of conceptual enactment to the fore. Conceptual activism may involve reimagining what it means to be play but, as this chapter explores, it can also involve reorganizing how what it is to be play materializes—something that changes across play's different conceptual moves, where realizing play as an aid prompts a different figuration from realizing play as a world or current. And since play is invariably about playing with concepts other than just play, conceptual activism draws on ways of understanding and accomplishing play to revise other concepts also.

I have come to play to consider what it brings to conceptual activism around gender. Mindful of the far-from-playlike experience of conceptual activism within contemporary gender politics, I want to consider whether something is lost when play is sidelined, and what play might, in turn, bring. However, following the last two chapters, where I approached gender through decertification, and then through public bodies' care-full and commonsense activism, I want to approach gender sideways by focusing on a conceptual analogue: property. There is a growing body of work on gender as property, but this is not my primary focus here.[1] Instead, I turn to property for the parallels to gender that it provides since both property and gender are polymorphic institutional concepts that sustain inequality in formal and informal ways. They are also concepts on which progressive transformative projects diverge when it comes to whether the aim is revision, abolition, reimagining, or redeployment.[2] But while property and gender share features, is property something to play with? As a concept of colonial and capitalist formation in the global North, property appears as play's antithesis—coercive, exclusionary, damaging, and violent.[3] At the same time, if the materializations of dominant property concepts are harmful, and if they are held—and held it would seem securely—through hegemonic social relations, what strategies and measures are available to counter their force? Sociolegal and social movement scholarship looks to law reform, sociopolitical activism, and everyday practices of disavowal and reinterpretation, as well as governmental projects, counterinstitutions, and creative arts, to resist and change how property works, and to revise what it means to be property. In among these processes, play can play a part. This part is recognized within some strands of political and cultural scholarship. Play is valued, even at times romanticized, for its help in countering infrastructures of domination thanks to play's capacity (built into its very definition) to seduce, dissemble, subvert, and loop around powerful structures and agents. The twisty character of play is an important feature of how it imaginatively and materially organizes meaning—typically of other concepts rather than of itself. In this chapter, without romanticizing play or amplifying its power, I center the twistiness of play in considering how play engages gender and property.

I start by introducing play and then turn to a series of different property plays based on the moves explored in chapter 2 as both property and play move between the conceptual figures of cell, current, aid, and world. After discussing different entwinements of property and play, I consider what they offer for thinking differently about gender play—in ways that foreground gender's institutional character. In concluding, the chapter addresses the conceptual figures to emerge from different forms of property and gender play in a dance that moves between pleasurable immersion, resisted currents, playful repurposing, and experimental creation.

Play

Play's weight and gravity have long been subject to debate. While for some, play is a lighthearted mode of action—whose rationale and purpose lie simply in its own enjoyment—for others, play is an important, outward-facing or functional practice, fulfilling socially necessary purposes. Disciplines from philosophy and education to sociology and play studies stress play's importance for human and societal development; its role in individual self-discovery and education; its necessity for collective flourishing in conditions where people play agentically and voluntarily rather than as others' play objects; its use as a medium or register for innovation, planning, and development; and its cathartic value as a "harmless" yet vital outlet for social conflict—vital in part because it seems harmless.[4] Writing on play, Rachel Shields (2015, 314) draws a distinction between two "contradictory versions." One "focuses on the social functions of play, play as learning, and play as a rule-bound activity"; the other focuses "on the creative and imaginative effects of play, play as freedom, and play as divorced in some way from a given reality." Shields's sketch of these two versions is helpful for thinking about play's relationship to conceptual activism. While Shields depicts these versions as "contradictory," what is important for conceptual activism is how play moves between and combines them, meshing—even as it devises a separation between—the rational and irrational, rule following and transgression, the planned and improvised, fictive and actual, and instrumental and expressive.

Play is a concept with multiple meanings, some merging and overlapping, some kept distinct and apart. In this discussion, play holds the following together (in a loose and changing form): (1) creativity and mimesis, as play involves explorations, activities, and ways of doing things that are expressive, (internally) purposeful, and often imitative; (2) electivity, as those undertaking play do so willingly; play might not be fun, but it is expected to be satisfying or worthwhile for its players—if not necessarily for those played with; (3) normative, as play invokes rules and norms (explicit or tacit) that are followed, asserted, circumvented, realized, replenished, and rejected; and (4) twists and movement—play works through stretches, reversals, and paradoxes as contradictions are, accordion-like, pulled apart and scrunched together.[5]

This last dimension of twists and movements is of particular importance for the property and gender play discussed in this chapter, with its evocation of fluidity, resistance, and transgression, as play condenses and moves between oppositions. We might think here of Gregory Bateson's (1972, 186) evocation of play as the nip that "denotes the bite, but it does not denote what would be denoted by the bite" (see also Nachmanovitch 2009). In other words, the nip represents the bite while refraining from realizing the biteyness of the bite (a biteyness that could involve deliberately causing pain, aggressive attack, or simply hunger). Play may realize itself (at least in part), but in relation to other concepts it is often a shadow practice that, characteristically, avoids realizing what it depicts by moving between, constructing a break, and knotting together alternatives—what seemed and could have been a bite is properly a nip, merely represents a bite, is both bite and nip, and has an element of undecidability—which is it? In play, subjects act *as if* the elements and context that give acts meaning and make them ontologically true were present—the toy gun shoots ammunition, the dolls' tea set contains hot tea—while relying on the notion, which may be explicitly shared or left uncertain, that the "real" affordances conjured up by what is done are (safely) absent. As a depiction of something else, a something performed as if it were the thing that the performance claims to be, pretend play produces surplus representational meaning—put another way, it produces ontological lack when it comes to, say, the propertyness of property or the biteyness of the bite.[6]

Play is a way of representing, deploying, or misrealizing (or rerealizing) concepts in ways that emphasize elasticity—stretching away from and toward imagined ontological referents.[7] Nachmanovitch (2009, 15) writes, "In playing, we are fluidly changing definitions of things: the piece of rubber is a sword, the sword is a penis, ad infinitum."[8] Play's elasticity, reversals, and knots of symbolic meaning are familiar to everyday interpersonal practices that don't set out to be play. We can see strains of play in the long-term couple's bickering, for instance, with its uncertainties, equivocations, and reversals, as it mixes and moves between serious annoyance, gentle sharp ribbing, and the performance of serious annoyance (which may or may not be entirely felt). The elasticity of play, as it stretches away and back toward what it represents, can also take more publicly political forms, where material props support new or altered imaginaries of concepts (see Giddings 2024). Playing at statehood or law, for instance, with objects such as postage stamps, passports, and legislative texts, uses the claimed status of the state to challenge (seriously? playfully?) what it means to be one. Material objects draw others into the play too, including opponents, whose participation, paradoxically, may emphasize the make-believe character of the state or law thanks to them acting as if it were real.[9]

And yet, because it is play, a protective cloak is available; what is enacted is to some degree safer due to its fictive status. This is not a law, state, or money; its currents are pretend ones, lacking the force of the "real" thing.[10] When institutional structures such as statehood are re-presented and deployed in play, the sandpit of play provides a bounded space, if also mobile and evolving, that stops radical ideas from being perceived as a genuine threat. A more complex version of this process happens with political satire, where uncertainty about who or what is pretending comes to the fore.[11] On the one hand, pretense is offloaded, being explicitly attached to the targets of the play whose actions are deemed to fall short in conditions where their staged utterances on democracy, freedom, fair exchange, and equality, for example, diverge significantly from how these concepts are materially realized. On the other, satire, in "the key of the clown" (Bogad 2016, 2), assumes a self-conscious register of pretend play as those playing assume the pretense (or at least its costume), drawing on carnivalesque resources of foolery, outlandish costumes, wit, laughter, and temporary status inversions to establish and counter the severity of what is at stake: from nuclear weapons and domestic military repression to state disregard for people's well-being and corporate power.[12] Satirical play involves opponents even as it may lightly mask or play with the antagonisms that it aims to reveal. But play is not always adversarial or competitive, as pretend play, serious play, and cooperative play demonstrate, and attending to different forms of play—with enemies, adversaries, fictive competitors, and collaborators—means attending to different kinds of spaces and different kinds of boundaries.[13] Satirical or playful confrontations between political opponents (see also J. Edwards 2013) often occur in public and civic spaces—the streets, media, parliament. Recreational or staged competition, such as sports, debating societies, or board games, typically take place in demarcated play spaces—a field, stadium, university auditorium, community center, café, or living space. Cooperative forms of play also tend to take place in organized communal or residential play spaces. At the same time, they are intended to reach further—to socialize people, for instance, into cooperation by practicing its forms, to counter social and ecological crisis outside play's "magic circle."[14]

The relationship of play to other social activities and arenas is a crucial issue for conceptual activism. If new meanings emerge during play but are contained by play's boundaries, their impact seems limited. This may, of course, be desired when it comes to oppressive meanings—stopping them from entering play and stopping them from exiting. The problem of unwanted social relations entering play has been a concern in many areas of play studies, including online and tabletop role-playing games, where gendered, racialized, and disablist norms feed through into the overrepresentation of white male imaginary figures (avatars, roles, etc.) and problems of sexist, racist, and disablist discourse and behavior within the structured play.[15] Yet the effects of social relations enacted in play on those playing, on audiences (if there are any), and on social life beyond the play are harder to assess.[16] Writing on the presence of slavery and holocaust play in sadomasochism, Margot Weiss (2006, 240) describes how even when sexual play does not directly reference wider power relations, it is shaped by them, *and this is integral to sadomasochism's erotic charge.* Weiss (238) identifies play as "a transformative, active process of engaging with the world and re-imagining, tweaking or recreating it." Yet this may say more about how play enacts the world than about what remains after the play. While research may study what is left—or rather created—by play, oftentimes play's leftover effects are asserted—hopefully or worriedly—rather than being things that are confidently known. Emancipatory play may seem to produce emancipatory outcomes and vice versa, but what follows from play's practice appears less linear and predictable. This complicates concerns about what playing with dangerous concepts does. Discussing children's toys and play, Seth Giddings (2024, 68), for instance, describes "imaginative play" as "a dynamic and nonlinear flow of embodied ideas, images, behaviors, and performances, . . . in which subjects and objects . . . are generated, circulate, and mutate, without ever condensing into phenomena amenable to straightforward cultural-political judgment and diagnosis" (see also Ketterling 2023).

In the discussion that follows, I consider what play does in conditions of uncertainty, where the celebration of playworlds as spaces of catharsis, cleansing, and change, able to shape and reframe life, may assume too much confidence and knowledge about what play accomplishes. If we tone down our expectations, without relegating play altogether to the social basement, cubbyholed from the main floor of politically meaningful life, and if we recognize play as a versatile, polymorphic concept and not just as a defined activity, what can we find play doing? The discussion that follows traces four ways that play supports progressive conceptual activism around property before turning to gender.

Property Play

Property play conjures up some very specific images—of owned things, such as sports equipment, board and video games, and toys, being used for play; or speculative financial play through the stock market and other investment gambles—but these are not the forms I want to explore. Working with play's elements of creativity and mimesis, satisfaction and electivity, norms and rules, and twists and movements, I want to consider how conceptual activism engages, politically, with property through play. These forms of play involve adversaries, strangers, and acquaintances—as well as, sometimes, friends—and public bodies as well as community groups and individuals, while drawing on the different conceptual forms discussed, of aids, worlds, cells, and currents. Chapter 2 approached these forms as dance moves for the concept, but of course concepts don't dance alone. Chapters 3 and 4 introduced conceptual partners, without focusing on the shape of the dance steps. In this chapter, I take up the concepts partnered with play, attending to the different combinations of shapes and moves to tease out some diverse ways that play entangles with first property and then gender. In relation to property, the four moves discussed are the property pleasures of immersive playworlds, play as an aid to resist property's inequalities and modes of domination, play currents that redirect and rechannel property uses, and the replenishing, bodybuilding, and immunity work that play undertakes within new property worlds.[17]

Pleasurable Immersion in Propertied Playworlds

Taking shape within a defined space of activity, play can reveal and counter capitalist and imperial relations, while prefiguring more communal and just ways of living. This prefiguring may come from improvised make-believe where play incubates new imaginaries, including for more generous, public, and cooperative property relations and regimes, or from structured games, such as Commonspoly and Eco.[18] Games like these two are often framed in educative terms, justified by their capacity to cultivate the sociopolitical imagination; to improve understanding, knowledge, and empathy; and to practice more cooperative ways of being, thus rooting the benefits of play in what is carried outside and beyond the play space.[19] Yet, as well as incubating social and ecological justice values, play also establishes special worlds of antinormative activity, where the self-perceived "guilty" pleasures of hazardous or nonegalitarian imaginaries, associated with war, conquest, and capitalist property relations, can be indulged (see also Fair 2022). This is a form of conceptual activism that utilizes the immersive character of playworlds to materially contain how dangerous or risky institutional concepts are manifested.

Representing and enacting conventional property concepts form a mainstay of many play spaces. These include the spaces of children's role-based but open-ended make-believe play where everyday things (grocery store items, for instance, or train tickets) are exchanged, sold, or lent, as well as rule-based games like Monopoly.[20] Somewhere between the rule-based board game and improvised practices of "let's pretend" are online virtual worlds of commercially designed play. In these digital play materializations, such as *Second Life*, complex forms of ownership are enacted, as vertically imposed, nonnegotiable game code meshes with user practice.[21] People buy, sell, and manage what can be done with what they virtually "own" through a network of property performances that contribute to bringing evolving game worlds into being. But property can also escape its virtual world. The capacity to trade and accrue value that places like *Second Life* have made available, as property and money move between game and nongame world, is an important caveat to the notion that online play spaces function as "magic circles."[22] Yet, for many players, property's transferability is a negligible or disregarded part of the game. The playworld is enjoyed as a space in which not only are "external" inequalities of property ownership bracketed (or, more accurately, "disentangled"; see Blomley 2014), but the idea and manifestation of property can be replayed as a safe pleasure. Here, play provides (or, at least, seems to provide) a materialization that *represents* property relations without *realizing* them—or realizes them within an institutional ontology that is degraded, or regraded, as both being and being contained by play.[23]

Containing power concepts, such as capitalist property (or exploitation, war, and sexism), within a game or playworld seems a good idea. Within the playworld, property can be enjoyed—the socialists and anarchists who relish buying up houses and hotels during a game of Monopoly, for instance. However, the inequities of unequal ownership vanish once the game is over. Bankruptcy and forfeiture in Monopoly end when defeat is acknowledged or when the board is folded up and stuck back in a drawer or on a shelf. Property inequality in a board game playworld is typically fleeting and insignificant. Unlike more explicitly improvised play forms, property in board games is dependent on in-game formal rules of recognition and enforcement to exist, and these are contained by the game world. Since it is unlikely that the property inequalities they establish will seep out to shape or reinforce other social practices, a board game appears to be a safe place to experience the thrill of money, ownership, and bankrupting others.[24] But are property norms also left at the borders of the game? Playing and enjoying property games may not convert participants to dominant property ideologies, but the calculations, discourse, and logic of games based on accruing commercial value, shrewd profit-seeking, transacting, investing, managing money, and calibrating sustainable debt create, if not an intimate relationship with complex market transactions, then at least an everyday acquaintanceship (or habituated fit) with basic capitalist forms.[25] While I want to leave open the question of what play does, turning to play as a good place to materially lodge dangerous concepts (that continue to exert allure) seems a strategy with risks—if not the risks of catastrophic breakdown, then those of normalization through sometimes familiar pleasurable acts.

Resisting Property with Play's Help

In his book *Play Anything: The Pleasure of Limits, the Uses of Boredom, and the Secret of Games*, Ian Bogost (2016, chap. 4) explores how playing embraces things as they are—where what *is* forms the rules, tools, and stuff of play, and where play's fun lies in doing what we can with what we are given.[26] Unlike the playworld that is entered, with its own specific norms, rules, and ways of acting, here it is the world, as it is, that becomes the terrain on which play happens. Playing with what is given (or at hand) does not necessarily mean social compliance and conformity. Play can work deliberately against property's currents, where currents signal the climatic force that concepts, such as property, assume as they move people, systems, and things in certain directions rather than others (see chapter 2).

Deploying play to resist dominant property currents operates across a wide swath of activities where play is used to roll over property to deny or diminish its power. Take mass trespass across owners' fields, where playfulness and the prefigurative "right" to enjoyment get mobilized to defy private property claims to control access to rural space.[27] By acting as if private property rights can be trumped by ethically superior property-forming claims, such as the right to roam, participants use discourses and manifestations of play to advance an alternative propertyscape through its "premature" enjoyable enactment. A different example of play's deployment to resist property is graffitiing. While graffitiing may be undertaken for many reasons, like mass trespass it can embody a playful affect as it plays with property. Graffitiing both claims and disdains property's normative order. In Sarah Keenan's (2010) terms, it constitutes a subversive property practice, countering the network of relations and practices that maintain conventional ownership. Like the guerrilla gardening discussed in chapter 2, graffitiing cultivates space against the grain of mainstream expectations of whose it is and what it is for. In the act of spray-painting buildings, informal property rights to the public visual landscape are asserted and prior ownership claims are studiedly disregarded as the wall becomes a canvas for private, communal, or public forms of recognition and address.[28]

Graffitiing and mass trespass show how play can operate as a discursive and material resource to oppose, withstand, or sidestep the force of dominant property currents.[29] Like elves dancing in the streets to oppose militarization

(Romanienko 2007) or teddy bears picnicking within a military base, play functions as a self-authorizing, bold, sometimes humorous tool of opposition.[30] Yet while play can be deployed knowingly and tactically, the currents of property can also be countered in less deliberate ways. Here play is tacitly rather than explicitly deployed to resist property norms, being taken up instead to pursue other goals, such as fun and mischief. Elsa Noterman and Nicholas Blomley (2024) suggest there is much to be learned here from the property practices of young children who have not yet absorbed and fully incorporated private property rules. They write, "For children, . . . property boundaries are still in the realm of open make-believe where they can become invitations, openings, and climbing frames" (237). Noterman and Blomley (249) continue, "Children's geographies show us that boundary-crossing, far from being reducible to 'trespass,' can be fun, creative, and free us to enact different ways of organizing ourselves in relation to land and each other." Engaging in play in ways that resist property relations can produce different outcomes. Sometimes, playful disregard of formal ownership is ignored; it may even, at times, be welcomed, as with community forms of guerrilla gardening to cultivate a vacant lot (Farran 2016). Other times, challenges to property relations lead dominant forms to reassert themselves, including with force. Because property is performative, it works through repeated actions.[31] Occasional disruptions, then, can be managed or dismissed. If play is to resist how property is materially organized in any significant and enduring way, it needs to be sustained. This doesn't necessarily mean staying still. Sustained resistance may move around and across property regimes, finding new and different crevices as toeholds for action, as I go on to explore.

How Play Carries Property's Repurposing

Play can be used as an aid to counter dominant property currents, but the conceptual figures can also be reversed so that property becomes the aid or tool to advance social change, while play currents shape property's deliberate reuse.[32] This reversal is not exact. Property is not being used here to resist play's currents. Rather, what I am interested in is how play carries property's repurposing through waves of enthusiastic energy as currents of pleasure, laughter, and well-being take hold, even as others may seek to escape.[33] Property's playful repurposing is often small-scale, as illustrated by PARK(ing) Day—"an annual, global, open-source event in which participants appropriate parking spaces and temporarily transform them into spaces that are more sociable and sustainable" (Thorpe 2018a, 742). PARK(ing) Day is a witty concept in which a payer puts money into a parking meter, then utilizes the parking space for a defined and limited period for nonvehicular uses, typically with others—such as creating a temporary recreational parklet (see Thorpe 2018a, 2020). Writing on PARK(ing) Day, Amelia Thorpe describes how play repurposes the property gained by the parking permission to support community well-being and to develop (and assert) relations of belonging to the neighborhood and its streetscape. PARK(ing) Day events reclaim space for the commons and, through the assertion of both informal and formal property rights, property itself is reclaimed (Thorpe 2018a, 2020).[34]

Property play can also center other relations that get institutionally treated (and deployed) *as if they were property*—gender identities, for example, or religious beliefs—to reframe and rescale their use, power, protection, and reach. This application draws on the liberal notion of the possessive individual, the person who owns themselves cut off from others, and so can come to own, or at least have nonalienable property in, their social identity statuses as that which attaches them to the social world and through which they acquire capabilities and value.[35] Sarah Keenan (2010, 423–24) writes, "Property happens when a space holds up a relationship of belonging, whether that relationship is between a subject and an object or between a part and a whole. This spatialized understanding of property means that being white, hetero/homosexual or other such social characteristic generally associated with identity politics can be understood as having property in the same way as owning a mobile phone can." Property operates as a conceptual device of recognition and facilitation that enables social identifications to bear unequal value and so act differentially in the world, while securing legal protection as "belonging becomes a belonging" (Keenan 2010, 427).

If identity status is propertized, questions of redistribution also arise (see also Goldberg-Hiller 2023; chapter 3). This is where equality law enters as a technical structure to manage and regulate the property rights that identity statuses bear. British equality law, for instance, bestows some protections on both dominant and subordinate identities through establishing, recognizing, and defining what belongs (when it comes to gender, for instance, or one's religious beliefs) and by structuring the scope and limits on how such belongings can be manifested.[36] The characterization of identity status as social property can be seen as a form of (academic) conceptual activism that deploys and tracks a property logic across different contexts to see what it gets used to do.[37] This recognizes that property in identity may materialize in ways that give performance rights to social groups, including to manifest gender-critical beliefs at work, but how do play's currents support such use? Legal and policy redistributions of how property in beliefs and social statuses operate certainly appear far from playful as chapters 3 and 4 explore; yet we can find currents of play surrounding and carrying social property's redeployment, including in ways I have elsewhere characterized as free-running the state (see Cooper 2019a, 124–27). Stephen Saville (2008, 892) describes free-running as "highly skilled . . . bodies overcoming the constraints of the environment." Refusing to be alienated or subdued by prevailing regimes of power, free-runners move playfully as they combine different possibilities for action in a "flowing dance" (Saville 2008, 899; see also Højbjerre Larsen 2021). In a performance of courage (or heroism) staged before others, activists treat the public body as a playground of possibility (see also O'Grady 2012).[38] Here, obstacles become points of contact as activists clamber, swing, and scale hostile governmental structures to find crevices and spaces where they can make contact and have traction.[39]

Chapter 1 traced sex realists' attempts to restructure state-recognized property in sex and gender (and to raise the value of sex) by countering the notion that sex could change informally or that more than two sexes are possible. Seeking to determine how key Census questions (and guidance) would be framed, gender-critical feminists and allies drew on professional, political, and legal resources as they free-ran the state's Census machinery. Adopting collectively learned and familiar moves (see also O'Grady 2012), they looked for points of vulnerability and for footholds in the material infrastructures, moving swiftly, energetically, and confidently, to promote and secure women's property in their sex.[40] This was a form of play with little explicit relationship to fun or pleasure. Indeed, conceptual activism around sex and gender, during this period, seemed far more stressful and fraught than playful.[41] However, play currents materialized in the plasticity of governance—its actions and machinery—as something produced through the interplay of officialdom and gender-critical activism. In other words, the play was not just in the give of the governance machinery but in the agonistic relationship of bodies moving in purposeful, creative, improvised ways through and against a governance terrain, as gender-critical activists responded to the recommendations, research, and reports emanating from the governmental Office for National Statistics (ONS). Attending to concerns raised by transgender organizations and activists, the ONS attempted to protect trans people's property in their sex and gender, to maintain a space—albeit one that kept shrinking—for self-identification, while simultaneously resisting compelled disclosure of trans status. By 2021, however, the force exerted by gender-critical free-running was such that property in sex had become reframed—repurposed to support a sex-realist agenda that restricted trans people's property in their sex, while establishing property in being trans as a legitimate target for data-collecting (see chapter 1).

Play's Value in Creating New Property Worlds

Play can provide currents of pleasure and determination that invigorate property's reuse—repurposing and revaluing property, whether it is property in a parking ticket or property in a social identity. But play can also be observed in the nourishing and fortifying of new property meanings. Exploring play's presence within changing property landscapes brings the complex relationship between imagining and materiality to the fore. Both property and play may seem, here, to revolve around acts of reimagining, as in the utopian novel where characters' play reveals the propertyscape of the new, fictionally envisioned world.[42] But play can also be a way of materially enacting new or counterhegemonic imaginaries of property, including as shards of activity that help to enrich and secure alternative property forms.

As a conceptual undertaking, remaking the propertyscape can center different aspects of what it is and means to be property. It can center the things recognized as falling within property categories (identities as well as objects and promises); the elements that contribute to making property up and how they fit together; the rights, powers, freedoms, and obligations that property makes available; what property is for; and the kinds of authority that property has and that it depends on.[43] Reimagining and redesigning the propertyscape also means reimagining who has access to this conceptual world and in what ways, the relationship between formal and informal property practices (and regimes), the place of property resistance, and what it means to lack property or be subject to it. Property scholar Margaret Davies (2021) proposes a reimagining of property as relational, reciprocal, and networked, where owning carries responsibilities of stewardship to others and the community more generally, and where property in land, especially, is tied to habitat—a densely meshed locale that sustains multiple forms of life.[44] Focusing on stewardship can bring property conceptually closer to governance, undoing the deeply scored liberal notion that relations of property and political government—of dominium and imperium—are distinct (not least because one is presumed to be private and the other public). Approaching property relations as governance relations, with important public qualities, can help property lean toward democratic accountability and responsibility rather than toward rights to control and exclude. It can also cause property to lean toward relations of belonging—where property identifies a mutually constitutive relationship between "part" and "whole."[45] Together, these conceptual moves bring common and public forms of property to the fore as property's reimagined paradigmatic form.

Redesigning property, deciding what goes here and there, can seem an imaginative escape from the dominant propertyscapes that we inhabit. However, reworlding property is not just an exercise of the imagination—speculating on a future when other ways of understanding property align with, and can be extracted from, the social practices of a far-off then. Communes, ecovillages, democratic schools, and other intentional communities forge new ways of doing property (e.g., Sargisson 2010), cultivating and tending them from a place of immersion that also entails play, including in the pleasure of building, gardening, and renovating a new physical propertyscape. Here, things are shared and gifted, and personal ownership no longer does the work of developing selves or parsing affective relations (or does so to a far lesser degree). For this normative property world, play may offer both nourishment and defense. This was something I observed while conducting research at Summerhill, the groundbreaking democratic residential school established by the educationalist A. S. Neill in the 1920s and still operative today (Cooper 2014; see also chapter 2, notes 33 and 38). At the school, pockets of play worked to fortify an approach to property that was flexible, pluralistic, and one that sought to reflect the school's commitment to individual freedoms within community.[46] Play at Summerhill also showed how the work done by property in conventional liberal orders could be sidestepped, as autonomy and social ties were seemingly forged in ways other than through ownership.

A different process takes place when play is used to stretch and secure fragments of more communal property relations within mainstream property worlds.[47] One example is the play that takes place on public streets—as dance, music, children's games, and scavenger hunts—reclaiming them as spaces of civic pleasure and belonging. Here play seems to forge and amplify progressive property concepts within a heterogeneous propertyscape; but play can also give rise to competing worlding accounts. One example comes from Nicholas Blomley's (2005) research in a Vancouver, Canada, neighborhood. The research examines residents' property narratives in responding to neighbors who had cultivated the grassy border between road and pavement, exemplified by one household that had placed a bathtub filled with flowers in this space. Some residents described it as a playful act that nurtured the communal character of the street; others saw it as an improper act of privatization—claiming the common verge through a bathtub-as-art-installation. Recognizing how the same material practices can be flagged to support different property imaginaries is important. It shows how instances of play do not simply sit inside particular property worlds but also contribute to their framing, depiction, and constitution, as people struggle to claim the meaning of a playful act.

Institutional Play as Conceptual Activism: Moving from Property to Gender

Property-based conceptual activism depends on property's capacity to be imaginatively and materially reorganized. So far, this chapter has explored play's contribution to this process, focusing on different moves that property and play, when partnered together, may make, drawing on the conceptual figures introduced in chapter 2. In the first, property assumes the figure of the cell whose presence sustains and nourishes its inhabited world of play. In the second, play provides an aid to resist the force and currents of dominant property regimes and practices. In the third, it is property that assumes the figure of the aid or tool, redirected and repurposed to accomplish other value-based outcomes, and carried on play's currents to do so. And in the final set of moves, property emerges as the reconceived and tended world supported by moments (but also structures) of play that work to nourish, sustain, protect, and steer it. These sets of movements, in practice, are not this distinct. They merge and combine in intricate ways. The moves discussed in this chapter are also not exhaustive; there are other steps and other combinations—for instance, developing playworlds may necessitate resisting property relations that structure access and use, such as through subscription fees. However, my aim in teasing out these four moves was to identify some forms that conceptual activism takes when it approaches property critically through play. What does this, then, offer and mean for gender—the primary institutional concept of this book? I stated at the start of this chapter that my aim in exploring property was to provide a parallel concept that could help us to explore what play might bring to progressive conceptual activism around gender. Focusing on property as an analogous institutional concept was a methodological gambit to decenter the more immediate examples that come to mind when gender play directly comes to mind.

For when it comes to gender and play, two accounts, which are connected accounts, seem to dominate: playing with gender and doing gender through play. The first foregrounds ways of enacting gender that rely on exaggeration, disorientation, and fluidity, where playing with gender means redoing gender, to "excite" its "system," in Alister Wedderburn's (2021, 173) words, so that nothing about gender is settled or certain. The excitement of gender may take place in organized playworlds, including where avatar proxies allow participants some freedom from their own gendered subjectivity (or, at least, presentation). But this kind of gender play also spreads through and across other sites. For if gender is performatively enacted everywhere that people are present, the potential for gender play to happen everywhere is also present. The second account concerns how gender shapes play. In the case of children's play, this may confirm or counter how gender roles, identities, and conduct are assigned and (un)done because children do gender when they do play.[48] Discussing gender as played with and play as gendered, the focus typically lands on individuals as carriers of gender and play; I therefore want to draw on my discussion of property play to consider forms of gender play that center gender's institutional qualities.

Let us start with gender housed by play as a way of enjoying gender, akin to the property enjoyment of games like Monopoly. We might speculate about a future where gender is confined to play, but gender norms are not yet that contained, and we are not at a time where the notion of confining gender to play seems plausible. More currently feasible is to see the defined playworld, of games and improvisation, as one where new gender ways can be tried and incubated. This immersive redoing of gender happens across a range of spaces, including queer community and arts-based ones, and to the extent that these spaces are not bounded, what gets practiced within them may circulate more broadly even as such practices become reinflected and, at times, resisted as they move into and through different mainstream sites.

As well as providing a creative space for new social relations and norms, play can also help to resist hierarchical gender currents, akin to the operations of property play witnessed in mass trespasses and graffitiing. Play here may take the form of obstruction, of refusing to perform gender or recognize its norms. Women's sex and labor strikes are an example of this, placing women's work at the heart of gender relations—sometimes playfully, sometimes not.[49] Playful or satirical modes of resistance to legal decisions that introduce and codify new gender settlements, such as *For Women Scotland Ltd*,[50] also illustrate play's deliberate use to criticize or upend objected-to new settlements (e.g., see Grabham 2025). When used to resist gender norms or the wider gender landscape, we might think of play refusing to be seduced by (normative) gender. At the same time, resisting gender, like resisting property through trespass or "defacements," tends to involve entry—wading into gender's currents, which may also be legal, domestic, or medical currents, in the hope that play can thwart or lessen them. One way that play does this is through exposure. Mass trespass and graffitiing demonstrate the power of current regimes of property through the intense, sometimes juridical, sometimes militarized reactions that transgression receives. Exposing this power is not always transgression's primary aim, but for gender play, including through participatory art and performance, exposure comes to the fore, driven by the need to critique the normalization that makes gender's institutionalized hegemony recede from view (see Fletcher 2020).

Arts-based practices of estrangement and disorientation reveal the violences and inequalities of both historical and contemporary regimes as critical mimesis makes the currents of the gender order known and felt. An example here is *The Touching Contract*, a twenty-first-century immersive performance work by artists Jesse Jones and Sarah Browne, addressing Ireland's patriarchal history in relation to women's sexuality, reproductive choices, and bodily autonomy. In this performance work, contract was deployed—indeed it was *played with*—as audience members signed a Declaration of Consent, part of the "legal 'score' shaping the performance" (Enright 2021, 31) as audience members agreed to be touched in countless, not fully enumerated, ways. Máiréad Enright (2021, 36), who collaborated with Jones and Browne in designing the agreement, describes how it made informed consent impossible (also see Enright and Kinsella 2023):[51] "The performers here chose modes of touch that . . . suggested inspection, examination, stopping and searching, detaining, herding, and categorisation." Exposing the legacy of gender's patriarchal currents, the production refigured an assemblage of medical, institutional, and religious touch that was unsettled and disturbing. Enright (2021, 36) writes, "It was confusing not knowing whether to feel reconciled to the performers, cared for by them, or somehow invaded. Discussing it afterwards, my friends and I could not agree. There had been tenderness, but there was no moment of accountability in which the performers or the artists explained what had been done." I return later to both uncertainty and unaccountability as features of play, suggesting they make play a productive but also risky register for progressive conceptual activism.

Play can act as an aid—deliberately deployed to critically depict and counter the gender order—but it can also generate currents, as an ethos and activity that energizes participants, carrying their conceptual activism in ways that impede opponents' ability to object. Earlier, I described how property play during PARK(ing) Day events redirected and repurposed property, taking up the legal permission encoded in paying a fee to create temporary community spaces that were charged by the playful, upbeat atmosphere, which developed and carried them. Redirecting and repurposing gender roles and values can also be carried through play as the mother, goddess, witch, slut, hag, and other familiar gendered figures get refueled, satirically, joyously, to take back the night, protest nuclear weapons, or for other gender uses. Sometimes, it is the gender categories of state processes that are playfully repurposed—a strategy deployed at different times by both sex-realist and gender-(as)-diversity protagonists. Sarah Pedersen (2023) describes the tactics that some gender-critical feminists used to demonstrate their opposition to the more informal approach taken to the sex category in the Scottish 2022 Census guidance, compared with the legally imposed, restrictive settlement in England and Wales. Tactics included writing "believer in biology" in response to the voluntary religion question, and "using the paper form and envelope to disrupt the smooth administration of the census and make gender-critical opinions clear, including creative uses of ribbon and glitter in the suffragette colours of green, white and purple, and folding the form multiple times to make it difficult to be machine-read" (Pedersen 2023, 5; see chapter 1). Here, the currents generated by a mischievous form of play were used to carry a sex that had been conceptually repurposed by gender-critical feminists as binary and immutable. Reversing the flow of bodily movement that free-running entails, sex-realist actions aimed to trip up the smooth flow of administration.

Finally, play exists as moments within gender's conceptual worlding. Like episodes of play within the alternative propertyscapes of everyday utopias or the play that erupts within heterogeneous propertyscapes to strengthen desired, and often dissident, property norms, play secures and enriches new gender concepts that are in the process of being inhabited and cultivated. Scholar and artist Ace Lehner (2022) describes the performance of community norms in relation to *Barbershop*, an "installation/performance/social practice project" in which participants were invited to queer the space by getting a clipper-style haircut.[52] While Lehner (2022, 109) describes the piece as a "trans praxis of failure,"[53] through its performance "the space comes playfully alive with the ephemeral creation of an alternative world."

Performance art may work to sustain alternative gender worlds, but it also can pull at possibilities within mainstream gender worlds. Akin to the flowers in the bathtub discussed by Blomley, play may be a way of cultivating a more feminized, less androcentric environment, as with yarn-bombing, where homemade knitted objects are draped over urban spaces and street furniture.[54] Other examples include play activities that educate children and young people about trans diversity to normalize a different genderscape.[55] Disturbing gender's prevailing meanings also arises in speculative academic play that recruits different histories and futures, what Ben Golder (2025, 2) describes as jurisprudence in its subjunctive sense, establishing "a consciously fictive jurisdiction to create law and generate legal concepts." Rewriting legal decisions troubles the worlding efforts of prior judgments, which have, over time, contributed to the organization of gendered meanings in relation to parental leave, pay, sexual consent, and more. By using past moments where gendered practices, policies, and relations came up for determination, feminists playacting judges lay down a different set of legal building blocks—fictively inhabiting gender's legal apex to prefigure other meanings as if they could be retroactively established and grown.

A different way that legal play supports new normative worlds is through law proposals that fictively enact future reform. Like the nip that signifies the bite without seeking to realize the bite, the speculative legislative proposal can signify law reform without straightforwardly seeking to accomplish it.[56] As chapter 3 explores, decertification was not intended to be read literally as gender's best future—at least, not conclusively. In developing a proposal that one may not (entirely) propose, speculative legislative designs, such as dismantling legal sex status, give rise to moments of academic play. These play moments erupt, move about, and cluster as they prompt new methods and new lines of analysis. At the same time, they protect the gender meanings being cultivated—which are, after all, just play. This means they are not just about to pass through Parliament and so can be more ambitious, experimental, and uncertain. Play here may stimulate alternative gender imaginaries, including imaginaries that diverge from the designed proposal of what law might become and, also, what it should not or cannot become. Designing a proposal that is not proposed is an example of play's surplus—the proposition that overreaches what is done or even sought.[57] Yet while play may journey through the genderscape to nourish and protect gender's reconceptualization, this does not mean that play is necessarily or always helpful. Play may lead the conceptual genderscape it resides in to decline, including, sometimes, through play's overproduction. Alternatively, play itself may contract and wither, failing to replenish itself, as it gets replaced (or not) by other conceptual supports.

Reimagining, repurposing, resisting, enjoying, and reenacting gender often appear in tension. Yet exploring play shows how these different modalities can flow into each other and how a single practice may combine several. For instance, witty street signage, redesigned traffic lights, and yarn-bombing use play to resist dominant heteronormative and androcentric norms at the same time as they use gender to enact, through micropractices, an urbanscape that is softer and more diverse. Art installations and performances also combine witty disclosure—filleting dominant gender relations and hierarchical gender regimes—with newly created spaces where other relations can be explored and sometimes thrive. And because such initiatives are often challenged, play cells move into and through these other intervening institutions, as the example of the *Ladies Lounge*, and the litigation it led to, illustrates.

The *Ladies Lounge* was installed in 2020, at Mona, a prominent private art gallery on the outskirts of Hobart in Tasmania. As an artwork, it established a bounded area that only "female-identified" people could access to enjoy a selection of works from the gallery's collection. Jason Lau, who was unable to enter, challenged the restrictive access policy on the grounds it discriminated against him because he was a man.[58] In response, the artist, Kirsha Kaechele, explained that the purpose of the art was to demonstrate and counter—in effect, to play with—the routine exclusions from privileged spaces and opportunities that women experience and for women and men to experience power being "flipped."[59]

While the court eventually found in her favor, the Tasmanian Civil and Administrative Tribunal, which first heard the case, rejected the claim that the playful character of the installation (designed with butlers and high tea) fell within the remit of the Anti-Discrimination Act 1998, section 26, which allowed for an equality of opportunity exception.[60] Kaechele responded, playfully incorporating the ruling as "the living expression of the art."[61] But art-as-play also entered the courtroom, unsettling its gendered dignity, as the tribunal ruling describes:

> There is one further matter that I should address. Ms Kaechele was accompanied to the Tribunal by a group of about 20 supporters, . . . dressed similarly to her in a conservative business style of similar colour. They sat in the back of the hearing room during the hearing, largely very still. . . . I understand that that stillness was punctuated every few minutes by the group shifting their posture in common and in unison in a coordinated manner. . . . One of the group was pointedly reading feminist texts. After I retired . . . the group left the Tribunal in a single line in a slow march led by Ms Kaechele to the sounds of a Robert Palmer song. . . . At the very least it was inappropriate, discourteous and disrespectful, and at worst contumelious and contemptuous.[62]

Play had transgressed, entering and subverting the gendered courtroom through a spectacle of choreographed gestures by attending members of the public that annotated and contested judicial control. This is one of play's powers: to remake (or at least unsettle) where agency, cultural status, and attention lie.

I do not want to suggest that play is or should be a primary or preeminent register for conceptual activism. For play itself can be a hazardous concept—elusive, light, overly confident, sometimes annoyingly idiotic and irresponsible. Enright's description of the unaccountable touch experienced in *The Touching Contract* underscores play's unnerving qualities even for those who support or are involved in its production. In ways that contrast with the care-full activism of public bodies, play often refuses to attend to competing agendas (see chapter 4). While it may move around, adopting and advocating for different things, it lacks the steadiness and conciliatory character of the activism described in the previous chapter. This also means that the pursuit of what play pursues can fail to adequately recognize other social relations and inequalities. This is a criticism sometimes made about feminist forms of play that, in seeking to counter an androcentric world of war, violence, and hard surfaces, a middle-class white femininity is unthinkingly privileged.[63]

Play is one register of conceptual activism among others. Yet, with all its limitations, it also makes a distinct contribution. Like other concepts, play takes on different forms in different contexts; but what is specific to play is its centering of twists, feints, reversals, paradoxes, and humor. This can make play an uneasy and disquieting register for political projects, but it also gives play qualities that can be helpful in conditions of conceptual conflict where other methods fail, and where argument meets argument in a seemingly endless flow of reciprocating rebuttals. In recent years, scholars and others have looked to drama and art as media through which conflict can be explored, countered, understood, and, on occasion, resolved. Play provides a similar expressive form (drama and art, as this chapter illustrates, can also be playful). But alongside its facility as a mode of creative and participatory expression, play brings the tangents and unpredictability of improvised action into a scene or struggle. In other words, play is not a game to be set up and run, where conflicting views face off against each other, but a mode of engagement that, without necessarily seeking to resolve conflict, can divert subjects from their own (preformed) agendas and from what they thought the agendas of their opponents were, and this may shift the conflict or open new lines of disagreement. One-sided play, however, can be destructive (irritating at best), in conditions where opponents are operating in other modes. The challenge is for the play of political contestants to meet and tangle, including in ways that remain attentive to the risk of injury, and the need for care.

Concluding Remarks

Gender play is typically understood as a kind of play that twists, stretches, inverts, and sometimes simply replicates conventional gender relations, attentive to the identities, expressions, and statuses that gender invokes and the embodied codes of masculinity and femininity that get performed in heightened, diminished, or unconventional ways, including through their mixing. Bureaucracies can be playfully confronted, and bureaucratic gender regimes playfully resisted, but this is often in service of subjects' freedom to do gender and do it differently. To supplement this account of gender at play, this chapter has reached for property as an institutional analogue, to change the examples folded into conceptual activism's imagining when conceptual activism around gender is imagined. Property is helpful because it offers a concept more readily associated with societal structures. Partnered with play, property offers a set of moves that discussion of gender play may miss but can also adopt, as gender gets reimagined, repurposed, resisted, and, also, confined.

This last, the confinement of gender through (and to) play, was the starting point for this discussion. Adopting the influential idea of play's "magic circle" as a distinct and bounded domain, I wanted to consider whether play could be a place where undesired gender concepts (or undesired concepts like gender) could be confined, recognizing that since concepts are material as well as ideational, this confinement does not relate only to abstract things—to gender's naming and categories—but also to how relational forms of unequal difference are made and used. If gender can be confined, the pleasures it generates (for some) can flourish and be secured. This is a form of conceptual activism in which imaginaries of gender as dangerous or risky, predicated on its presence and consequences as an oppressive and hierarchical order, leverage gender's playworld confinement. But such an approach has problems. Aside from disagreement over whether gender should be confined to play, and what conception of gender should be so confined (and to what conception of play), such a politics must grapple with the complex ways that play evades enclosure, how it leeches into wider social soil through the norms, practices, experiences, and modes of understanding and knowing that it rehearses. Play also is far more socially enmeshed than an image of leeching suggests. And this chapter has explored some of the forms this enmeshment takes, focusing on four significant ways that conceptual activism plays with property to think further about what conceptual activism through play means for other institutional concepts, particularly gender.

Play is an important register for conceptual activism thanks to its unexpected moves and returns, creativity, sticky touch, and sense of fun or irreverence (which may be explicit or tacitly found in the refusal to give existing rules absolute authority).[64] At a time of urgency and horror given global and domestic crises, progressive forces can feel the pull to mirror and replicate the hard, combative, (even) militaristic style of opponents, including in the practical ways that conceptual meaning is (re)organized. In such conditions, play can seem too soft, trivial, or feminine (even). Yet play's value comes from its refusal to compete with powerful interests on their own terms. Play does not seek to "win" by using the same kinds of power that hegemonic forces deploy and then defeating them with it. Rather, it operates by inverting these powers, by exporting them to other terrains where their realness is called into question, and by mixing them (up).[65] Oriented to juxtaposed meanings that are materially enacted, play responds to—although is not determined by—what is out there. It is attentive to the potential that small-scale moments offer for stretching and replaying social life and its landscape, and to fast acts that support slow activism (see chapter 4).

Deliberately contesting or complicating the literal is a key feature of play and an important aspect of conceptual activism. This is something that nonplay activism may dismiss (or miss). The conceptual activism of policy practice, described in chapters 1 and 4, does not aim to play with meaning or to put forward meanings that it does not support. While achieving buy-in from divergent constituencies can affect the meanings advanced, as demonstrated by the conflict over the Census sex question and policymakers' responses to nonbinary and trans gender identities in conditions of growing gender-critical opposition, the aim is to achieve a good, viable compromise that can be (legally) defended. Developing policy depends on commitment. Play's exploratory and experimental character may also carry commitments, including to specific concepts. Yet the elastic attaching conceptual commitment to what is done gets stretched and inverted—as play determines what else can be done, sets the stakes and costs in doing what is done, or simply does something else.[66]

In this chapter I have focused on the versatile form that play can take when partnered, conceptually, with property and then gender, where the figures of world, aid, cell, and current reveal different kinds of movements and encounters. In attending to the distinctions between these moves, I have sought to unsettle their rigid compartmentalization. Play can materialize in the same event as a cell of activity to observe and as a current to feel. Play also operates in hybrid ways as world-aids, aid-currents, and so on. But it is with the connections between moves that I want to end, with dance as a frame for exploring how property play and gender play connect playworld pleasures to practices of resistance, repurposing, and reimagining.[67] Too frequently, the conceptual moves discussed in this chapter get pitted against each other, as resistance and repurposing, for example, become framed as opposing options. In other words, gender (or property) is something to counter *or* something to use for other ends, but it cannot simultaneously be both (see also chapter 3). Too frequently, also, these moves focus on the question of conceptual meaning at the expense of conceptual form (or what it is to be a concept). This is something this chapter has countered, building on the book's earlier discussions to trace the flow and interplay between different property and gender play forms. These are not just speculative or ideational connections. The links between resistance, repurposing, and reimagining already exist and materially exist. Often, they converge on the same activity, as in PARK(ing) Day events where dominant property forms get resisted, reutilized, and reimagined through play. Yet while they already exist, we might also approach these connections as connections to develop further (rather than oppositions to choose between or contradictions to expose), because it is by building connections between different conceptual activist moves that dominant regimes get caught.

This chapter opened with the divisiveness of contemporary gender politics, caught between the drive to abolish and the drive to proliferate. To some degree, this conflict relates to different conceptions of gender, or at least different conceptions of which kind of gender should be given priority. Approaching this conflict through gender's dance with play, however, suggests ways that these different political projects could be manifested *in relation to each other*, where resisting gender oppression connects to enacting new gender imaginaries (which may be genderless or dissident imaginaries), and to utilizing gender for other progressive ends. Undertaken literally, the contradictions between these different approaches surface as problematic sticking points. But play flourishes when there is uncertainty, change, and equivocation, and as a kind of political cartilage, it supports connection, bringing conceptual activist projects together in ways that enable different meanings, priorities, ambiguities, and contradictions to live.

Conclusion

Gender's Conceptual Morphologies, Methods, and Dances

Conceptual activism can involve many things. It can involve critiquing and unsettling dominant understandings as critical academics and activists routinely do, and it can involve proposing or campaigning for meanings to change (such as how sex is defined in law). It can involve telling a different story or history of what a concept means or how and why it emerged, cutting some ties and asserting others, as historical sociologist Gurminder Bhambra described in relation to citizenship and the importance of colonialism to its development (see chapter 2).[1] Conceptual activism can involve authoritatively enacting new meanings in law, policy, and other institutions against objections, and it can involve authoritative objections to new meanings being advanced, as witnessed in early 2020s Britain, where gender critics used the powers of courts, government, and regulatory bodies to resist gender-(as)-diversity's momentum. Conceptual activism can involve assuming (or being compelled to assume) responsibility for meanings that are objected to, and it can involve a shift in register so that concepts are deployed playfully rather than literally.[2]

Conceptual activism can take many forms, and, among them, one key form is the prefigurative: acting as if the meaning of terms, such as gender, the state, or property, has already changed or as if new concepts, capturing new claims, are already in place. Prefigurative conceptual activism can involve meanings that are critical of what is and what is emerging, and it can involve meanings that embody desired changes. While the first traces impending harms and catastrophes and makes them intelligible in ways that prefigure a future where such meanings will have become common sense, sought-after positive meanings can be enacted (as well as imagined) through material cuts and joins that give them ontological force—as in the policy concept of "lived sex." Dismissed by critics as nonsensical and irrelevant, this prefigurative form of conceptual activism sits at the heart of this book.[3]

In writing *Conceptual Activism*, I have focused on progressive variants of conceptual activism—recognizing that they might be staged in other terms, for instance as good sense or politically neutral, to allow their incorporation as professional commitments.[4] What counts as progressive is, inevitably, subject to dispute, as contemporary gender politics reveals. However, conceptual activism, including in its prefigurative form, does not belong to leftist agendas. It occurs across the political spectrum, and this is important to recognize. Rightist bodies and movements, from corporations and religious organizations to authoritarian governments and media personalities, undertake conceptual activism, using their varied powers to advance and secure new reactionary meanings. Opposition to these rightist forms often ends up (implicitly or otherwise) targeting conceptual activism as the problem. "Gaslighting" and "post-truth politics" frame contemporary liberal and left concerns that meaning has escaped (or is in danger of escaping) the reins of reality. Critics worry that reengineered concepts of freedom, democracy, and empowerment normalize and justify, more blatantly than ever, practices of hierarchy, exploitation, exclusion, and violence. In such conditions, critics suggest, claims about what is true, what is in fact taking place, become impossible to demonstrate or prove, and this is dangerous. Sex-realist feminists express concerns along these lines, as do those countering Trumpian and other rightist projects. And so, in opposing the conceptual activism of the Right, conceptual activism can itself become rejected as, at best, trivial and, at worst, harmful and dangerous. These concerns are understandable. However, this book works from the premise that progressive politics needs a conceptual imagination, including one under permanent revision. It needs this if it is to make critical sense of the world it objects to in ways that do not depend on the specific meanings of property, state, race, gender, law, and more, that dominant social relations currently anchor. And it needs this if it is to prefigure or anticipate a more socially and ecologically just society. In short, meanings matter. And since concepts are not only abstractions, categorizations, and slices of thought, since they also have a material life, how concepts are manifested—how meaning is *practically* organized—is centrally important as well.

Conceptual activism identifies a multifarious cluster of meaning-politics, intent on changing—and sometimes retaining—how meaning is materially and ideationally organized in conditions of resistance. As such, it is a central dimension of social struggles and sociopolitical change. Conceptual activism is not just about symbolic politics (symbolic politics is not just about symbolic politics); rather conceptual activism details a praxis intent on shaping the material and ideational cuts, joins, and members that the conceptual organization of meaning gives rise to: What counts as war, tariffs, or an election, for instance; what do peace, sustainability, and solidarity entail? This book has focused on institutional concepts (including gender, property, and certification), concepts that are typically deemed less normatively saturated and intrinsically contentious than the explicitly value-laden concepts of democracy, freedom, and equality around which political theory typically centers (see also Connolly 1993). Yet while institutional concepts may hide their sociopolitical investments, these can and do surface.

In this final discussion, I want to draw together the main threads of this book: the struggle for gender's future, the morphology of concepts, and methods for undertaking and studying conceptual activism. Through the course of this book, these threads have been tangled, separated, and changed as their imagined, but also material, relationships evolved. Here, I follow their knotted relationships as they ravel around and through each other.

Gender-Based Conceptual Activism Within Prefigurative Conceptual Studies

Overcoming and Diversifying Gender

Central to my discussion of conceptual activism has been the conflict between two prominent gender projects in early twenty-first-century Britain, gender-(as)-diversity and gender-critical sex realism: one a political project intent on accommodating and embracing diversity and fluidity in the name of gender; the other a project intent on battening down the hatches of sex, as a binary and stable structure of domination to be ameliorated and repaired. This book has centered on the dominant aspects of both within the public sphere, emphasizing their orientation to a liberal politics of individual identity, group membership, and entitlements that, particularly in the case of sex realism, has relied on establishing and policing the boundaries of its categories. Yet this book has also suggested that both political projects have elements that face toward an abolitionist or deconstructive politics when it comes to gender—where gender's dismantling is not simply a linguistic move to void the language of gender in favor of sex but a move to free people from gender's disciplinary and unequal organization.[5] In chapter 3, I identified some glimpses of this politics, of overcoming gender as an institutionalized structure of hierarchical difference, including through its de-production and overproduction, its disuse and overuse.

Overcoming gender and enacting dissident forms of gender diversity provide the more radical terrain for this book. While they can be read as two contrasting approaches, they also identify lines of (potential) alignment—complementary critiques and paths for radically changing what gender is, based on different but not irreconcilable conceptions of gender, engaging different foci, contexts, and scales. This does not mean tension between them dissolves; rather, the tensions between overcoming gender and enacting dissident forms can be helpful for a transformative progressive gender politics, especially when approached gently and generously. Perhaps we might think of the tension between gender's overcoming and its dissident enactment as something like the tensions, but also convergence, between political projects that seek to overcome organized established religion, with its power and institutionalization, and those projects that take dissenting and minoritized religious traditions in new progressive directions.

The tensions between gender dissidence and gender's overcoming can be played out in different ways. This book has focused on concepts, and in so doing has sought to counter three common perceptions. One is of concepts as trivial, peripheral, or irrelevant in the face of material concerns. Adopting an approach to concepts that encompasses and foregrounds their materiality, this book has shown how a conceptual approach can advance and be embodied in radical forms of practice as well as understanding. Concepts are materially expressed, they don't just hover in the ether; and it is this expression, in all its forms, that gives concepts their power. A second perception is of concepts as corresponding to what currently is. This book has focused, instead, on prefigurative forms of conceptual activism, where new meanings—associated with desired futures or rerealized presents—are enacted as if they were already valid. A third perception is that discussing concepts entails discussing substantive meanings. This book has explored different understandings of sex and gender, but central to its discussion has been the question of form—what it is to be a concept and what this contributes to conceptual activism. Approaching concepts as social phenomena that are mobile and plastic, this book has looked at how concepts move, dwell, evolve, get made, and are used.

The Morphological Life of Concepts

My starting point for exploring the morphological life of concepts, and particularly prefigurative concepts, was with the claim that concepts involve both the material and imagined organization of meaning (see also Holbraad 2020).[6] Approaching concepts as material as well as ideational upsets long-established understandings of what a concept is (and where it resides). As chapter 1 discussed, this approach is itself a conceptually engineered way of understanding the concept that chooses to place the relationship between imagining and materiality *within* the concept rather than outside it to foreground their dynamic relationship. This avoids the separation and distancing between imagining and materiality that comes when concepts are treated as ideational tools affecting or observing a separate physical or practical realm. And it avoids treating the imagining/materiality distinction, when it comes to concepts, as a settled ontological division instead of something that is contingent, constantly evolving, and contested. The dynamic relationship between imagining and materiality, and the different conceptual forms it takes, means that concepts are always in flux. Dominant meanings may seem to settle, and the deployment of institutional power can seem to temporarily pin down conceptual meanings, demanding that these be the meanings governing social life; but, as this book has explored, such pinned-down meanings are also evaded and challenged. Thus, even when gender-critical litigation pinned down the guidance on sex, for 2021 Census purposes, as legal sex alone, respondents filling in the Census survey had the practical ability to draw on and manifest other understandings.

The example of the Census conflict over sex demonstrates an important aspect of conceptual morphology: how concepts assume different forms involving different relationships and affordances. I have explored this as one of shape-taking and movement, focusing on the figures of worlds, cells, currents, and aids as some of the forms that concepts assume.[7] Concepts are typically assumed to be tools, classificatory linguistic mechanisms that academics use for formal analysis, and other people and organizational bodies use for other stuff. Yet formal analysis is not restricted to academia, and within academic work, concepts operate in other ways: as stimuli and experimental sites, places of comfort or distress, sites of community-making, targets for repair. This last speaks to the force of concepts as more-than-tools, thanks to the powerful networks within which they are embedded—take concepts of marriage, ownership, disease, and taxation, for instance. The force of conceptually organized meanings, present across diverse social environments, suggests there is value in approaching concepts in ways that are not just oriented to their deliberate utilization. For radical forms of conceptual activism, the capacity to create new conceptual currents as well as cellular clusters of meaning that develop and secure sites in sought-after ways is also key.

This book has explored the possibilities and challenges of different conceptual forms, for new emerging concepts, through play, policymaking, and academic research. The case of decertification shows how a new conceptual world can be created and tended during academic research; how it may overlap with other conceptual worlds, here deregistration and disestablishment; and how it can be subject to competing curatorial practices as it gets tethered to competing projects. Decertification was developed, as a research tool, to stimulate thinking about radical legal changes to gender as a regulatory category, and to act as a research prompt to understand current investments and current organizational practice. As such, decertification was subject to worlding practices that kept it flexible and open, with elastic boundaries that could remain sensitive to time and place. For opponents, by contrast, intent on using the proposal to demonstrate where the slippery slope of trans-positive law reform might lead, a shadow world was created—one that was, at times, overly rigid, and at other times overly amorphous. But what about other conceptual moves? Did decertification assume the form of a current or cell within the wider environment? As I explored in chapter 4, soft decertification operated in organizational practice, between 2018 and 2025, as some organizations treated legal sex status as something that could be sidelined—an archaic organizing principle that was being practically replaced, and not just in Britain, by a more flexible and plural understanding of gender.[8] However, organizational recognition of informal changes in lived sex and gender was vulnerable to pushback, as earlier chapters trace. The pressure placed on public bodies to revert to a binary and biological concept of sex can be read as a critical response to organizational currents perceived as requiring members to participate in the normalization and growing hegemony of gender-(as)-diversity. And it can be read as a move to reassert an alternative set of conceptual currents based on legal sex status. Soft decertification's contraction coincided with the rapidly diminishing achievability of law reform measures to decertify sex. As a proposal placed in the swirling seas of Britain's gender struggles, decertification may have precipitated minor waves, but the currents of its legal institutionalization felt far off.[9]

Did decertification also fail to assume the shape of cells? Securing and nourishing their host environment, the cell seems a move for hegemonic concepts—meanings that protect established arrangements, that can comfortably reproduce and proliferate and, where necessary, induce environmental change so that they become convergent with it. Take woman = adult human female, a conceptual cell whose material expression and ontological institutionalization spread rapidly in Britain in the early 2020s, prompting sociolegal changes, as this book has explored, which in turn helped it to become increasingly normalized. Concepts such as decertification, at odds with wider institutional currents, lack such a mutual reinforcement effect. As a result, their cellular presence may remain sparse.[10] But could they be present as a kind of sleeper cell, inactive until some future animation? Or as a pedagogic practice in which conceptual cells are forged for the learning they prompt without any expectation or requirement for their survival? Or is decertification an example of cellular challenge—causing us to consider the kinds of environmental changes that could enable decertification to thrive and to consider those contiguous concepts (deregistration, pluralization, perhaps) with greater present-day metabolic powers? One way of approaching these questions is through the figure of the dance.[11] Political work often seeks to identify the key question and the key strategy, but the figure of the dance is more pluralistic; different activist approaches enact different dances, and while they shape each other, conceptual activism does not demand that a single dance is preferred.

The Economy of the Concept

A different aspect of conceptual morphology—applicable to specific moves as well as to the relationship between them—concerns the concept's economic life. In chapter 3, I considered the economic life of decertification—as an imagined law reform proposal, as the reorganization of how gender categories are regulated in law, and as a broader future for what gender could become. The turn to economy was partly to rethink economy, to pull it away from the conceptual dominance exerted by market competition and capitalism. It was also done to provide an account of gender that foregrounded its societal production, acquisition, and use, to counter liberal accounts of gender that treated it as an identity or defining feature of groups and individuals. In the case of gender, an economy of the concept attends not only to how people and society become gendered but also to the contemporary processes giving rise to individual and group-based accounts of gender, rather than more systemic or institutional ones, as things that are made, held, and used—at least in the conceptual imaginaries dominating public utterances and inscribed in legal form (see chapter 3). Also central to an economy of the concept is how conceptual imaginaries get formed through material practices. For instance, in neoliberal conditions, the concept of gender, as individual or group property, acquires an onto-epistemic life (materially realized and understood) as something to possess, protect, invest in, exploit, and capitalize, even as this process may be subject to liberal mechanisms that attempt to modify whose genders get protected and recognized as property, along with what gender as property can be used to accomplish (see chapter 5).[12]

Conceptual economies, of course, apply to other concepts.[13] They also apply to counterhegemonic gender concepts, including ones that prefigure *what gender could become*. Conceptual economies make this prefiguring intelligible and material—as something made, distributed, held, and used (and not only in this order).[14] Concepts of agender and nonbinary can be approached in this way, as can concepts of gender dissidence and gender's overcoming.[15] While some forces may dismiss the capacity of such concepts to exist ontologically in advance of their wider realization, characterizing their claimed existence as illusory, distracting, and naive in conditions of patriarchy, or while they may attempt to eliminate their economies of making, holding, and use (at least in their public manifestation), radical gender economies are also more tenacious. Here, the prefigurative "as if" provides a register for action when it comes to making, acquiring, and using gender differently, living gender *as if* it could be sidestepped or overcome without depending on or pinning down what counts as real.

With its emphasis on responsible forms of possession and use, conceptual economy also provides a way of approaching troublesome concepts. These may be troublesome from mainstream or critical perspectives but, in both cases, dilemmas arise about whether their production should be halted or their use restricted. Chapter 4 explored the challenge that public bodies faced in managing the enactment of contentious concepts, such as realist concepts of sex. Attached to organizational members, such concepts often constituted unwanted presences, even as they were increasingly supported by legal judgments and political pressure. In such conditions, policy practitioners became compelled to find ways to hold undesired meanings without advocating for them, or to use them circumspectly, when legally or politically compelled to. But responsibility for objected-to meanings can also be understood as a way of doing activism as a public body. This complicates notions of possession or ownership that assume that what is held is desired, including when it comes to concepts. It also complicates notions of what good activism looks like.

A different response to troublesome concepts arises with play (chapter 5). Play offers a modality for troublesome concepts, such as gender or property, that allows them to be created, shared, and used, rather than eliminated or excluded, without the consequences and intentions usually associated with such actions. Yet play's safety depends on play operating as a contained space apart from other arenas of living. In practice, this does not happen. Bounding off troublesome concepts, containing their formation and use within play's "magic circle," is limited and often uncertain. This does not mean play is irrelevant when it comes to troublesome concepts, simply that its value is not primarily one of containment. While play itself is a versatile polymorphic concept that can be formed, held, accessed, and used in different ways, as chapter 5 explores, play also gets involved in the economy of other concepts. In the case of property and gender, it can unsettle and transform their production, acquisition, and deployment, causing hegemonic conceptual economies to stumble (at least briefly). For instance, playful trespass may undermine ownership of land and what ownership carries; while playful art installations unsettle the power associated with dominant gender acquisitions (what manhood, for instance, carries) or repurpose gender concepts for other uses. Play twists the conceptual economy of what is played with. But in another sense, we can think of play as a shadow, performing the conceptual economy of institutional concepts, such as property and gender, in a minor key.

Gender's Metacategories

Whether conceptual activism happens through play or other registers of action, it engages the metacategories of a concept. This proved a major aspect of the conceptual struggle around gender; yet the capacity of gender to sit within multiple metacategories was too often sidelined or disregarded in direct debate. Little public discussion took place reflecting on what gender *was* in ways that recognized it could be characterized in many ways and that none were definitively correct in ascertaining the only conceptual cuts and joins that were plausible. At the same time, different conceptions of gender shaped public discourse, and were enacted in practice. The conflict of this book centered on a disagreement between gender as a set of fictive stereotypical roles and preferences, on the one hand, and gender as a psychosocial identification and material way of living, on the other. Amid this two-sided struggle, other metacategories of gender also surfaced (often by implication), including gender as a class, a mode of expression, and a hierarchical (binary) order, along with the book's inclination toward an institutional account.[16] For each of these framings, different (imagined but also material) cuts and joins got made and identified that variously composed, included, excluded, or reorganized people, qualities, and things. Gender's metacategories are important when engaging with specific projects and politics, since they frame and shape gender's significance, flexibility, reach, and use.[17] What it means to overcome gender as a personal mode of expression is quite different from overcoming gender as a hierarchical order, for example.[18]

Gender's metacategories are also subject to the morphological turns discussed in this book. This is particularly evident when the metacategory is a distinctive one, such as "protected characteristics" in British equality law, rather than more generic metacategories of group, class, and structure. It then becomes possible to explore the economy of such metacategorical concepts—how they got made, acquired, used, and in some cases abandoned or depleted. It also becomes possible to trace the dances they perform, how a concept like "protected characteristics" takes shape, and moves through a changing sequence of shapes, as it works with the form and affordances of being an aid, world, current, and cell, settling sometimes as one and sometimes as another, depending on the context. Here, too, in relation to gender's metacategories, it becomes possible to explore minor and oppositional economies and dances (of the metacategory, and of gender within the metacategory)—for instance, of gender as a grammar or personal expression.

But is there a risk? This discussion suggests that the morphology of concepts is an important aspect of conceptual activism, that conceptual activism is not just about the specific meanings that specific concepts hold but the ways in which conceptuality imparts force, options, processes, capacities, even modes of care—the guerrilla gardening undertaken and observed, for instance, when dominant concepts, such as the state or gender, are reoccupied and cultivated to produce unexpected radical meanings. Exploring these moves in relation to conceptual activism around sex and gender, the contribution that conceptual morphology makes to understanding and doing conceptual activism surfaces. But in the process, is conceptual action left too knotted up? Does approaching concepts in these diverse, interacting, and intra-acting ways create confusion, blunting the ability of concepts to function as effective tools and mechanisms for advancing a progressive transformative politics?

In tracing concepts' complex morphology, I do not want to dull or diminish the contribution that the reorganization of meaning can make to transformative progressive politics. At the same time, I want to counter the fetishization of specific concepts or metacategories. Recognizing the ongoing relationship between the imagining and materialization of meaning; how concepts change shape in moving between cells, worlds, currents, aids, and more; and processes of formation, allocation, and use within conceptual economies underscores concepts' evolving and plural character. Dominant forces may seek to stabilize and fix how meaning is organized and to standardize it across different arenas. While they sometimes may also avoid both, efforts to pin down meaning, and to do so publicly, can be a powerful political move. Progressive forces often engage in similar attempts. Yet, as discussion of play in chapter 5 suggested, countering the attempts of powerful institutional forces to fix concepts by drawing on the same techniques may not prove fruitful. A more flexible approach may, instead, be more successful and may better prefigure what concepts should come to mean and be as provisional and contextual meanings. This also recognizes forms of conceptual activism that seek to disorganize and decommission concepts. Disorganizing meaning, or seeking to abandon and dismantle specific forms, is an important aspect of conceptual activism, as the decertification of sex and gender illustrates. But as other abolitionist politics (such as prison and border abolition) underscore, abandonment and disorganization are not the opposites of engagement and creation. They do not dismantle what exists to leave empty space. Rather, undoing and redoing emerge from the same practice and combine. This echoes a point made by Bonnie Honig (1993, 13) in her refusal to choose between "a politics of settlement and a politics of unsettlement, as if any politics could be one without the other." It also recognizes that the organization of meaning, when it comes to concepts like gender, is an ongoing project of organization and disorganization, as new metacategories are introduced and others rejected, and as people recognize and expose, but also introduce, gender in unexpected places.[19]

Conceptual Activist Methods and Other Dance Partners

Academic work relies on methods—ways of working that can be used and, also, countered. Methods are not necessarily recipes, nor are they blueprints. This book came out of the need to keep developing and thinking about methods for progressive conceptual work to complement (and supplement) the vast array of available critical methods, which may also be progressive methods. Too often, in leftist scholarship, the hopeful turn—if it has not been preemptively dismissed as naive—arrives as an urging or vision in the final pages, often with onto-epistemic commitments that seem in sharp contrast to those that have preceded it. But how might hopeful work be done in nonhopeful times; or to put it a little differently, how might we act if we acted as if hope remained an option?[20] With its focus on conceptual activism, this book has drawn on several methods to study and undertake such work. Building on previous approaches that I have explored, of conceptual inspiration from inventive progressive initiatives and the political prompts that conservative legal dramas can generate, this book has worked with the conceptual activism of academics and policy practitioners, foregrounding mainstream sites (local government, trade unions, national government agencies, universities, and community organizations) as places where conceptual activism happens and from where it can be observed happening. This relation between doing and studying, and the forms of enmeshment it entails, is a central methodological theme of the book. Here, different registers of doing—from speculative academic designs, to care-full policy work, to enjoyable play—offer modalities for the agonistic, solidaristic, and cooperative politics that conceptual activism enacts.

Conceptual activist methods do not belong to the academy. However, in thinking methodologically, this book has attended to academic work: how it undertakes conceptual activism by entering and cultivating the worlds that concepts give rise to—from property and play, to conceptual engineering and conceptual activism, to the very concept of the concept itself. It has addressed how academic conceptual activism deliberately and reflexively crafts new analytical aids; and how it prototypes things, such as speculative laws, to do analytical and experimental work. Across different academic methods for doing conceptual activism, a recurring concern is engagement. In interview, geographer

Kath Browne described how, without oxygen, new concepts die; Amanda Perry-Kessaris similarly talked about effective concepts being animated and lively rather than blobs (see chapter 2). Engagement seems an obvious claim: What kind of academic or intellectual work doesn't need it? But concepts are typically seen in less vibrant ways—as collecting or cataloging devices that stabilize and fix, mental gatherers imposed on a situation to make sense of or control it. In much academic work, concepts are overly designed and overly scrutinized. They are things that academics carefully and lovingly craft or carefully and lovingly observe. They are formulated as epistemic offerings, whose credibility comes from being accepted as they get passed from one academic to another. But the life of a concept is typically far less controlled. This book has approached concepts' academic life as more like a dance than an inheritance of precious porcelain—twisting, turning, expanding, shrinking, coming in close to its partner, moving away, as concepts get inhabited, used, felt, and observed. Concepts exist within, and take their shape from, imagined and material networks of meaning (and not just meaning). Gender, for instance, is composed of, and sits within, networks that also embrace concepts of work, public life, war, and care. But concepts can also be explicitly introduced to each other, or they can be brought together in less deliberate ways.

Finding new dance partners for concepts pulls concepts away from their taken-for-granted tramlines, to suggest or prompt new lines of development. While a critique of economy, as it is, emphasizes the presence and harms of exploitative labor, competitive markets, extractive production, and wasteful consumption, economy can be imaginatively and materially prefigured to foreground egalitarian and sustainable ways of making, using, and allocating social life's parts. This is something that work on alternative economies undertakes; however, it risks limiting its potential through (usually) unstated assumptions about what counts as economic goods. Broadening the concept of economy by partnering it with gender decertification (where economy tracks a set of dances that decertification might perform; see chapter 3) may seem risky, diminishing capitalism's prominence and so undermining its critique. Yet the value of such broadening lies in supporting different futures by showing the array of other logics and organizational forms that could be brought into economic thinking, including ones that are already active elsewhere. For instance, exploring how municipal and trade union gender policies are accessed, used, changed, and destroyed might suggest normative ownership structures for other goods. This move reverses the neoliberal tendency in which all kinds of social, cultural, and political processes get pulled into a profit-oriented market logic—witnessed with public-sector markets, competition between providers, and the proliferation of ordinal rankings for public goods. Instead, this move makes the countersuggestion that progressive social, cultural, and political processes might reshape how currently marketized goods (housing, food, travel, energy, finance, and more) are made, allocated, and used, anchored in values of democratic participation, accessibility, equality, creative development, kindness, and ecological responsibility.

What conceptually reimagining economy from the vantage point of decertification also demonstrates is how the establishment of odd (even queer) couplings changes the partners in the dance. Conceptual interchanges are often treated like billiard balls, ricocheting off each other as each ball, unmodified by the encounter, gets shunted in a calculable direction (and with calculable force). Instead, we might think of concepts being brought together in ways more akin to a meeting of cake and mud, moving against and with each other in an array of ways, evolving and changing in the process as they carry elements of the other with them. Utopian sociologist Lisa Garforth described this aspect of her own work in interview: "What I can do . . . is to put ideas next to each other that often aren't next to each other, and to try and make them talk to each other in interesting ways or to find resonances that feel a bit instinctive but can be drawn out. . . . And what comes out of that is very rarely a 'we should.' It's more often much more of a, 'Oh, you know, I think it would be useful.'"

The conceptual dance of this book resembles the conceptual conversation that Garforth describes, but in ways that foreground embodiment—as it relates to diverse material things (since concepts are not only expressed or lived as utterances) in motion with, around, and against each other. The dance also resembles methods based on refraction and diffraction (see Barad 2007), where the targeted concept is not only changed by the investigative encounter but carries some of this investigative machinery with it. These transfers of meaning can be seen in the case of gender and sex, a transfer that became the site of protest as critics argued that gender's "lived" dimensions had become troublingly stuck to sex (see chapter 1). Concepts are always in relations with others, but the deliberate creation of a dance pair, triplet, or ensemble changes all the parties. Gender, for instance, changes when partnered with economy or play. This affects how it is imagined and how it is enacted. Or, to take another example, the concept of activism changes when partnered with public bodies rather than grassroots social movements, prompting reflections about what good activism looks like, and the value of care-full activism that attends to different constituencies, alongside more adversarial forms (see chapter 4). In the case of decertification and economy, decertification pushes economy away from the conventional things and services usually deemed to make economy up—as a law reform proposal, regulatory structure, and social relationship become economic materials.

This changes the meaning of gender, sex, and their deregulation (or reregulation) through decertification, as it also changes the meaning of economy.

And yet we must ask, how significant are these dances—whether it is the solo dances of a concept (always mired in wider networks but that may dance as if it were distinct), or the dances in which conceptual partners, triplets, and more move center stage? In chapter 1, I addressed the skepticism of some analytic philosophers toward the resilience and significance of newly engineered meanings, recognizing their pessimism about the likelihood that such deliberately crafted meanings would be adopted by others or have any material impact. Advanced in the lab conditions of conceptual academic work, conceptual changes can falter as soon as the scheduled dance is over. Yet, in other contexts, and sometimes in academic ones also (particularly when academics are part of wider collaborations), new meanings take off, materializing in different and unexpected forms.[21] The question of conceptual activism's significance returns us to the materiality of the concept. If concepts are just ideational, new ways of sculpting meaning may seem phantomlike, nonexistent when they fail to be taken up. But concepts involve materiality—in their depiction, expression, use, signaling, realization, and more, however brief this may prove to be. Even a concept like ghosting is materially expressed, whether through signs and effects of an absence or through what should have happened and hasn't. Consequently, in considering what the reorganization of meaning does, the life of its material forms becomes important, as well as the movement of meanings across different material forms as conceptual meanings persist, and as they get brought back into play.

Conceptual activism is a method for undertaking change and for resisting it. It offers a concept for studying struggles over meaning, for examining how institutions advance and resist meanings, and for studying reflexively one's own engagement. And yet it is vital to hold on to the critical premise that counter-hegemonic registers of conceptual activism take place in conditions that are not of their own making. Powerful forces shape the meanings that prevail, and it is against these that progressive minor-stream meaning-politics struggles. As the conceptual conflict over sex and gender reveals, not everything is possible. Not only is room for maneuver constrained, but prevailing forces shape what meanings are desired, which are deemed plausible, and how they materially manifest—whether this relates to dominant meanings or the meanings that oppose them.

Yet, despite this, meaning-politics remains a key element in political confrontations and in attempts to live more justly and ecologically. Whether touched, heard, felt, or undertaken, conceptual activism happens. It happens in disputes over law and policy, in the dismembering of statues and in the renaming of streets, housing estates, transportation lines, and even seas. It happens when we imagine and describe the condition of our planet, and in the processes introduced to address these conditions. We do not know what conceptual activism will achieve, which meanings will take off, how they will be revised, and the material lives they may lead. This book has focused on the conceptual conflict over sex and gender, but it has done so mindful of conceptual activism in many other contexts, in the hope that the methods, questions, and issues explored here may provide fruitful dance partners for other political projects.

Notes

INTRODUCTION

1. The full title of Kuang's novel is *Babel: Or the Necessity of Violence: An Arcane History of the Oxford Translators' Revolution*.

2. See, for instance, *Phoenix v. The Open University* ET 3322700/2021 & 3323841/2021, para. 559, describing the claimant's gender-critical beliefs.

3. For Women Scotland Ltd v. The Scottish Ministers [2025] UKSC 16.

4. The term gender-(as)-diversity captures both the notion that gender gives rise to diverse subcategories (which, despite their unequal power, should be treated as equally legitimate) and the notion that gender itself is valued as an expression of diversity.

5. When concepts are depicted as purely ideational, the question of conceptual materiality sits outside the contours of the concept—often emerging as a question of implementation, with all the challenges that uptake of new meanings face (see chapter 1). If the concept, by contrast, is formed around and in the relationship between imagining and actualization, complex questions about materiality and materialization become constitutive of the concept itself. This becomes apparent in relation to conceptual activism. Reconceptualization is not an act of reinterpretation in which the targets of conceptualization form stable objects that are then viewed through a multiplicity of lenses. Reconceptualization reworks ontological boundaries, cuts, and joins also. This involves changes in understanding—collective as well as individual (or individual-in-relation). It also involves material social practices. The social fabric can be ideationally cut and joined in multiple ways (for instance, the elements deemed to compose sex), but material cuts and joins will also play a part here in shaping which imagined cuts and joins seem more useful or resonant, even as forces will disagree and struggle over what these are.

6. The relationship (including intrarelationship) of imagining and materiality developed in this book draws on Karen Barad's work: see Barad 2007, 2014; also Barad and Gandorfer 2021.

7. In this conflict, conceptual activism centers categories and boundaries, and how they are produced, accessed, gained, and used. At the same time, struggles such as this one

over categories and boundaries also draw in other aspects of how meaning is organized, including beliefs about the real, and how concepts are felt, heard, and seen.

8. For different perspectives on the British conflict, see Butler 2025; Cooper 2019b; Hines 2020; Pearce et al. 2020; A. Sullivan 2021.

9. I have briefly explained my use of gender-(as)-diversity in note 4. For gender-critical approaches to gender and sex, see, for instance, Lawford-Smith 2022; Stock 2021. Use of the term gender-critical to describe this politics is itself contested. Objectors argue that other feminist politics are also critical of gender and prefer to use other terms for sex-realist accounts. In this book, I use the term gender-critical when referring to proponents' self-identification. My use of the hyphen indicates a distinct political project rather than simply being a critical account of gender.

10. There is a rapidly growing literature on conservative antitrans politics—framed also as antigender or as "heteroactivism." See, for instance, K. Browne and Nash 2017; Butler 2025; Lamble 2024; Nash and Browne 2020.

11. See, for instance, Woman's Place UK, home page, accessed December 4, 2025, https://womansplaceuk.org/; Fair Play for Women, home page, accessed December 4, 2025, https://fairplayforwomen.com/; Sex Matters, home page, accessed December 4, 2025, https://sex-matters.org/.

12. For further discussion on gender as property, see Cooper and Renz 2016; Davies 1994; Decoster 2024. This line of thinking is indebted to Cheryl Harris's (1993) work on whiteness as property. For an interesting account exploring feelings of loss of power among those opposing gender-(as)-diversity, see K. Browne and Nash 2023.

13. See, for instance, Pedersen (2022) discussing the views and mobilization among Scottish feminists against liberalization of the procedure for gender transitioning in Scotland.

14. Meanwhile others have drawn parallels and connections between some strands of gender-critical politics and transnational, largely right-wing, "antigender" politics: see Bassi and LaFleur 2022; Hemmings 2022; Lamble 2024; Thurlow 2022. In Britain, rightist support for a binary, sex-based account of women and men got publicly demonstrated through conservative Christian litigation, government policy decisions, and coverage of gender-critical feminist perspectives in rightist newspapers and online platforms. For discussion of the links in Britain between gender-critical and rightist politics, see also Hines 2025.

15. Some trans activists also use the concept of sex but have interpreted it in more fluid and plural ways than sex-realist politics does; see also chapter 1.

16. On gender abolition and its stakes within left materialist and contemporary communist politics, see discussion in Belinsky 2019; Escalante 2018; Gleeson 2017. For other work on disrupting gender within gender-(as)-diversity politics, see discussion in Bey 2022; Wang 2023.

17. See Fairbairn et al. 2022.

18. See also Mermaids, an organization "supporting trans, non-binary and gender-diverse children, young people and their families," and Transgender Trend, a British organization that collates resources and produces materials offering counterperspectives to those seen as trans-affirming for children and teenagers: Mermaids, home page,

accessed December 4, 2025, https://mermaidsuk.org.uk/; Transgender Trend, home page, accessed December 4, 2025, https://www.transgendertrend.com/.

19. See Chua 2023; Garland and Travis 2025; Cass 2024.

20. Gender-critical beliefs have been legally recognized as "philosophical beliefs." This makes them a "protected characteristic" within British equality law, entitled to protection from discrimination and harassment (broadly analogous to religious belief). The leading case is *Forstater v. CGD Europe and Others* UKEAT/0105/20/JOJ; see also *Phoenix v. The Open University* 3322700/2021 & 3323841/2021; *Pitt v. Cambridgeshire County Council* 3311160/2023; *Adams v. Edinburgh Rape Crisis Centre* 4102236/2023 & 4103479/2023; *Esses v. The Metanoia Institute* 2206164/2021 & 2206708/2021; *Bailey v. Stonewall Equality Limited and Garden Court Chambers Limited* [2024] EAT 119, see also [2025] EWCA Civ 1662; *Orwin v. East Riding of Yorkshire Council* 6000146/2022; *Lister v. New College Swindon* 1404223/2022; *Ali v. Reason and Nott* J00CL858; *Meade v. Westminster City Council and Social Work England* 2201792/2022 & 2211483/2022. For discussion of newspaper support for gender-critical politics and academics in Britain, see Shaw 2023.

21. In relation to prison policy during this period, see *R (FDJ) v. Secretary of State for Justice* [2021] EWHC 1746 (Admin); see also Lamble 2025. On women's refuges, see Renz 2023.

22. For example, see "Brighton NHS Trust Introduces New Trans-Friendly Terms," BBC, February 10, 2021, https://www.bbc.co.uk/news/uk-england-sussex-56007728.

23. I discuss this further in Cooper 2022.

24. Opposition was expressed toward schemes run by Stonewall, an organization that advocated for equal rights for LGBTQ+ people, and Advance HE's Athena Swan, an accreditation framework to support and advance gender equality within higher education and research. For a critical account of Athena Swan's take-up of gender identity, as "policy capture" by activists, see Armstrong and Sullivan 2023; and for a critical account of participation in Stonewall's trans-positive scheme for employers, see Cunningham 2021.

25. See, for instance, the Supreme Court decision in *For Women Scotland Ltd v. The Scottish Ministers* [2025] UKSC 16.

26. For other accounts of gender in this vein, see Cooper 2020a; Lorber 2000; Risman 2004. Approached institutionally, gender coexists with other institutional concepts, such as law, property, and the state, which it helps to shape, is shaped by, and meshes with.

27. For a concept like gender, in contemporary Britain, it is more helpful to see institutionalization as a process that evolves, that is plural—with dominant and minor variations emerging—and that is held in place but also subject to destabilizations.

28. Conflict over conceptual meaning is explored through Gallie's (1955–56) frame of "essentially contested concepts" (e.g., see Reitan 2001). But it is also explored through other concepts and frameworks, including agonism, discourse, dissensus, and ideology.

29. In a footnote, Cantalamessa (2021, 57) notes that conceptual activism may also be done nonverbally.

30. Explored more fully in chapter 1, my approach to concepts and their development avoids treating them just as units of language or ways of using language. Concepts have a material dimension, as meaning gets enacted and manifested, while also being materially shaped, prompted, and pressed on by inequalities of power, exploitation, and oppression, as well as by resistance, political struggle, and prefigurative practices.

31. Viviana Asara and Giorgos Kallis (2023) provide a helpful account of key elements of prefigurative politics. These are (1) the refusal to divide means from ends. Political ends (or objectives) operate as means, while the means of sociopolitical change are lived as a kind of end. Prefiguration offers a counterpoint to the conventional political logic, exemplified by militaristic and vanguard strategies, that the ends can justify the means and so rationalize violent, cruel, undemocratic processes and practices. Prefigurative politics argues that the dangers of violent, cruel, and undemocratic "means" lie not only in how they damagingly shape what ensues but in how they cannot be distinguished from what ensues since there is no final "ends" vantage point from which prior action can be assessed. (2) The future can be rehearsed or anticipated. This typically involves small-scale or representational practices. (3) The present is lived as if it were otherwise. While the "as if" gestures to the fictive or simulated character of what is done, it also signals an assertive refusal to conform to and sustain hegemonic practices. Instead, the world that is sought is attempted. This is closely linked to the anarchist principle of building something new in the skin of the old. Rather than approach change as a top-down governmental process or as necessitating the direct dismantling of a society's established shape, new practices develop subdermally, causing the old skin of society to eventually wither and die as nothing within its casing any longer sustains it. In its place, a new societal skin emerges. For contemporary scholarship on prefigurative politics, see, for example, Ashar 2023; Maeckelbergh 2011; Monticelli 2022; Swain 2019; Yates 2021.

32. Tom Kemp (2023) develops a parallel analysis in his account of postrepresentational refugee detention politics.

33. Conceptual prefiguration could tie democracy to participatory rather than representative practices, or to lottery-based selections rather than elections (Gibbons 2024). It could revise the acts that constitute a democratic taking part or the scale and spatial boundaries of participation (extending electoral democracy, for instance, to all those affected by an election's outcome rather than those living in a narrowly defined territorial space). It might also extend democratic participation to nonhuman forms of life.

34. At the same time, conceptual engineering tends to rely on relations of correspondence (if not present, then optimistically anticipated) to explain what concepts are and do (see chapter 1).

35. We can observe something similar with the institutional concept of the state. If the state remains conceptually imagined as a hierarchical apparatus of governmental bodies within a defined national territory, it can be reformed, but more radical ways of doing government remain outside the conceptual parameters of stateness (see Cooper 2019a). Some may argue that this is right; that there is no good reason to draw more radical forms of governance into a state imaginary—better to abandon or limit the concept of the state and recognize radical governing possibilities in other ways. Yet established terms like the state—or gender or property—have authority and familiarity, and this can sometimes prove beneficial. Refusing to take up a revised concept of the state, for instance, for progressive politics may not only perpetuate a politics of purity (as concepts that are deemed contaminated become abandoned) but also romanticize the outside (civil society, grass roots) while depending on and reinforcing the distinction between state and nonstate. This leaves dominant concepts of the state, with all their power and eminence, free for

conservatives to monopolize. In analytic philosophy, some suggest that reconceptualizing produces new concepts and so, while the same term is used—for example, the state—this is not the same concept. I agree that, in reimagining the state, the concept of the state has changed; yet this state concept is not a bounded thing, sitting within a solar system of similarly bounded conceptual things. Concepts carry complex networks in ways that can make an investment in sharp boundary-drawing, between overlapping and changing concepts, unproductive. At the same time, when it comes to material forms of manifestation, such boundary-drawing is at the heart of many political struggles, as this book explores.

36. Jacques Derrida's work on unconditional concepts also reaches toward utopian notions of what concepts could mean—simultaneously depicting such limitless and unthinkable meanings as both impossible and necessary. In relation to justice and law, Derrida (2001) writes, "Despite this absolute radical heterogeneity between the two, they are indissociable. . . . Why? Because if you want to be just, you have to improve the law. And if you improve the law—that is, deconstruct the previous system—it is in order to be more just, to tend to justice." More generally, we might think of unconditional concepts as social imaginaries that guide, stretch, inspire, and counter the conditional practical ways in which certain normative concepts become operationalized or manifested.

37. Feminist writers and activists, for instance, have sought to redefine concepts, for reparative or ameliorative purposes, in ways that make negative qualities constitutive of what it is to be that thing. Sally Haslanger's (2000) subordination-based approach to what it is to be a woman is a good example of this, causing some to ask whether the UK's late Queen Elizabeth II would fall outside, and so not count as a woman (e.g., Carlson 2010, 63; see further discussion in chapter 1). Other feminist scholars, emerging from different traditions, have also treated oppression as determinative of the conceptual categories of woman and man. Monique Wittig (1996, 26), for instance, writes, "It is oppression that creates sex and not the contrary."

38. Importantly, a critical relationship to objected-to concepts is different from conceptual prefiguration undertaken by right-wing forces—who act as if the meanings that they seek (such as the neoliberal corporate state) are right and proper, as they combine new imaginaries and practical policy agendas. Prefiguration, it is important to note, is not the exclusive preserve of progressive or leftist forces.

39. Judith Butler (2004, 204) writes, "It is not a question merely of producing a new future for genders that do not yet exist. . . . It is a question of developing, within law, within psychiatry, within social and literary theory, a new legitimating lexicon for the gender complexity that we have always been living. Because the norms governing reality have not admitted these forms to be real, we will, of necessity, call them new."

40. This contextuality is commonplace for some social categories, such as disability; yet, as critics have argued, it has proved immensely harmful for people faced with nonhegemonic gender and sex identity statuses; see, for instance, Currah 2022; Spade 2015.

41. Kathleen Stock (2022, 41) proposes instead that sex-based concepts are needed "as traditionally understood, for efficient causal explanation and prediction."

42. These material processes include the vast networks of things that shape academic work, from places and temporal rhythms to news stories, events, and dreams. This book, however, focuses on created academic data, particularly empirical data—including

interviews, observations, legal judgments, and the experience of producing a speculative legal proposal.

43. These ideas are also developed in work on the utopian imagination; see, for instance, Salmenniemi et al. 2024.

44. The account focused on English-speaking common-law jurisdictions. A small handful of cases also arose in Australia and South Africa. See Cooper 2019a.

45. For further discussion along similar lines, see Locke 2007.

46. Interviewees varied in their methodological orientation, and not all undertook empirical research. Conversations with them do not appear, in this book, as findings that bring us closer to the truth of academic or policy practice, but as stimuli to think with and alongside—a method indebted to John Clarke's (2019a) "critical dialogues" project.

47. The main body of interviews are now in the public domain. See Cooper et al. 2023.

48. Publications from the project included two special issues, one in *Feminists@Law*, the other in *Feminist Legal Studies*: see Cooper et al. 2020; Cooper and Renz 2023.

49. See, for instance, Cooper 2016, 2019a.

1. MATERIALIZING THE CONCEPT

1. See also English 2025; A. Sullivan 2021. And see Vivienne et al. 2021 on how other contemporary censuses are approaching sex and gender.

2. See "Question 2—Your Sex," 2011 Census in England, National Archives, https://webarchive.nationalarchives.gov.uk/ukgwa/20110324104313/http://help.census.gov.uk/wales/help/help-and-information/Aboutthequestions/Individualquestions1to15/Topics/Question2Yoursex_U0002B.html; see also Duke-Williams, n.d.

3. See "Information Pertaining to the ONS Roundtable on 24 June 2020," ONS, August 12, 2020, https://www.ons.gov.uk/aboutus/transparencyandgovernance/freedomofinformationfoi/informationpertainingtotheonsroundtableon24june2020.

4. This chapter draws primarily on more general work on conceptual engineering rather than discussions specific to concepts of woman, gender identity, sex, and so on. For further philosophical discussion within this vein (and related ones) on who counts as a woman and how woman is defined, or otherwise approached, see, for instance, Barnes 2019; Haslanger 2000; Jenkins 2016, 2023; Simion 2018a. There is also a contemporary literature on how to define and conceptually approach gender identity: for example, Cosker-Rowland 2023.

5. For further discussion on the challenges and value of "conceptual disruption," see Löhr 2022; and on concerns about "linguistic confusion," see Mikkola 2009, 569–72.

6. Mona Simion (2018b, 924, 921) suggests one solution is to "give[] primacy to epistemic normative constraints in setting the normative boundaries for the ameliorative ambition." She writes, "If the conceptual engineering program is likely to leave us with concepts that fail us epistemically, devoid of representational devices that we can employ in exploring the world around us, then maybe we should set our engineering ambitions aside. What the program needs is a normative limiting recipe." However, Simion recognizes that social justice reasons for engineering cannot always be disentangled from epistemic ones since injustices typically shape our conceptual repertoire and perspectives.

Other conceptual engineers take up this point, advocating for conceptual revisions that are counterintuitive—whether deliberately or simply in practice. Robin Dembroff (2018, 42) suggests that emancipatory meanings may appear "false and largely unintelligible" since they counter the normalized meanings that dominant social relations produce (see also Belleri 2021). Dembroff's interest is in genders that do not yet seem to exist. Sally Haslanger (2000), by contrast, attends to gender as it currently exists, yet adopts a counterintuitive conception of woman anchored definitionally in subordination; see discussion in Simion 2018a; also Barnes 2019; Jenkins 2016; Mark Pinder 2022; Thomasson 2020.

7. Here conceptual activism is concerned not only with how conceptual imaginaries account for what already exists ("a partition of logical space" in Sally Haslanger's [2020, 240] terms) but with what else concepts (can) do.

8. On the implementation challenge for conceptual engineering, see also Queloz and Bieber 2022.

9. Changing a concept's meaning is identified as particularly difficult when the existing meaning seems stable and well understood. Sigurd Jorem (2021, 194) refers to this as "standing meaning"—"the meaning a word has in a language" that is "stable across speakers, times and places." Allison Koslow (2022, 18) suggests that some ways of engineering concepts are likely to be less successful than others. She describes hurdles for "the would-be conceptual engineer": "They tell against proposals that involve introducing homonyms of stably used expressions. They tell against proposals that involve replacing a usage sustained by communicative desires by one that does not better satisfy those desires. They tell against proposals that involve broad use of a word-meaning pair that will paint someone in a political light that some people are keen to be seen in and others are loath to be seen in. Finally, they tell against proposals that require speakers to use more epistemic effort to successfully apply an expression."

10. Limits on state law's capacity to control conceptual engineering are demonstrated, if paradoxically, with "legal fictions." Here, the law recognizes a thing as coming within a category that it is not properly seen as belonging to because category membership (from the perspective of law) largely takes place on other planes; I explore this further in Cooper 2024.

11. Emphasizing the legal incapacities of informal or everyday conceptual engineering can underestimate its occurrence, along with the consequences that may follow a term, such as marriage, being conceptually reengineered in the vernacular—not only for the communities in question but also for how legal authority is subsequently determined. In part, this is because the effects of conceptual engineering on how bodies assume and enact rights, powers, and statuses are not predetermined. This is addressed further in chapter 4, where I explore public bodies' conceptual activism—how they adopted new approaches to gender and sex categories in ways that were efficacious despite the meanings they enacted diverging, at times, from the assigned binary ordering of state law. In the case of the Census, the contrary judicial outcomes between England and Wales, on the one hand, and Scotland, on the other, where a more flexible approach to sex category identification was legally permitted, illustrate how the informal take-up of lived statuses is not necessarily doomed to failure; see Petition, *Fair Play for Women Ltd v. Registrar*

General for Scotland [2022] CSOH 20, esp. para. 55; and *Fair Play for Women Ltd v. Registrar General for Scotland* [2022] CSIH 7, para. 23:

> The census form is, perhaps more than any other official document, a public facing one, seeking responses from the populace about a whole raft of things, some of which may . . . contain to a greater or lesser extent subjective elements. It is to be expected that the language used, and the meaning to be attributed to the words used, are to be interpreted according to their popular and common meaning, not according to a specialist, restricted definition which may be adopted where matters of status and rights may be in issue. . . . We do not think that the question "what is your sex" should be interpreted as meaning "what is the sex registered on your birth certificate (or GRC [Gender Recognition Certificate])."

For discussion of the Scottish case, see also Tickell 2022.

12. A key issue here is what Karen Barad (2003, 804) describes as "representationalism"—"the belief in the ontological distinction between representations and that which they purport to represent; in particular, that which is represented is held to be independent of all practices of representing. That is, there are assumed to be two distinct and independent kinds of entities—representations and entities to be represented."

13. For one account of a closer, more knitted-together relationship, see Herman Cappelen and David Plunkett (2020, 12), who write, "Some concepts (or our use of them) can be constitutive of some element of non-conceptual reality . . . [and so] can change the nature of the relevant part of social reality."

14. For further discussion, see also Eklund 2024; Jorem 2021; Löhr 2022; Thomasson 2025.

15. Within work in conceptual engineering, there is some recognition of the interplay between ideational meanings (concepts) and material worlds. For a causational account, see Podosky 2018; and for a brief discussion on the capacity of reengineered social concepts to reshape the world, see McKenna 2018.

16. Conceptual activism, as Cantalamessa (2021, 54) describes it, involves deliberate, calibrated assessments: "Conceptual activists want to use language to get audiences to react in a certain way in order to get them to reflect on some aspect of word use in order to instigate conceptual revision and, by extension, social reform."

17. A different approach to the material expression of concepts can be found in a current of anthropological work that approaches concepts materially and ontologically rather than as interpretations of a distinct and separate social world; see discussion in Henare et al. 2007; Holbraad 2020; Holbraad and Pedersen 2017. Thus, for gender-critical feminists, this would suggest that their concept of sex as immutable biological sex is not an *interpretation* of physical or reproductive embodiment but what physical or reproductive embodiment gives rise to. Martin Holbraad and Morten Axel Pedersen (2017, 218) write, "With what other 'stuff' can things feed their conceptualizations, after all, than the very stuff that makes them what they are, as 'things'? So, the data that make a (conceptual) difference, in this case, are no longer what people say and do around things, but rather what we hear, see, smell, taste and touch of the thing as we find it (heuristically) as such."

18. Realization of new material ontologies has a specific place within transformative conceptual activism—in some respects it is the keystone—since materially producing

new kinds of states or gender relations, based on new imaginaries of what it is to be a state or gender, fulfills conceptual activism's promise: for instance, that the state is now caring and egalitarian; that gender identity is now elective and multiple. However, what counts as *realizing* the material ontology of a concept rather than just *using* or *depicting* conceptual meaning varies, particularly when concepts are subject to fraught disagreement; see Cooper 2024. Policies on nonbinary prenatal care, for instance, may shape how gender is imagined (as plural, distinct from sex, etc.) in ways that *contribute* to new gender ontologies, without policies in themselves necessarily being deemed part of gender's ontology. Institutional accounts of gender, however, approach gender's ontology differently, and so may identify policy on nonbinary prenatal care as a contributory part of gender's ontology. The stakes in this distinction can be observed in the case of gender-critical feminists, for whom an artwork that depicts sex as fluid and multiple or a local government policy that assumes people can self-identify their sex is a *representation* of sex (and indeed a misrepresentation of sex); these enactments are not deemed part of sex's ontology because this ontology is strictly defined as being forged on a distinct plane, namely of reproductive biology. For others, (re)presentations and policy discourse help to make up what sex is; they are not just the relations of production that bring sex into being or depict it. Determining what constitutes the ontology of a concept is important when it comes to identifying (and struggling over) its normative worth, and whether it is something to create, protect, or dismantle. If gender is imagined as a structure of domination, its maintenance has a different normative value than if gender is understood as part of a person's sense of self with no inherent relationship to inequalities of power; for further discussion, see chapters 3 and 6.

19. Barad's dynamic materialist account of concepts is informed by the theoretical physicist Niels Bohr, whom Barad (2003, 820) describes as offering "a new epistemological framework that calls into question the dualisms of object/subject, knower/known, nature/culture, and word/world. . . . Bohr's insight that concepts are not ideational but rather are actual physical arrangements is clearly an insistence on the materiality of meaning making that goes beyond what is usually meant by the frequently heard contemporary refrain that writing and talking are material practices."

20. ONS, home page, accessed August 3, 2025, https://www.ons.gov.uk/aboutus.

21. For a useful discussion in the US context, see Waldman 2024; and for different perspectives on designing sex and gender categories, see, for instance, Bittner and Goodyear-Grant 2017; Westbrook and Saperstein 2015.

22. According to Jane Clare Jones and Lisa Mackenzie (Jones 2020, 24), "Trans ideology posits gender identity as the essential *truth* not only of someone's gender, but, in fact, of which sex a person 'really' is." See also A. Sullivan 2021.

23. On the importance of attending to what follows from conceptual choices and decisions, see also Jorem and Löhr 2024.

24. Context shaped the conceptual conflict over sex and gender census categories, including in relation to the rationalizations deployed. Here arguments resonant with world-to-mind engineering in the form of prioritizing "objectivity" (A. Sullivan 2021) combined and sometimes clashed with pragmatic concerns to do with buy-in, intelligibility, and the negative symbolic consequences of presenting sex and gender in biologically inflexible ways. Those in favor of less tightly circumscribed categories suggested sex questions

should not be posed in ways that threatened the privacy or validity of transitioning or that disregarded people who identified as nonbinary. Meanwhile, sex-realist feminists worried that many respondents would be confused by questions asking about gender identity, and they worried that data would merge or confuse sex and gender, compromising possibilities for comparative and historical statistical analysis.

25. I have critiqued this proprietary account further in Cooper 2019a, chap. 4.

26. On the parallel conflict in Scotland, where litigation on whether the sex question legally required respondents to identify their legal sex held that it did not, see *Fair Play for Women Ltd v. Registrar General for Scotland* [2022] CSIH 7; see also Murray and Blackburn 2019 for a critical historical account of the Scottish government's approach; and Cowan et al. 2021 for a response.

27. In December 1998, the ONS responded to a query from a campaigner for Press for Change (a transgender law NGO) about how to answer the Census sex question. The ONS responded, "Should there be the traditional question on the individual's Sex in the 2001 Census, it would be reasonable for you to respond by ticking either the 'Male' or 'Female' box whichever you believe to be correct, irrespective of the details recorded on your birth certificate." Diversity Solutions Consultancy 2008, 8.

28. "Question 2—Your Sex," 2011 Census in England.

29. On developing a gender identity question, see ONS 2016b.

30. For a discussion of gender-critical beliefs and sex realism, see the introduction. Although there is a strong overlap between the two, some sex-realists (e.g., gender conservatives) may not be gender-critical. This discussion is predominantly focused on gender-critical sex-realist enactments of what sex means.

31. But see ONS 2016a, 15: "Sex, as biologically determined, is one of the most frequently used and important characteristics the census collects as it is used in most multivariate analysis of data and feeds into the UK population projections. It is critical that the collection of information on gender identity for a small population (estimated to be less than 1%) does not jeopardise the quality of data collected on sex for the population who don't have trans identities or the protected characteristics of gender reassignment."

32. "Gender Identity Update," ONS, January 2017, section 3, https://www.ons.gov.uk/methodology/classificationsandstandards/measuringequality/genderidentity/genderidentityupdate.

33. "Sex and Gender Identity Question Development for Census 2021," ONS, June 2020, annex 4, https://www.ons.gov.uk/census/censustransformationprogramme/questiondevelopment/sexandgenderidentityquestiondevelopmentforcensus2021.

34. "Qualitative Research on Gender Identity: Phase 1 Summary Report," ONS, September 2017, section 4, https://www.ons.gov.uk/methodology/classificationsandstandards/measuringequality/genderidentity/qualitativeresearchongenderidentityphase1summaryreport. The ONS considered gender identity to be a concept that could support data on trans people since asking about "gender reassignment" (the term used in the Equality Act 2010) was seen as outdated and unacceptable. Thus gender identity became, at times, a proxy for trans people rather than a typical feature of contemporary personhood: "Data users showed a clear requirement for information on gender identity for policy development and service planning.... This focused on a need for data on a population comprising less than one per cent of the population at local authority level.... There is a user need

for data about gender identity . . . to support interventions for this community. The user requirement for data on those with the protected characteristic of gender reassignment is strengthened by the Equality Act 2010. Hence, ONS plans to take forward work on gender identity." ONS 2016a, 18, 21.

35. "Qualitative Research on Gender Identity."

36. This was informed by reluctance among some trans test respondents to be visible or, alternatively, to be invisible according to how they answered two separate sex and gender questions; see "Qualitative Research on Gender Identity."

37. See "Sex and Gender Identity Question Development"; also UK Government 2018. The Census (Return Particulars and Removal of Penalties) Act 2019 amended the Census Act 1920 so that penalties would not apply if respondents failed to answer the gender identity question.

38. "Guidance for Questions on Sex, Gender Identity and Sexual Orientation for the 2019 Census Rehearsal for the 2021 Census," ONS, September 2019, https://www.ons.gov.uk/census/censustransformationprogramme/questiondevelopment/genderidentity/guidanceforquestionsonsexgenderidentityandsexualorientationforthe2019censusrehearsalforthe2021census (italics added).

39. The ONS reported that "respondents understood 'non-binary, transgender or . . .' to suggest that the terms are mutually exclusive. It was felt they should be separated with an and/or. As this is not possible for a screen reader to deal with, the Office for National Statistics (ONS) is using 'If you are one or more of . . .' The term 'variations of sex characteristics' was welcomed. . . . References to 'consider' (and 'believe,' which was used in a previous version of guidance shown to respondents) were strongly disliked and considered inaccurate. We are using 'whichever answer best describes your sex.'" "Guidance for Questions."

40. Woman's Place UK also suggested that the guidance provided in 2011 for transgender people (on how to answer the sex question) be removed for the 2021 Census: "WPUK Submission to UK Statistics Authority: Phase 1 Assessment of 2021 Census," Woman's Place UK, March 30, 2020, https://womansplaceuk.org/2020/03/30/wpuk-submission-to-uk-statistics-authority-phase-1-assessment-of-2021-census/.

41. Quoted from the letter sent to the directors of the UK Census authorities, the First Minister of Scotland, and Prime Minister, December 18, 2019, National Records of Scotland, https://webarchive.nrscotland.gov.uk/3/archive2021.parliament.scot/S5_European/General%20Documents/CTEEA_2019.12.18_Sullivan.pdf. In her article, Alice Sullivan (2021, 646) also describes concerns and expectations expressed to the ONS from statistical regulatory and expert bodies (the Office for Statistics Regulation and the Methodological Assurance Review Panel) in autumn 2020.

42. R (Fair Play for Women Ltd) v. UK Statistics Authority [2021] EWHC 940 (Admin), paras. 4–5.

43. R (Fair Play for Women Ltd) v. UK Statistics Authority [2021] EWHC 940 (Admin).

44. This was, however, complicated by the legislative premise, accepted by the court, that a person's gender could be the same (or not) as their registered birth sex. Yet if gender and sex are not synonymous concepts, what does it mean to say that gender is the same as the sex at birth? The only way of making sense of this equivalence, if it is not a causational relationship, is through the presumption of a category correspondence or

alignment between a certain birth sex and a certain social status, role, or identity—where the male body gives rise to the social character of being a man, for example. While this is not inevitable, the notion that this is a "cis" outcome suggests a presumptive alignment or shared set of qualities between being male (sex) and man (gender).

45. The ONS suggested that some households may have already completed the Census ahead of the Census date, but the court did not consider that this justified not amending the guidance; *R (Fair Play for Women Ltd) v. UK Statistics Authority* [2021] EWHC 940 (Admin), para. 25. For a contrasting approach, see the Scottish decision in *Fair Play for Women Ltd v. Registrar General for Scotland* [2022] CSOH 20; *Fair Play for Women Ltd v. Registrar General for Scotland* [2022] CSIH 7.

46. Approaching sex and gender as institutional concepts suggests their ontology is formed, at least in part, by bureaucratic action. For further discussion of this approach, see Cooper 2024.

47. R (Fair Play for Women Ltd) v. UK Statistics Authority [2021] EWHC 940 (Admin), para. 16.

48. "Office for National Statistics Withdraws from Census Guidance Case; How Best to Respond," Gendered Intelligence, March 17, 2021, https://genderedintelligence.wordpress.com/2021/03/17/office-of-national-statistics-withdraws-from-census-guidance-case-how-best-to-respond/.

49. See, for instance, "Census Guidance on the Sex Question Ruled Unlawful," Sex Matters, March 10, 2021, https://sex-matters.org/posts/data-and-statistics/census-guidance-on-the-sex-question-ruled-unlawful/.

50. Sex Matters to Ed Humpherson, OSR, November 14, 2023, https://osr.statisticsauthority.gov.uk/wp-content/uploads/2023/11/Sex-Matters-to-Ed-Humpherson-letter.pdf. See also analysis by Biggs 2024.

51. Sarah Pedersen (2023, 9) describes how, in Scotland, some gender-critical feminists showed their opposition to the legal ruling that allowed guidance on the sex question to include self-identification through their own conceptual activism in completing the census form—for instance, writing "believer in biology" in response to the question about religion.

52. Sex Matters to Ed Humpherson, OSR, November 14, 2023 (italics added).

53. "Gender Identity, England and Wales: Census 2021," ONS, January 6, 2023, https://www.ons.gov.uk/peoplepopulationandcommunity/culturalidentity/sexuality/methodologies/sexualorientationandgenderidentityqualityinformationforcensus2021.

54. The question of conceptual continuity is a recurring theme in conceptual engineering—namely, when does revising a concept lead to a new concept, and when does it simply amend it? For discussion on this point, see Köhler and Veluwenkamp 2024; Prinzing 2018. This book offers an alternative way of addressing this question.

2. HOW CONCEPTS DANCE

1. I explore what conceptual activism is and the relationship between imagining, materiality, and the reorganization of meaning in some depth through the course of this book. In brief, conceptual activism involves reorganizing meaning to advance change or to protect existing meanings in conditions where they are perceived to be under threat.

Conceptual imaginaries relate to the beliefs, values, feelings, principles, and knowledges that hold up and compose meaning, while materiality relates to how meaning is practically represented, expressed, constituted, enacted, and realized.

2. My approach to these interviews was inspired by John Clarke's (2019a, 2) "critical dialogues" project, which aimed to make the process of "'thinking out loud' more visible and more audible" as "intersubjective," "dynamic," and collaborative. See also Werron et al. 2024 on "practices of theorizing."

3. This chapter draws on a selection of the interviews. Of the twenty-three conducted, about half were with interdisciplinary sociolegal scholars. This created a body of interview data from scholars working with broadly shared foundational concepts and methods. Other interviews were with interdisciplinary scholars in geography, politics, critical race studies, governance studies, and sociology who work on meaning politics—most (although not all) through a mix of empirical and theoretical research. Academic research discussed in interviews related to Australia, Cyprus, Egypt, India, Ireland, South Africa, the UK, and the US. Interview questions and discussion evolved over the course of the research as lines of analysis emerged, but broadly interview prompts concerned interviewees' relationship to conceptual activism, the challenge of developing and using concepts in counterhegemonic ways, what concepts did, concept formation and change in relation to community praxis, and how the form or shape of the concept was imagined.

4. Sociolegal scholar Bronwen Morgan, for instance, resisted the figure of the balloon—one I had introduced into our discussion based on an earlier interview. She said, "What I was visualizing when I was speaking earlier was almost like grass weavings or something. . . . It wasn't balloon-like, it was more like lots of threads interwoven. . . . Although it would be quite beautiful from a distance, it might be quite messy close up."

5. Dilip Gaonkar makes a similar point in Calhoun et al. (2015, 192), commenting on "the tension and the alignment between the 'third-person' objective point of view and the 'first-person' insider point of view" in relation to social imaginaries.

6. Conceptual attachments, however, were not always experienced positively. Geographer Craig Jeffrey commented on "how people discard concepts when they cease to become useful or feel embarrassed that they once used them. Again, it's this very affective response to intellectual work."

7. Interviewees described how concepts provided "out there" objects of study as well as "in here" commitments (see also Connolly 1993), as emancipatory perspectives, like feminism, connected personal academic experiences to wider struggles in ways that supported a critical conceptual politics. Public policy scholar Janet Newman commented, "I came into political life through feminism. And that of course upended a lot of concepts, much like postcolonial theory. You have to go back to the beginning and say, 'Where does this idea come from? What it's about? Why is it useful, or wrong?'"

8. However, this can be hard work and take time, as geographer Peter Kraftl described in relation to a group of children he was working with on a project about play. The children talked to the researchers about spaces of racism, poverty, and poo:

> In one particular community, [they] began to tell us about how they felt disadvantaged compared with others living in other places in the city, and for us they were actually conceptualizing themselves or kind of co-producing, . . . in some entirely

unexpected ways, some concepts. One concept was that the groundwater, the water that flowed through the community, was racist. . . . Another was the presence of duck poo everywhere on one playground. . . . We called it "smearing" because there was this sense in which they were conceptualizing this space as just being smeared with duck poo. . . . For us, what was striking was that this was totally unexpected. . . . It actually took us ten years to write about this because we didn't know how to respond or what to do with these data and what we thought, you know, children were trying to tell us. (See also Horton and Kraftl 2018)

9. Janet Newman helpfully described one instance of this more equivocal conceptual location through the notion of the edge: "Borders and boundary work are, I think, interesting because feminism is on the periphery of the academy and women have been on the periphery of organizations, and those borders I think are very productive. . . . I was an activist worker in local government . . . on the edge with a few other women. And that was a very productive place to be. . . . We were on the edge of what the mainstream was, [and] on the edge of what theories about local government were at the time. . . . Being on the edge can be a very vulnerable place to be, but it can also be a very political place to be."

10. For further discussion see Patton 2006; also Derrida 1974.

11. In other words, concepts' take-up of these forms contributes to what it means to be a cell, current, and so on. Max Black (1993) suggests that when two things are linked by metaphor, this is not a one-way relationship of importation, although this may depend on the relative stability of meaning of each term. This relationship is also addressed in work in organizational studies on "conceptual blending"; see Fauconnier and Turner 1998; and see also Cornelissen 2006; Weick 1998. I have said the figures offer "loosely patterned forms," drawing on Evelyn Fox Keller (2002, 120), who suggests that imprecision and ambiguity can be important aspects of metaphor.

12. For further discussion, see also Cornelissen 2004, 2006, developing Karl Weick's ideas; and Reynolds 2018.

13. On concepts as tools, see also Köhler and Veluwenkamp 2024; Marchiori 2025; Nado 2021; Wolfe 2014.

14. Discussing the use of sex and gender categories in American state agencies, Paisley Currah (2022) adopts a similar approach. Against calls for sex and gender to be seen as having true or real meanings, Currah argues that their meaning varies according to the context of their deployment as regulatory concepts.

15. For a useful discussion on the functions and affordances of concepts—what they should and can do—see Marchiori 2025.

16. For a helpful account of the challenges and translation practices that conceptual coproduction can entail, see Quintana et al. 2022.

17. Examples include public statements at the start of cultural, educational, and other events acknowledging that they take place on (unceded) Indigenous land.

18. For an interesting account of the apology in relation to extinct animals, such as the great auk, see Craps 2026.

19. Others, such as Sara Ahmed, have also explored how concepts like apology, equality, and diversity can be enacted in ways that undermine their realization (e.g., Ahmed

2020). In other words, such concepts function as counteraids—to obstruct or resist rather than realize the commitment they express. Alternatively, we might think of such concepts as being *realized*, but what is realized or materially enacted is a different conception of the concept—one that sees realization as happening through, and being accomplished by, what is written or said. Disagreement, then, is not about whether materialization has happened but about the kinds of materialization that concepts such as apology and diversity ontologically require for their realization and what such realization does (or accomplishes).

20. This "many worlds" approach also draws on the concept of the pluriverse. Maggie FitzGerald (2023, 253) writes, "The pluriverse is a dual assertion: it reveals that a one-world ontology underpins the modern world (in both theory and practice), and, in pointing to other actually-existing multiple worlds . . . by which I mean co-constitutive ontologies and epistemologies that are together enacted through collective practices and thereby constitutive of forms of life—it demonstrates that this one world assumption is false."

21. See also Bey (2022, 62), who argues for a Black trans feminism that refuses this territorial move.

22. Academics come to the concepts that they inhabit in diverse ways. Morgan described the part played by a transition network in prompting her interest in the concept of social enterprise:

> I ended up getting involved in non-academic networks around transition, just transitions and climate action. And there I found that people were really working with an effort to shift things in paradigmatic ways that involved, amongst other things, conceptual imagination. So, I think that was the first place where I came across people talking about social enterprise. . . . I could see that these people were connecting quite radically different imaginations of how they would live their daily life in terms of powering, you know, creating power, but also making something that could provide an income stream. And so things that I had essentially sorted in my head into, "This is what public government would do and this is what private enterprise would do," were being mixed up in very interesting normatively attractive ways. . . . I would sit there and listen. . . . It's definitely something about the stakes of all of that coming alive that made me much more invested in exploring that.

For further discussion of how economy and government might conceptually mix, see chapter 3.

23. Important here is the ongoing praxis of walking and landscape-changing as "intertwined paths give their shape to spaces" (Certeau 1984, 97). Here, Michel de Certeau (97) cautions against a survey that just notes the formal lines that have been left, rather than the ongoing process of their creation, where "the trace left behind is substituted for the practice."

24. On reimagining leftward what it could mean to be a state, see Cooper 2019a; Cooper et al. 2019; Newman and Clarke 2014. Feminist artists Sarah Browne and Jesse Jones (2019) capture something of this last archiving possibility in their "post-patriarchal archive," a place for depositing the hazardous sexist stuff of contemporary life that will have become obsolete. This is a prefigurative participatory art project that wittily

anticipates an imagined future and uses it to identify patriarchal objects (and other features) of the present that should be confined to the archive. For further discussion along these lines, see chapter 5.

25. Discussing the tending or care work needed for the concept of depletion, Shirin Rai remarked, "Care takes the form of being aware of the limits, it also takes the form of continually revisiting and expanding [the] concept too . . . but I think care must mean [for] concepts to let go. You know, that's what I mean about travel" (see also Rai 2024).

26. In work on conceptual engineering, questions of novelty and innovation are examined as writers disagree about what it means and what is involved in inventing concepts—and whether conceptual engineering is about revision rather than invention (e.g., see Eklund 2024). Guerrilla gardening concepts presuppose that concepts are entered, reappropriated, and adapted (including radically) rather than invented anew because the historical arc of their conceptual development is an important part of their meaning and effects. Conceptual histories (with all their contestations, side streams, multiplicity, and flux) are often underattended to in conceptual engineering scholarship, leading concepts to appear temporally flat, as synchronous meaning displaces diachronic meaning.

27. For further discussion and different perspectives, see Comaroff and Comaroff 2001; Keenan 2025; Mottier 2008.

28. See Adams et al. 2014; Hung 2017; also Richard Reynolds's guerrilla gardening website, accessed August 6, 2025, https://www.guerrillagardening.org/.

29. See also Köhler and Veluwenkamp (2024), who emphasize that the question of conceptual continuity relates specifically to the normative functions of the concept.

30. Many interviewees felt strongly that concepts could not act independently and that it was important to attend to how conceptual currents were generated and deployed by wider social forces. Ballakrishnen said, "Yes, there are gusts of winds, there are currents, there are ways in which concepts float and become important and get taken on, but . . . it's not happening completely in a vacuum, it's not just happening as a natural force . . . it's almost like a stagecraft, like there's a theatre of it in terms of how it works." The take-up and use of currents in relation to play is explored in chapter 5.

31. Discussion of atmospheres also gives rise to a similar conceptual network "of concentration, diffusion, sedimentation, coherence, mass, expansion, and movement" (Sloterdijk 2009, 47) that impresses upon actions and objects. Such networks do not reside exclusively within specific concepts; rather, individual concepts operate, in Bhambra's words, as "shortcuts" or as nodal or entry points into wider networks that act.

32. Focusing on the institutional concept of gender, Renz identified the value in diminishing its force. Her account of gender as something that can fluctuate in intensity contrasts with conventional understandings, which treat gender as a structure or subjectivity that is normatively constant and stable. Individuals may transition and the meaning of gender is subject to historical shifts, but gender is not treated as being like illness or disability, that is as something which can be subject to "chronic flare-ups, [or] going into remission" (Renz interview; see also Renz 2019; Renz and Cooper 2022).

33. A small-scale example to illustrate this point concerns the concept of "laws" as imagined and enacted at Summerhill School, established by the educator A. S. Neill in Suffolk, England, in the 1920s and still active today. Summerhill School is famous

for its commitment to democratic, participatory community government that involves children, as well as its policy of elective class attendance (see Neill 1968; also Appleton 2000). At Summerhill, laws refer to the many rules that the community has introduced (and sometimes wholesale abolished; see Appleton 2000, 112–15) concerning rights, prohibitions, and regulatory expectations placed on both child and adult members—from laws on bedtimes, to going downtown, making noise at night, and sharing (or gifting) personal things. The concept of laws works to delineate and underscore the (evolving) norms that are identified as necessary for community well-being, and the sanctions that are applied when laws are not complied with. As such, the concept of law provides an imagined and enacted tool for community members in their interactions with each other. At the same time, school laws function as currents affecting community members, since all are subject to law's force (although some laws apply only to certain groups, and specified individuals may be formally exempt from a particular law's scope). Despite law's force, noncompliance and transgression occur (see Appleton 2000, 96–97; Neill 1968). Being caught up in the current of laws does not render school members docile. Rather, their entanglement gets expressed through participation in designing and voting on the laws at school meetings, adjudicating cases, determining fines, and hearing appeals, as well as in remarks made by children to each other, something I witnessed while doing field research at the school, that they would "bring them up" at the school meeting if the offending (or annoying) behavior did not cease.

34. See, for instance, N. Brown and Nettleton 2017; E. Cohen 2009; E. Martin 1990; Reynolds 2007, 2018.

35. In doing so, I reverse the gaze adopted by Andrew Reynolds (2018), where he traces more than three centuries of change in the social figures drawn on by scientists to explain the biological cell (itself a term drawn from its social application), including citizens, the factory, state, and society. As understandings of both biological cells and society have evolved, so have the figures used to depict how cells live and work (Reynolds 2018). See Daniel Nicholson (2019) also for a critique of the machinic figure of the cell in favor of a more plastic, dynamic, less determined understanding.

36. This reactivation was consolidated in the Supreme Court decision in *For Women Scotland Ltd v. The Scottish Ministers* [2025] UKSC 16. For critical discussions of the weaponization of safeguarding, and of the sexual exceptionalism in carceral politics, see Bower-Brown 2024; Lamble 2025.

37. For Renz, these concepts were ones you might step on and find as shards in your feet—"like, you know, if you step on a sea urchin" (interview).

38. For further discussion, see Cooper 2014. At Summerhill School, concepts of democracy and freedom also traveled through the school's capillaries, from children's right to participate in decisions about the school, to exercising their personal freedom to miss classes without sanctions, to misbehaving and being "fined" (see Appleton 2000; Neill 1968). In the operative context of a school community, liberal concepts of freedom and democracy became radicalized. Approaching freedom through the figure of the cell attends to how it materialized (including in laws, community member utterances, children's decisions and choices about how to live, school publicity, and narratives of the school's origin and ethos), and what such materialization accomplished—from fighting off alternative concepts (or alternative conceptions of freedom, such as individual liberty) to

sustaining the school through the presence and manifested vitality of children's freedom (Appleton 2000).

39. Cells, for instance, can also be aids, as Reynolds (2018, 141) discusses in relation to their reengineering.

40. My use of dance in this way is indebted to dance studies, including work on conceptual dance; see, for instance, Berleant 2004; Bieszczad 2022; Brannigan 2018, 2021; Fabius 2012; Lepecki 2004; Pakes 2019; Novac 2022. While conceptual dance is approached as a form of dance practice that reflexively challenges and reenacts what dance is and does (by stretching, interrogating, and abandoning key elements, including sometimes movement itself), its enactment and the discussions surrounding it are helpful for thinking about other kinds of expressive patterning in which plasticity, movement, and change but also fixity and stillness take place, including the expressive patterning of conceptual form.

41. See also Mulcahy 2021 and Ramshaw 2023 on the research process as one of dance.

3. SPECULATIVE IMAGINARIES

1. Other members of the research group were Robyn Emerton, Flora Renz, Elizabeth Peel, Emily Grabham, Hannah Newman, and Jess Smith.

2. The project was titled the Future of Legal Gender and funded by the Economic and Social Research Council (UK). Its aim was to design, analyze, and critically explore a speculative law reform that would dismantle sex and gender as legally established, acquired, and regulated statuses in Britain ("decertification"), explore informal decertification by existing agencies, and deploy decertification, methodologically, as a critical aid to understand diverse contemporary perspectives on sex and gender regulation. The project led to a number of publications, including two special issues (in *Feminists@Law* [2020] and *Feminist Legal Studies* [2023]), and a final public report; see Cooper et al. 2022; see also Cooper and Renz 2023.

3. Participant in a thread discussing the research project on a web-based platform (not named to protect anonymity).

4. Interview with trade union official.

5. This chapter foregrounds the *imagined* dimensions of conceptual meaning. The material accomplishment of new conceptual meanings and the challenges this entails are addressed more fully in the next chapter.

6. For further discussion, more generally, on the governmental and legal challenges and changes in how gender categories are used, see Jessica Clarke 2015, 2019; Currah 2022; Currah and Moore 2009; Holzer 2018; Katyal 2017; Saguy and Williams 2024; J. Williams 2026. I explore these issues further in Cooper 2022; Cooper and Emerton 2020; Cooper and Renz 2016.

7. I use the phrase sex-gender to indicate the formative relation between sex and gender, where acquiring a legal and social sex categorization is expected to give rise to, and is aligned with, legal and social gender membership. The converse, gender-sex, indicates contexts, such as transitioning, under the terms of the Gender Recognition Act 2004, where change of legal gender (predicated on a change in social gender) allows for a change in legal sex. This chapter draws on interviews conducted before the Supreme

Court decision in April 2025 in *For Women Scotland Ltd v. The Scottish Ministers* [2025] UKSC 16, which held that sex for Equality Act purposes was biological sex—that is "the sex of a person at birth" (para. 7).

8. For further discussion, see John Clarke 2014; Pryke 2007; Robertson 2012; S. Sullivan 2010.

9. Processes of making may valorize equality (as with antidiscrimination law) even as their own relations of production may prove far from egalitarian.

10. On the importance of access to "sharing" economies, and the problem of unequal distribution, see L. Richardson 2015; see also Bardhi and Eckhardt 2012 on car sharing; and Morgan 2024 on commons-based sharing economies and digital platforms.

11. For an interesting discussion of individual utopian consumption, see Atanasova 2021; for a critical discussion of the concept of consumption and its expansion, see Graeber 2011.

12. This is also explored in political economy and economic sociology through the language of "prosumption," where active consumption, purposefully engineered by producers, adds commercial value to what is made; see Comor 2011; Roberts and Cremin 2019. The difference here is that the contribution that use makes to production is not necessarily driven by profitability or commercial sustainability.

13. However, work in policy and implementation studies has long countered this linear model; e.g., see Barrett and Fudge 1981; Lipsky 2010.

14. Capitalist relations exert force, but they do not fully determine the meaning, effects, and value of alternative economic practices and circuits. At the same time, alternative economic circuits and forms, such as the cooperative, commons, and sharing economies, may draw on and sustain social differentials of gender, race, education, and wealth; see Bledsoe et al. 2022; Schor et al. 2016.

15. Writers working in this field don't always agree on the terminology. For instance, some argue that the term alternative reinforces the normative status of capitalist economics. However, conceptual disagreement over these terms is not germane to my discussion here.

16. For examples along these lines that also point to more expansive understandings of economic goods, see, for instance, Chatzidakis et al. 2014; Narotzky and Besnier 2014; Power 2004.

17. See, for instance, the organizing categories used by Gibson-Graham (2008, 616) for "diverse economies": "transactions," "labor," and "enterprise."

18. For broader approaches that target what counts as an economic thing, see Arnould 2022; Bossy 2014; Hong and Vicdan 2016.

19. In choosing the figure of the dance, my analysis is indebted to Karen Barad's work on concepts and diffraction (see also Thiele 2014). Drawing on physicist Niels Bohr, she (2007, 142) writes, "Apparatuses are not passive observing instruments; on the contrary, they are productive of (and part of) phenomena." Barad's work is helpful in identifying how apparatuses (as material-discursive practices) form part of the object studied, the possibilities for reversing the apparatus-object frame, and the contribution that apparatuses make to the cuts that distinguish apparatus from studied object. Although Barad does not develop the figure of the dance, her discussion of the relationship between apparatuses and the phenomena studied evokes a similar idea when she (2007, 146) writes,

"Apparatuses produce differences that matter—they are boundary-making practices that are formative of matter and meaning. . . . Apparatuses are themselves phenomena (. . . part of the ongoing intra-activity of the world)." Thus economy is part of what gender decertification is and does, and decertification is part of economy, while each also contributes to the onto-epistemic cuts that differentiate them. Approaching dance as patterned movement offers a counterpoint to a conceptual account that treats relations as rigid and fixed when it comes to the primary concepts of this chapter (decertification, sex/gender, and economy); the economic features of making, acquisition, and use; and the social forces engaging with decertification.

20. My understanding of conceptual dance is indebted to work in dance studies; see Berleant 2004; Bieszczad 2022; Brannigan 2018, 2021; Fabius 2012; Lepecki 2004; Novac 2022; Pakes 2019.

21. On the controversial place of stillness in dance, see Lepecki 2006, 15–16.

22. I am grateful to Bonnie Honig for this point.

23. For discussion of the maker movement, see, for instance, Ferretti and van Lente 2022; Marotta 2021; Schor et al. 2016; T. Smith 2017. I return to craftivism in relation to property and gender play in chapter 5. For an innovative example of how making and exhibiting can be used to support legal research, see Perry-Kessaris and Barnes (2025) on "fantasy legal exhibitions" as a design-based prefigurative method.

24. On feminist judgment writing, see, for instance, Davies 2011; Gayoye et al. 2021; Golder 2024; R. Hunter et al. 2010. On other judgment writing projects, see, for instance, Ferreira et al. 2025; Rogers and Maloney 2014, 2022.

25. Other examples include peoples' tribunals, where the architecture of staged legal inquiry holds political and corporate elites to account (Byrnes and Simm 2018), and feminist legislation-writing projects (e.g., Batagol et al. 2024). These examples demonstrate how simulations-with-revisions are not juxtaposed to the real. Rather, they deploy forms that critically mirror what is, rehearse a different real, and realize this something else in a register of academic and grassroots experimentation (see chapter 5; see also Mitchell 2008, 1119–20).

26. See, for instance, Cooper 2023, 2026; Grabham 2020, 2023.

27. On the neoliberal university, see, for instance, Burton and Bowman 2022; Gupta et al. 2016; Loveday 2018. For an interesting small-scale study of academics undertaking "unfunded" research within a neoliberal context, see R. Edwards 2022.

28. In contrast to the Australian feminist legislation project, which focused on legislative drafting and parliamentary lawmaking (see Batagol et al. 2024), our closest formal comparator was the law commission. This invokes an earlier lawmaking stage, allowing for greater abstraction and prefigurative utopianism in the prototyping carried out. On the British Law Commission, see Lee 2023.

29. Interviews were conducted with staff in local government, independent statutory bodies, government agencies, umbrella bodies with public responsibilities, trade unions, nongovernmental organizations (NGOs), schools, and women's service providers, as well as with independent experts, academics, lawyers, legislative drafters, and the general public. The survey generated over three thousand responses. For further discussion and analysis of the survey specifically, see H. Newman and Peel 2022; Peel and Newman

2020. Workshops were held with lawyers, legislative drafters, trade unionists, NGOs, graduate students, and regulatory bodies.

30. I explore the methods and challenges in crafting a legal text further in Cooper 2023. Counterintuitively, perhaps, the legislative prototypes we developed moved from greater to lesser specificity; for the final text, see Cooper et al. 2022, 37–39.

31. Trans men who give birth are currently deemed mothers for the purpose of their child's birth certificate; see *R (McConnell and YY) v. Registrar General* [2020] EWCA Civ 559.

32. We interviewed several rabbis from different denominations. One from a more progressive denomination described how they were introducing new practices to recognize nonbinary congregants but suggested that, in general, sex/gender difference was not particularly relevant to their work. Another rabbi we interviewed remarked, "I think it would be possible to preserve the right of religious bodies to define legal maleness and femaleness, even if the state doesn't have that requirement or doesn't assign people's gender or sex in that way at birth. So, there could be a right for religious organizations to do so. In fact, there might need to be a right for religious organizations to do so, because they are not all liberal and many would, I suspect, completely reject the idea that it would become impossible to assign people a gender identity or affirm sexual identity." For further discussion on the wider point of devolved authority for sex and gender ascriptions, see Jessica Clarke 2015; Cooper and Emerton 2020; Cooper and Renz 2016.

33. The individualist and group-based paradigms dominating public discourse also crowded out more systemic, structural, and institutional understandings of gender, as I discuss later.

34. These concerns are explored in more detail in Cooper 2022; Cooper and Emerton 2020; Emerton 2023; Peel and Newman 2020; Renz 2023.

35. See, for instance, Susan Dalgety, "Abolishing Legal Status of Sex Would Rob Women of Sex-Based Rights and Protections," *The Scotsman*, May 20, 2022, https://www.scotsman.com/news/opinion/columnists/abolishing-legal-status-of-sex-would-rob-women-of-sex-based-rights-and-protections-susan-dalgety-3702218.

36. One trade union official suggested in their interview that the project survey was being used by critics of trans rights, who were encouraging supporters to respond, since the timing of the survey coincided with the UK Government's consultation on reforming the Gender Recognition Act 2004; "Consultation Outcome: Reform of the Gender Recognition Act 2004," UK Government, last updated October 19, 2018, https://www.gov.uk/government/consultations/reform-of-the-gender-recognition-act-2004.

37. While critics did not have the right to destroy the proposal, the capacity of us, its designers, to do so was also limited—both by the difficulty in eliminating an idea once put into circulation and, more practically, by the conditions of production of externally funded university research.

38. This approach to property complicates and disperses sovereign ownership by identifying and separating out rights—or, more precisely, permissions, powers, responsibilities, obligations, and freedoms—to do different things. Property "sticks" may be held in combination or distributed among different subjects. They may also be held informally—as well as formally—with property sticks seized, assumed, used, and gifted in ways that may not be officially permitted but prove practically efficacious. Worth noting, however,

is how, in other contexts, the unbundling of property sticks can support more intensive forms of commodification and marketization and can disregard the necessary ontological connections between different sticks (e.g., see Robertson 2012, 393–94).

39. As with sharing material on social platforms (e.g., John 2013) or peer-to-peer lending (e.g., L. Richardson 2015), the intention is to avoid vertical relations of bestowal. Goods are not directly and explicitly gifted to another but are made available for others to use if they choose to. Acquiring access and use through an invitation to consider or take up a thing can prove less directive in *how* things are to be used. In interpersonal gifting, there is an unspoken expectation or assumption that the thing will or should be used according to the ascribed uses carried by the object, unless these are explicitly overridden in the act of giving or by an up-status repurposing (using gifted things in ways that increase rather than decrease their status)—an ashtray as a flower holder but not a flower holder as an ashtray. Making things available for unnamed others, through an open invitation to take them up, carries less explicit injunctions regarding use. This works for speculative things, such as imaginary laws, particularly in conditions of conflict where the thing may be deliberately used in counterintended ways. Critics, for instance, as I discuss, used decertification to demonstrate the extent of opposition to liberal gender transitioning reforms, and to expose what they claimed was the "real," if covert, endpoint of liberalization (see also Peel 2025).

40. See Fairbairn et al. 2022 on the UK Government's consultation. The Scottish consultation led to legislation to liberalize gender transitioning; however, it was stopped by the Secretary of State for Scotland, under section 35 of the Scotland Act 1998, from being submitted for royal assent on the grounds that it exceeded Scotland's devolved powers, a decision that was upheld in court; see *Scottish Ministers v. Advocate General for Scotland* [2023] CSOH 89; also Torrance and Pyper 2023.

41. The notion that self-identification actually "makes" gender comes largely from critics who argue that when self-identification prevails, gender becomes reduced to what a person claims or presents themselves as being. This self-presentation does not just mistakenly depict the category a person fits in, but remakes what it means to be a category of gender.

42. In other contexts where identity categories are in dispute, "living as" may be a relevant test of category belonging that is tied to community recognition. In other words, a person acquires and holds membership in a group because the community recognizes them, while living as a member of a group may also generate community recognition.

43. See "Apply for a Gender Recognition Certificate," UK Government, accessed December 19, 2025, https://www.gov.uk/apply-gender-recognition-certificate/what-documents-you-need. This hollowed-out approach avoids stereotypical demonstrations of sex and gender by simply requiring evidence of sustained use of the "correct" new gender-sex names, honorifics, and category selections. However, in conjunction with required medical confirmation, it risks reaffirming substantive gendered assumptions about what women and men are like. The official presumption, between 2018 and 2025, and one made explicit for those transitioning, was that gender-sex should signal a stable commitment. Section 2(1)(c) of the Gender Recognition Act states that the panel must be satisfied that the applicant "intends to continue to live in the acquired gender until death." However, in practice sex and gender categories, during this period, could be acquired and

held in overlapping and discontinuous ways. Someone could be a woman for sex-specific hostel provision, nonbinary within community networks, and male when playing sports. This tells us something about how sex and gender got institutionally produced in conditions where the binary, largely fixed categories of formal state law could be overridden or displaced by other principles and criteria.

44. For sex-gender, a state-enforced system of birth-certified sex became pockmarked by a series of permitted (and less legal) exceptions, and by informal arrangements that disregarded the certification work done by state law. In sports, this tended to resurrect biological sex—specifically, a testosterone-fueled account of biological sex—as something that could trump legal sex when the two were deemed to diverge. In other British contexts, many municipal councils, trade unions, NGOs, and regulatory agencies leaned toward self-identification in the late 2010s and early 2020s, recognizing that identifications could informally change, and that people might identify as neither women nor men. In the following chapter, I explore this policy landscape and the opposition it encountered.

45. Withdrawal is a well-established epistemic technique that denaturalizes and makes visible taken-for-granted features of everyday life through the prospect of something being withdrawn (see also Honig 2021). Sometimes withdrawal is a practical accomplishment, as with strikes and boycotts, but it can also involve speculative ideas or unachievable proposals. By focusing on what might be lost or removed through decertification, contemporary gender regimes and the regulatory categories they rely on surface, along with the stakes, investments, and contrasting feelings of optimism and anticipated loss; see, for instance, H. Newman and Peel 2022; Peel and Newman 2023.

46. Critics presented sex certification as exclusively beneficial to women since men did not need it. In Britain, men's power did not come from their legal status, and decertification would therefore not reduce it. A women's rights expert commented, "I think one of my real anxieties is that you would end up recommending that women would lose their sexed status. And I think the only people who would lose from that would be women. Men wouldn't . . . They would still be seen as men. They will still act out masculinity because that's been really successful for many years."

47. On the history of birth registration and recording of sex in a British context, see Higgs 1996; also Basten 2006; Cullen 1974; J. Smith 2023.

48. On the work done by certificatory processes, see, for instance, Bartley 2003; Goodman 2004; Munasinghe et al. 2021; Schroeder 2010; Schwarzbach and Richardson 2014.

49. Because of this, some trans rights activists and organizers also defended certification for the security it offered them as vulnerable subjects. One interviewee remarked, "I think that a lot of trans people use legal status as a way to prove that they have the right to access really basic amenities and to be [able to say] well, actually, I am this and the law states this, and no matter what you say, the law is on my side."

50. For further discussion, see Cooper 2022; Cooper and Emerton 2020; Grabham 2023; Renz 2023.

51. Reliance on certification is commonplace. Yet the common-sense status of many certification processes can deflect attention from the politics and power relations that structure sectors and the place, uses, and consequences of certification within them; e.g., see S. Brown and Getz 2008; Spiegel 2015.

52. For further discussion, see, for instance, Bartley 2003; Spiegel 2015.

53. On certification's constitutive work, see Munasinghe et al. 2021, 254; Mutersbaugh 2002.

54. My thanks to Bonnie Honig for suggesting this point.

55. Approached from a conceptual engineering perspective, this raises questions about conceptual continuity—where the same term is used to characterize something that has substantially altered; for further discussion on this point, see chapter 1.

56. There are echoes here of Julia Black's (2001) discussion of the move from "command and control" to decentered regulatory forms. Black's (2001, 105) account of the former resonates with criticisms of how legal sex and gender status is regulated, with "poorly targeted rules, rigidity, ossification, under- or over-enforcement, [and] unintended consequences."

57. As with other forms of denationalization, this could also privatize gender. I explore some implications of this in Cooper 2020a.

58. Gender abolitionism approaches gender as a socially made thing whose harmfulness derives, in part, from its role in making other things, including war, exploitation, aggression, and ill health. Gender is not just—or even principally—from this vantage a benign resource for developing selves and communities, as gender-diversity politics may suggest; its systemic significance and impact are far greater and more troubling. Gender abolition here is not about abolishing the term gender so much as it is about abolishing the relations, processes, and practices that gender is deemed to entail; see also Cull (2024, 158), who describes the latter as metaphysical rather than conceptual abolition.

59. See, for instance, Rai 2024; Walby and Shire 2024. These are uses, of course, that can outlive gender, and so continue to draw (or intensify how they draw) in and on other social relations, including poverty, national status, geography, ethnicity, and age, to manage the gaps or changes caused by gender's productive decline or disuse (at least in certain contexts).

60. This may suggest that gender should be overconsumed, turned into waste, and jettisoned by a society that no longer wants or needs it, like the objects placed in the postpatriarchal archive, devised by artists Sarah Browne and Jesse Jones (2019), to hold the remains of a faulty world that has been superseded. Talk of gender waste, however, risks attaching waste to certain gendered subjects rather than others, especially those whose lives appear more marginal and unconventional, and so precarious.

61. For a helpful discussion of the relationship between disuse, nonwork uses, and transformative reuses, see Honig 2021.

62. For further discussion, see also Bey 2022, 67; Weltman 2024.

63. On craftivism, see, for instance, Bratich and Brush 2011; Vachhani et al. 2025. For a discussion of gender and complex systems analysis, see Walby 2007.

64. Gender-critical feminists objected to individualistic and voluntarist accounts of gender, but their emphasis on class-based relations of domination meant more structural accounts, attuned to gender as a complex landscape of tangled interconnections and, at times, contradictory relations of power, often got shelved.

65. My thanks to Donatella Alessandrini for helping to clarify this point.

4. COMMON SENSE AND FACING BOTH WAYS

1. The councils abolished were higher-tier urban authorities and included the Metropolitan County Councils of Greater Manchester, South Yorkshire, and West Midlands. They were abolished under the Local Government Act 1985.

2. For discussion of municipal socialism and the new urban left in 1980s Britain, see Saunders 1984; Gyford 1985; Lansley et al. 1989; see also Cooper 1994, 2017.

3. I explore how councils positioned themselves in relation to narratives of illegality and defiance in Cooper 1996.

4. My use of the term *care-full* draws particularly from Miriam Williams's work; see Williams 2017, 2020, 2022.

5. In investigating how public bodies used policy practices to introduce new gender categories and meanings in Britain in the late 2010s and early 2020s, this chapter focuses on those doing the practical work. This includes organizations as well as individual employees within them (see also Olsson 2009; Pettinicchio 2012), deploying their agency or discretion—"slack" in William Connolly's (2013, 185) words—as "institutional engineers" or, as Frances Cleaver (2002, 17) prefers, "do-it-yourself bricoleurs." See also Abers (2019) on "bureaucratic activism." Policy workers have historically pursued initiatives, in this field, with little or no organizational support. However, my discussion focuses on work that was desired or, at least, tacitly accepted by the host organization rather than on defiant or overtly noncompliant practices. Officials engaged in supporting equality governance did not present themselves as work-based activists, although they were undertaking activism as the concept is used here; see also Bobel (2007) on activism by social movement actors who disavow the title of activist.

6. I use the term policy practice to foreground the materialization of gender concepts in how policy is made and carried out without relying on a clear separation between the two. Policy practice includes writing and disseminating texts (reports, agendas, recommendations, etc.); it also includes speech (in meetings, in frontline services), as well as the ways that bodies and resources move and the ways buildings are constructed and organized (adapting changing rooms in leisure centers offers a very vivid example of how new ways of understanding gender were materializing). Conceptual activism through policy practice is interactive, innovative, and repetitive, and it relies on institutional legibility, reason, and materials; see also Freeman et al. 2011.

7. Conceptual activism is as much concerned with what is done as it is concerned with how meanings are imagined in an analysis that treats meaning change not as the precursor to new forms of practice but as bundled up and coconstituted with it. The doings addressed in this chapter are governmental (rather than grassroots) doings, and the kinds of materials at stake (policy reports, funding allocations, access to public services, etc.) mirror this. These are also doings that contribute to gender's production as an institutional assemblage composed of norms, rules, strategic moves, roles, deportment, labor, evaluations, the allocation of power and resources, and more (see P. Martin 2004). In other words, policies, funding decisions, job ads, and such do not just support or respond to gender as a social quality of human subjects; they also help to make up gender as an institutional formation.

8. In Britain, public opposition to gender-(as)-diversity activism did not come primarily from conservative opponents (e.g., Lombardo and Meier 2022), although conservative Christian litigation organizations did engage in legal action. The most visible opposition within mainstream and social media, as well as within public-sector organizations, was from gender-critical feminists; for further discussion, see introduction and chapters 1 and 3.

9. For Women Scotland Ltd v. The Scottish Ministers [2025] UKSC 16, para. 7.

10. Referring to these relationships as attachments moves away from the tendency to see attachments as desired or favorable (even as they may also be damaging); see also Anderson 2023. The concept of attachment here draws attention to the ways in which organizations became legally bound to gender-critical meanings through cases brought against them, which established the duties of employers when it came to gender-critical staff manifesting their beliefs.

11. For examples of cases, see *Meade v. Westminster City Council and Social Work England* ET 2200179/2022 & 2211483/2022; *Fahmy v. Arts Council England* ET 6000042/2022; *Phoenix v. The Open University* ET 3322700/2021 & 3323841/2021.

12. See Fish et al. 2018; Goldstein 2020; Horton and Kraftl 2009; Tironi 2018; Vachhani et al. 2025. For further discussion, see Soaita (2024, 1423) on the everyday "more concealed" activisms of housing tenants; on the "makeshift activism" of refugee organizations as the small-scale, reparative "patching together of solutions," see Lanari (2024, 187).

13. For further discussion, see also Bobel 2007; D. Martin et al. 2007.

14. A similar premise underpins the assumption that prefiguration takes place *outside* state bodies since prefiguration also presumes that desired objectives are unachievable at the time of action and so are merely represented, rehearsed, or piloted; for a different perspective on institutional prefiguration, see Cooper 2020b.

15. See also Risberg and Corvellec (2022) on the place of "trying" in organizational diversity work given the obstacles and restraints present.

16. For further discussion, see Bey 2021; De Jong and Kimm 2017; K. Thomson 2020. I have explored elsewhere the complex processes through which radical sexuality agendas get "softened" through state incorporation; see Cooper 1994, 1995.

17. Projects for change may involve collaborating or liaising with grassroots social movements but also may not; see Abers 2019. Activism here is not a synonym for statecraft (e.g., L. Weiss and Thurbon 2021), with its emphasis on careful, muscular governmental action. While activism may involve the craft or art of governing, it signals a mode of public action that is sociopolitical, outward facing (extending beyond governmental self-care and self-empowerment), and explicitly or tacitly agonistic.

18. State and nonstate (including grassroots) bodies must be sharply differentiated, bearers of contrasting logics, if only the latter (by definition) can do activism.

19. This recognizes that how various kinds of state boundaries are defined and understood, as well as how they materialize, is temporally and geopolitically contingent and so not helpful to pin down abstractly.

20. For further discussion and examples on this point, see Cooper 1995; Cooper and Herman 2020; O'Brien et al. 2023; Rich 2019; Verhoeven et al. 2022. Institutional

decoupling can allow more contentious aspects of public bodies' practice to operate by being kept apart from what are deemed to be core or official structures and processes; for instance, in *R. (JHRW) v. Leicester City Council* [2016] EWHC 1512 (Admin), para. 46, and [2018] EWCA Civ 1551, para. 10, the court held that council chamber resolutions in favor of the movement to boycott, divest from, and sanction Israel could be valid (as undertaken and discussed by representatives) since they were properly and sufficiently kept apart from the council executive's procurement and contracting policy.

21. Explicit state activism, for instance, may involve the creative development of new powers or take-up of existing ones for unexpected or improperly perceived ends (see Joubert 2023), such as the creative accounting techniques used by 1980s new urban left councils in Britain to release funds for public expenditure given the severe constraints imposed by central government at that time (A. Clarke and Cochrane 1989; Stoker 1991). In their showier activism, public bodies, such as radical municipal government, may assume powers and roles deemed to belong to other authorities, which, in a hierarchically structured system, often includes roles or powers associated with superordinate bodies (e.g., see Cooper and Herman 2020; Malen 2003). In the quieter activism explored here (see also Pottinger 2017), councils, regulatory bodies, and trade unions relied primarily on conventionally accepted resources and powers in giving shape to new gender meanings in their services, funding, rules, and policies. For further discussion, see generally Abers 2019; Buchter 2021; Olsson and Hysing 2012; Pettinicchio 2012.

22. Public bodies' approaches to sex and gender categories have been radically unsettled by the Supreme Court decision in *For Women Scotland Ltd v. The Scottish Ministers* [2025] UKSC 16. Thus this chapter offers a picture of public bodies' activist practice in the seven years leading up to this judicially imposed resettlement.

23. Common sense can also be unsettled, dismantled, pushed to the side, or reappropriated. Claims of "loonyism," "extremism," and, more recently, "wokeism" counter attempts to procure a new common sense by marking new meanings as outlandish, dangerous, excessive, or otherwise wrong.

24. In the process, new meanings slid from political-seeming attempts to counter an injustice, not yet accepted as existing or as wrong and in need of repair, to becoming part, in Jacques Rancière's (1999) terms, of the police order, with its stabilized partitions and distributions.

25. The leading case to decide that gender-critical beliefs are protected under the heading of religious and philosophical beliefs in British equality law is *Forstater v. CGD Europe and Others* UKEAT/0105/20/JOJ.

26. Another official described a dilemma being faced by housing officials, in relation to nonbinary children, in complying with provisions under the Housing Act 1985, section 325(1), which treats young people of "opposite sex" who are over ten and not married or civilly partnered and who must share a bedroom as falling within the statutory definition of overcrowding. They said,

> Basically, there is a housing allocation policy, where if a family has two children, a boy and a girl, they would be given separate rooms. . . . A family come forward to say they have got a nonbinary child and they don't know, should they be given a

separate room? Obviously, when we've got limited housing and limited-size housing as well . . . we know that the number of . . . young people identifying with non-binary is increasing. And we would say very legitimately increasing. We don't think this is a dodgy thing or a phase. . . . But we would also have people who would jump on that bandwagon and say: fantastic, my child is nonbinary. And it would need some definition as to what can you do? But equally, what we don't want to do is medicalize it too much so that they have got to come away from somewhere with a certificate.

The tension identified here between the requirement for definition and evidence to manage scarce resources, on the one hand, and concern about the overformalization of sex and gender, on the other, is explored in chapter 3; see also Cooper 2022.

27. On vagueness and sex from an analytic philosophical perspective, see also Daly 2015.

28. On isomorphic institutional pressures, see DiMaggio and Powell 1983. Regulatory and certifying bodies have here played an important, if at times contentious, role in defining "good" or "best" practice, generating new normative standards and templates (see Bartley 2003; Schneiberg and Bartley 2008; Wedlin 2007), and encouraging organizations to converge around a norm (see also chapter 3).

29. See also *R (JHRW) v. Leicester City Council* [2016] EWHC 1512 (Admin), upheld on appeal, *R (JHRW) v. Leicester City Council* [2018] EWCA Civ 1551, where the applicant argued along these lines to oppose municipal government's participation in the pro-Palestinian movement to boycott, divest from, and sanction Israel (see *R (JHRW)* [2016], paras. 3, 5), although they lost their case for judicial review.

30. The tension, such as it exists, between being impartial and taking a policy stance that aligns with one side rather than another in a conflict is not necessarily a bad thing; for scholarship on agonistic politics, see, for instance, Connolly 2002; Glover 2012; Honig 1993.

31. See, for instance, *R (Smith) v. The Chief Constable of Northumbria Police* [2025] EWHC 1805 (Admin), which held that the chief constable's decision to authorize the visible participation of police at a Pride event, given the event's support for "gender ideology and transgender rights" (para. 135), could be perceived as breaching a duty of impartiality, and therefore was unlawful.

32. Partisanship is routinely associated with activism. Indeed, it is often treated as activism's quintessential and necessary quality—assertively supporting an agenda, politics, or group, knowing others have different views, yet with no mandate or obligation to embrace them. In conventional accounts of activism, responsibility to opponents is bracketed. Far from being a relationship of accommodation or transpartisan accountability, the friend/enemy logic of activism constitutes it as a relationship of combat, competition, and sometimes destruction (or elimination) as sides seek victory over each other. Commonplace in grassroots politics, intensified adversarial engagement can also be found in ideologically explicit state activism, such as the 1980s municipal activism in Britain with which I began this chapter.

33. On "heteronymous" forms of conceptual engineering, see Chalmers 2025; chapter 1. In her work on "care-full justice," Miriam Williams (2017, 2022) describes the responsibility that people have for others thanks to their mutual interdependence. Williams's work

attends to everyday practices, such as alternative food provisioning. She argues that care needs to be done justly, while justice should be undertaken caringly.

34. Another union official remarked that the provision of "gender neutral facilities" should not be "at the expense of single sex facilities" and "neither should be mutually exclusive."

35. See also Strunz (2012) on how terms' different meanings may be more (or less) distinct and separable from each other; see also Viola (2019, 236) on vagueness, pragmatism, and "essentially contested concepts"; and Hodges (2008) critiquing the drive for precise definitions in conceptual development.

36. Vagueness elicited different opinions (see also Emerton 2023, 104). One city official said, "We always make the argument the risk to us is far higher the more vague we are because it's more likely that people will make mistakes and that we could then be subject to judicial review or legal challenge." Other have also argued that, while vague concepts may be inclusive, thin shared meanings can make concepts inadequate as guides to action (see Hamilton-Jones and de Groot 2021). Yet this seems to assume a specific sequencing, in which the concept as cognitive aid or template clarifies in advance what should be done. What vagueness entails and what it does depends also on the form that concepts assume (as cells, worlds, and currents, as well as aids). Vagueness, or lack of definitional clarity and precision, may arise as concepts move between these different forms—for instance, when conceptual currents, are taken up as aids (see chapter 2).

37. See, for instance, *Meade v. Westminster City Council and Social Work England* ET 2200179/2022 & 2211483/2022; *Fahmy v. Arts Council England* ET 6000042/2022; *Phoenix v. The Open University* ET 3322700/2021 & 3323841/2021.

38. In chapter 3, I considered what ownership looked like within economies of speculative lawmaking, reregulation, and gender futures. There I adopted a distributed property model in preference to one of dominium or mastery. Yet when it comes to political and legal discourses on possessed belief, a model of dominium or mastery is tacitly adopted. Limits may be imposed on what propertied beliefs can do, but beliefs are seen as fully owned by those who hold them. The distributed property model introduced in chapter 3 offers a different approach. Jane Baron (2013, 58–59) writes, "Seen as a bundle of rights, property is not monolithic but is composed of pieces (. . . 'sticks') that are combined together but can be disentangled." In the case of care-full activism, how sticks are distributed, held, and used within organizational conflicts comes to the fore. Turning to the concept of property does not resolve social justice concerns (see also Pateman 2002); however, what a "bundle of sticks" approach to property here offers is a fine-grained set of technologies based on divisible rights (including powers, responsibilities, freedoms, and prohibitions) among bodies in relation to things, such as contentiously enacted concepts of sex and gender.

39. For careful attention to the temporal mix of hegemonic and counterhegemonic processes, see also Stubbs 2018.

40. Slow activism can make space, as one interviewee put it, for "debate, analysis, research to get us to a nice place where there is a legal framework that not everybody might agree with, but [where] people understand the journey and the reasons we have the law as it is" (quoted in Emerton 2023, 113).

41. I explore this further in Cooper 2026. There are similarities here to nonreformist reforms; e.g., see Akbar 2022. These are reforms intended to contribute to transformative processes rather than tamping down the desire and momentum for change.

42. See also the discussion in Ozturk et al. (2025) on slow incremental policy change around nonbinary inclusion and equality.

43. Writing on prefigurative law, Amy Cohen and Bronwen Morgan (2023, 1065) describe a modality of legal engagement framed as "any how and in case." This modality does not assume that sought-after changes will necessarily follow what is done but acts on the off chance that they might or out of a refusal to withdraw and let reforms fall into disuse because success appears unlikely. This less instrumental approach to law also aligns with slow activism.

44. In many respects, the gender meanings that got manifested in equality governance policies were not new. They were not new to the community groups and individuals who lived gender-(as)-diversity, and they were not new to officials developing services and policies who had long assumed self-identification would be relied on when it came to gender (or sex). However, the explicit emphasis on trans inclusion, banning gender and sex category assumptions in frontline service delivery, and the expressed need to recognize nonbinary constituents were striking and innovative aspects of British public governance during this period.

45. Certainly, this happens thanks to hegemonic forces, logics, and discourses. At the same time, new or minor-stream agendas are pursued—their characterization as activist comes from the conditions of opposition, resistance, and containment that they encounter.

46. I explore this relationship of governmental ventriloquizing further in Cooper 2013.

5. PLAYING WITH HAZARDOUS CONCEPTS

1. On the relationship between gender and property, see, for instance, Davies 1994; Decoster 2024.

2. Property can be understood as a practice, sociolegal object, idea, regime, and set of relations (see also Layard 2020). Given its take-up here as an institutional analogue to gender, I approach property, in institutional terms, as an assemblage of rules, roles, spaces, relations, things, moves, norms, beliefs, and orderings. Institutional status may seem to suggest an enduring formation with coherence, stability, and force, but it is important to recognize that institutional diversity exists in conjunction with institutional change; see chapters 4 and the conclusion.

3. See, for instance, Blomley 2003; Keenan 2017, 2019.

4. For different perspectives on play's rationale and purposes, see Bogost 2016; Dittmer 2013; Huizinga 1955; Kane 2011; Lehner 2022; Trammell 2020; Vervoort et al. 2022.

5. These different features suggest different kinds of imagined boundaries to what is and is not play. Conceptual activism can also involve deliberately bringing play into domains where it is not supposed to be (or perceived not to belong), such as military sites, in ways that (temporarily) change the materialized meaning of the domain or practices undertaken there; see also Wedderburn 2021.

6. It is important here to recognize that questions of ontological lack depend also on how concepts are imagined. Thus, the propertyness of property according to one imaginary may be (at least partially) realized, while for another imaginary it is only playfully simulated. I explore this further in Cooper 2024.

7. See Consalvo (2009), discussing Goffman and Fine on "key" changes as ways of moving in and out of a gameworld.

8. This movement uses objects, sites, and subjects (participating, watching, objecting); it also has its rhythms. On play as a toing and froing, see McDonald 2014.

9. I explore this further in Cooper 2019a, 2023.

10. Margot Weiss (2006, 240) makes a similar claim, "Play is also disarming; because it is just play practitioners can play with dangerous 'taboo' topics more explicitly than one can in real life. In some ways, the bracketing function . . . provides an alibi to make reenacting power plays safe."

11. On political satire, see, for instance, Bogad 2016; Romanienko 2007; Shepard 2009; Tunali 2020.

12. Lisiunia Romanienko (2007, 144) describes how in the city of Wrocław, in late 1980s Poland, "Orange Solidarity members arrived at scheduled and unscheduled spectacularized public protests . . . dressed in orange elf costumes. . . . They frolicked around Soviet tanks, they sang nursery rhymes through streets blocked by overturned trams, they danced around burning military vehicles, . . . they even held hands and sang songs . . . in front of menacing weapons positioned on heavy military vehicles engaged in crowd control" (see also Misztal 1992). Related uses of political play are described as taking place at Greenham Common Women's Peace Camp, established at the military base near Newbury, Berkshire, in the 1980s, about fifty-five miles west of London. Writers describe how protest campers breached the perimeter to picnic on the base and dance there; and how they dressed as teddy bears, witches, and more to symbolize their opposition to nuclear weapons, assert women's power, and ridicule the military logic of security; see also Feigenbaum 2008; Feraro 2016; Roseneil 1995, 2000; Welch 2010.

13. This has been a site of continuing discussion within play studies since Johan Huizinga's (1955, 28–29) early depiction of play as "temporary worlds within the ordinary world, dedicated to the performance of an act apart."

14. Huizinga (1955) introduces this concept to studies of play.

15. Emma Vossen (2018, 206, 210), for instance, has written on rape speech in online play, arguing that the wider social context and power relations mean that even where the same speech is used by men and women, the meaning and effects can be unequal (see also Vella et al. 2020). Aaron Trammell (2020) discusses how racism conditions play to be hurtful, toxic, and brutal, to exclude or objectify those who get played with, while also providing material for the play itself. On the relationship between white heterosexual male gamers and the men's rights movement, see O'Donnell (2020); and see Goudet (2024) critiquing the absence of certain gender identities in online games and their racialization.

16. See, for instance, discussion in Malaby 2007; M. Weiss 2011.

17. In turn, these different material instantiations of play contain, resist, redeploy, and reinvent (or reform) the cuts and joins that make up property concepts, where property's conceptual cuts and joins are both imagined and material, and tied up with each other.

For instance, imagined cuts can be materially enacted (such as imaginaries of landlord behavior that get played out in Monopoly), while material cuts or imagined notions of salient material cuts form and consolidate conceptual imaginings (for instance, the lines drawn to indicate a parking space or, rather, a temporarily licensed area, deployed in PARK(ing) Day events, as I discuss later). For other work on cuts in this vein, see Barad 2007; Blomley 2011; Strathern 1996.

18. For a description of the cooperative board game Commonspoly, see "Gaming for the Commons—Commonspoly," CreaTures, accessed January 2, 2026, https://creatures-eu.org/productions/commonspoly/index.html; on Eco, see "*Eco* (2018 Video Game)," Wikipedia, last edited September 11, 2025, https://en.wikipedia.org/wiki/Eco_(2018_video_game).

19. For further discussion, see, for instance, Fjællingsdal and Klöckner 2019; Gugerell 2023; Petz et al. 2024; Morgan Pinder 2024. Interestingly, the website for Commonspoly, a board game described as recapturing the initial impulse of Monopoly's ancestor, the Landlord's Game, describes itself as celebrating "those moments of collective joy that bloom when a group of people share a common understanding of what it means to actively and truly participate in society" (accessed January 2, 2026, https://commonspoly.cc/). The Landlord's Game was created by Elizabeth Magie and intended as a critique of monopoly power; see Pilon 2015. My thanks to the anonymous Duke University Press reviewer for directing me to this history. In their discussion of utopian pedagogy involving arts-based methods and play, Suvi Salmenniemi, Pilvi Porkola, and Hanna Ylöstalo (2024) also emphasize its value as collaborative, immersive, embodied, and nonlinear, facing toward what could be while also tangled with everyday life.

20. Several writers have explored Monopoly's value, including pedagogically, teaching students about capitalism, for instance; e.g., Shah 2022; see also Seto (2008, 1039) on Monopoly as an example of "non-redeemable, non-convertible currencies."

21. For further discussion, see, for instance, Jagoda et al. 2015; Lastowka and Hunter 2004; Lim 2010.

22. In several online multiplayer games, including *Second Life* (*SL*), game-world property relations seep out. This may conflict with the intentions of game designers, be permitted in part, or, as in *SL*, explicitly be promoted to generate "first-life" economic value for regular players and for companies who use virtual worlds to sell brands; see, for instance, Goggin 2012; Lehdonvirta 2005a, 2005b. The play principle of maintaining uncertainty and open-ended outcomes, and of constraining those with too much power or capacity within the playworld (for instance, through use of handicaps), drastically shrinks when digital playworlds present themselves as reliable, investible places for first-life wealth creation.

23. At the same time, unlike horizontal forms of play or board games that make cheating and other transgressions possible, even if they are formally forbidden, the governance of online play spaces structures and constrains the forms and relations of property that can emerge. In digital playworlds, inventive and progressive forms of property-making can be rendered impossible through code—for instance, game software that makes players unable to hold property in common, make property public, redistribute, or tax it. Code does not turn subversive property relations into trespass or theft; it simply stops them

from taking place. More generally, games and play simplify property relations, giving rise discursively and narratively to a model of sovereign ownership rather than disaggregated property rights, although, in practice, especially with rule-based games, there are often strong restrictions on what can be done with things owned.

24. But, of course, this depends on the limited scope of the play life as well as its reach—if lives are largely lived in a game world, what happens there may matter more.

25. Something of this premise runs through Elsa Noterman and Nicholas Blomley's (2024) discussion of how children learn property norms and conventions through play.

26. Bogost (2016, 92) describes play as the opposite of irony since irony involves relations of distancing, while "in play we draw them close."

27. In Britain, an iconic mass trespass of privately owned land took place at Kinder Scout, in the Peak District, in 1932. This act of civil disobedience led to the organizers' imprisonment, but it has also been heralded as helping to prompt national policy changes, including the National Parks and Access to the Countryside Act 1949, and as providing a symbolic historical referent for the Countryside and Rights of Way Act 2000; for a modest account of the trespass's impact, see Hey 2011. In other contexts, beaches have been spaces of regularized and performative trespass to preserve community use and enjoyment; see, for instance, Azcárate 2025.

28. For further discussion, see Assaf-Zakharov and Schnetgoke 2021; Farran and Smith 2021; Halsey and Young 2006, 280–81; McAuliffe 2012. A related disregard for prior ownership claims, by enacting alternative informal ones, occurs in the outdoor sport of parkour or free-running as participants run, tumble, and move, in an often spectacular stream-like flow, through the physical urban landscape. We can understand urban free-running as an example of conceptual activism—as property's meanings become (if briefly) materially reenacted. Free-running, like graffitiing, also generates an anticipatory conception of the space, anchored in its imagined future use. Mark Halsey and Alison Young (2006, 286–87) describe how graffitists view surfaces as structures waiting to be written on.

29. For a different example of play's deployment to counter hegemonic property regimes, see Alice Proctor's description of Uncomfortable Art Tours and badges with the printed words, "Display it like you stole it," to counter museums' depictions of objects as if they belonged to them and were properly (and naturally) in their rightful place; The Exhibitionist, home page, accessed January 2, 2026, https://www.theexhibitionist.org/. My thanks to Sarah Keenan for directing me to this initiative.

30. On the teddy bears picnic at Greenham Common Women's Peace Camp, see the documentary film *Carry Greenham Home* (1983), directed by Amanda Richardson and Beeban Kidron. For a helpful discussion on the ecopolitical possibilities of incongruity-based humor that works by crossing human/nonhuman divisions, see Tønder 2026.

31. For further discussion, see also Blomley 2013, 2014; Decoster 2024.

32. Graffitiing and mass trespass also provide examples of this reversal as play currents carry property's repurposing—for instance, to support more democratic relationships to cities and the land. My aim, however, in identifying different kinds of property play is not to create a taxonomy—with different instances allocated to different boxes—but to draw out the many ways that property play can take shape within progressive conceptual activism.

33. See, for instance, Marsh and Śliwa (2021) on the Orange Alternative in Poland; their analysis suggests waves of play, humor, and laughter can be deliberately forged and intensified to disorient opponents.

34. Another example, explored by Thorpe (2018b), concerns community-based repossession of vacant sites in Montreal for recreational and urban agricultural uses. Here the affordances of play encourage people to get involved, while the prefigurative elasticity that play espouses and practices (acting as if unauthorized rights have force or as if counterhegemonic rationalizations prevail) generates confidence in taking up and repurposing spaces, which may also be used expressly for play.

35. For further discussion, see Bey 2022; Decoster 2024; Macpherson 1962; Nedelsky 1990; J. Richardson 2010.

36. Property logics help to structure juridical assessments of what counts as the propertied res, the scope of protection, and what the propertied object, such as a religious belief, may be permitted to accomplish (Cooper 2019a, chap. 4; Cooper and Herman 2013). In the case of gender and sex, as earlier chapters explore, proprietary conflicts have centered on who can claim a relationship of belonging to the category woman, in what circumstances, and with what consequences.

37. This discussion, along with earlier work on this topic, is indebted to Cheryl Harris's (1993, 2020) work on whiteness as property, in terms of the entitlements, expectations, changes in value, and relationship to other capitalized forms of status, such as socioeconomic class, that whiteness carries.

38. There are echoes here of Hannah Arendt's (1958) account of public action in bravely, adventurously creating new meanings, practices, and relations (and, in some cases, sustaining older ones) through action in front of (and with) others; see also Butler 2015; Honig 1995.

39. Writing on dance and law suggests some similar practices in terms of the embodied movement through which conflict, scrutiny, and adjudication take place; see, for instance, Mulcahy 2021; Mulcahy and Seear 2023.

40. Dominant conservative forces also regularly play with resources, rules, tactics, expectations, and norms, as they undertake calculated activity to circumvent or undermine progressive laws or anticipated legislation that conflicts with their self-identified interests. In cases of free-running, however, state bodies may not make themselves easily available to be used by the forces free-running across them. Indeed, it is this resistance and the tension it generates that motivate and enable political free-running.

41. It also does not resemble the concept of "serious play"—a term used to identify the creative development of policies and products or the playful achievement of work objectives; e.g., Statler et al. 2011.

42. Here, both property and play are manifested, but these manifestations are purely textual.

43. On contestations around these aspects of property formation and recognition, see Bruun et al. 2018. An example of the contestations that can arise over how property cuts are made, in terms of whether relations and practices are recognized as property (and what kind of property), is the litigation over virtual land in *SL* in *Bragg v. Linden Research, Inc.*, 487 F. Supp. 2d 593 (E.D. Penn). In an act of conceptual cutting intended to bear legal force, the makers of *SL*, Linden, argued that virtual land

was not land that one could acquire title to as property. Virtual land, rather, was "a license of access to Linden's proprietary servers, storage space, bandwidth, memory allocation and computational resources of the server, which enables the experience of 'land' and the things that one can do with 'land' on the Second Life platform" (quoted in Lim 2010, 315).

44. For further discussion on property's relationship to habitat, see Davies et al. 2021.

45. For further discussion, see Cooper 2014; Davies 2020; Keenan 2014.

46. Integral also to this process were instances of play against and at the boundary of the democratically designed school laws, as play demonstrated how property relations and property limits worked by mischievously and inventively countering them; Appleton 2000, 29–30.

47. Within *communally designed* property worlds, heterogeneous property relations also arise—of individual financial reserves held back from the community, things wasted, and members' economically unequal opportunities and futures. These can endure even as communities try to equalize or manage their effects.

48. See, for instance, Heikkilä 2022; Mulvey and Killen 2015; Wohlwend 2009, 2012; Yuen and Shaw 2003.

49. See, for instance, Goldberg-Hiller 2023; Morales 2013; Paxton 2024.

50. For Women Scotland Ltd v. The Scottish Ministers [2025] UKSC 16.

51. The contract devised by Máiréad Enright in conjunction with the artists who wrote the piece, Jesse Jones and Sarah Browne, stated, "You will be Touched by one or more female Performers. . . . However, the Touch(es) Administered maybe be experienced as having one or more of the following qualities . . . sensations of embarrassment (e.g. blushing, sweating, shaking); . . . feelings of bewilderment or boredom; . . . outbursts of emotion (tears, rage, confusion, laughter); panic attacks; . . . onset of spontaneous civil disobedience; risk of radicalisation; hypersensitivity to the future touch of the State." "The Touching Contract," Artangel, accessed January 2, 2026, https://www.artangel.org.uk/in-the-shadow-of-the-state/the-touching-contract/.

52. "Barbershop: The Art of Queer Failure," Ace Lehner's professional website, accessed January 2, 2026, https://ace-lehner.com/barbershop.

53. This failure is associated with the absence of a commercial transaction, limited haircutting skills, and a queer open-ended antisuccess aesthetic.

54. Yarn-bombing has been well studied academically; see, for instance, Haveri 2016; Mann 2015; McGovern 2019; Price 2015.

55. One example is the "genderbread person" or "gender unicorn," which playfully and accessibly represents aspects of sexual and gender difference (e.g., "Gender Unicorn," Trans Student Educational Resources, accessed January 2, 2026, https://transstudent.org/gender/), a framing that has been actively opposed by conservative Christians and other sex realists.

56. When legislative proposals are crafted, they are expected to express the best outcome imagined as possible: what gender could become, for instance, as those crafting the text determine it. Yet the speculative law reform proposal explored in chapter 3 was designed for an open-ended mix of purposes, including as an intervention in a conflict and as an attempt to stimulate discussion about gender's future.

57. I explore these themes further in Cooper 2023, 2026.

58. In *Lau v. Moorilla Estate Pty Ltd* [2024] TASCAT 58, the Tasmanian Civil and Administrative Tribunal found an act of direct discrimination had taken place. This was overturned in the appellate court; see *Moorilla Estate Pty Ltd v. Lau* [2024] TASSC 49. See also Banks et al. (2024), addressing the argument that Lau experienced (and so had access to) the artwork, the *Ladies Lounge*, even if he could not access the art contained within it.

59. Moorilla Estate Pty Ltd v. Lau [2024] TASSC 49, para. 22; see also para. 30. In this appellate judgment, the Supreme Court of Tasmania stated, "The Ladies Lounge is a participatory installation. The process of being admitted or refused admission and the participation in the Ladies Lounge is part of the art itself" (para. 3).

60. Lau v. Moorilla Estate Pty Ltd [2024] TASCAT 58, paras. 33, 38–59, 69, 74.

61. See "Interview with Kirsha Kaechele About the Ladies Lounge," Mona, May 7, 2024, https://mona.net.au/blog/interview-with-kirsha-kaechele-about-the-ladies-lounge. Kaechele described how the installation could fit various exemptions that permitted a woman-only space (under the Anti-Discrimination Act 1998, s. 27), including on religious, educational, or use of a facility grounds.

62. Lau v. Moorilla Estate Pty Ltd [2024] TASCAT 58, paras. 77–78.

63. For discussion of this point in relation to yarn-bombing, see Close 2018; Hahner and Varda 2014.

64. While games typically involve formal rules, play leans toward more informal ones—that is, toward norms and agreed rules that are emergent, shapeshifting, and experimental, and that move in and out of sense (or deliberately assert multiple kinds of sense). In play, formal authority or the authority and rules of the play's instigator may also be disregarded and evaded.

65. In some cases, play defers to formal structures and order (see also Huizinga 1955, 10), even as it simultaneously resists, counters, and ignores them, like the child who plays with the parental instruction to stop playing and get ready for bed as an instruction they both note and simultaneously refuse to notice.

66. In the process, play may also enact a mode of social proprioception in determining the boundaries and landscape of the social. In many ways, play offers a sensitive, sometimes less risky, rapid-fire way of determining, through testing, where the normative, prohibitive, and permissive parts of the social fabric lie, including their capacity to withstand or change under different kinds of contact or pressure.

67. Interestingly, play and dance converge in the proto–West Germanic word *spilon*, which means "to play, dance, move"; for further discussion, see Sutton-Smith 1997, 182–83, quoting Gadamer 1982 on "spiel."

CONCLUSION

1. Telling a different conceptual history can also broaden and reclaim a concept. In interview, sociolegal scholar Bronwen Morgan described the importance of revisiting both the history and future of the concept "market" to tell a story that did not focus on profit-making: "It's trying to break open that assumption that markets are tied to capitalist accumulation and bring back some sense of . . . use value."

2. Conceptual activism can also involve relinquishing play for a more literal, even monosemic register.

3. Conceptual prefiguration can seem an instance of fast activism, of controversial meanings deployed and bedded in, despite being out of joint with the commonsense understandings that surround them. But conceptual prefiguration also demonstrates slow activism in the sedimentary shifts of meaning it supports; see chapter 4.

4. Public bodies' conceptual activism has been a major part of this discussion. An important feature of this conceptual activism is its deployment of bureaucratic and statist material resources to enact new meanings (see chapter 4). For instance, rather than advocate or campaign for nonbinary recognition or trans women's inclusion in female residential spaces (hostels, refuges, room-shares during school trips, etc.), public bodies such as local government, trade unions, and schools may enact such meanings in their policies and provision. In this sense, public bodies may seem prefigurative actors extraordinaire—able to operationalize the sought-after future rather than merely desire and aspire to it. At the same time, it is in their limited ability to operationalize new meanings that the prefigurative status of their actions can be found. Bodies remaking gender categories faced constraints and pushback from protest politics, government departments, and litigation that undercut the growing normalization of sex and gender as plural, fluid, and self-defined, leading normalization measures to become, instead, a contentious acting "as if." This is a much less attended-to form of prefiguration, in which prefiguration names a reduced status rather than an expanded one. Reconstructing meaning as prefigurative through initiatives that derealize it, forcing it to contract so that it no longer manifests new meanings at scale, attacks both the emerging (promised) conceptual imaginary and its materialization. While sex-realist critics targeted objected-to meanings—of gender as plural, mutable, and as trumping sexed embodiment—what actually got attacked was the manifestation of such meanings in public policy practice; in the inclusion of trans women in women's sports, prisons, and affirmative action initiatives; and in data-collection categories that departed from binary birth sex.

5. In early 2020s Britain, abolitionist and deconstructive tendencies in both camps had a negligible public presence—unsurprising, perhaps, given the centrality of law, policy, and institutional sectors such as schools and prisons to the conflict. Instead, sex realism and liberal realist approaches to gender diversity held center stage as the main projects visibly opposing each other across different public arenas. One area where a liberal approach to gender diversity was expressed and also resisted concerned the treatment of nonbinary identities. See, for instance, the decision of the financial ombudsman to award damages to a nonbinary complainant who was compelled to identify themselves within binary sex categories of female and male to use a car insurance price comparison website (Fiona Mallinson, Ref. DRN-4915750, Financial Ombudsman Service, 2024, https://www.financial-ombudsman.org.uk/decision/DRN-4915750.pdf). Central to the ombudsman's finding was a recognition that nonbinary discrimination falls within the ground of gender reassignment as a protected characteristic. A different outcome, however, was reached in the case of a legally nonbinary Californian who sought a Gender Recognition Certificate registering them as nonbinary in the UK; this was held not to be possible since the British system only recognized categories of male and female;

R (Castellucci) v. Gender Recognition Panel [2025] EWCA Civ 167; see also *R (Elan-Cane) v. Secretary of State for the Home Department* [2021] UKSC 56, which denied the applicant the right to have a passport indicating their sex/gender as X. Interviews with equality governance staff adopting a gender-(as)-diversity approach revealed an empathetic attention paid to nonbinary as an emerging conceptual category in contrast to other research; e.g., Ballakrishnen 2025. Nonbinary can be accommodated within gender/sex classificatory frameworks; see J. Williams (2026) on its potential here as a category to challenge gender norms within law and policy; and see H. Newman and Peel (2022) on views among nonbinary survey respondents on abolishing legal sex or adding an additional category.

6. In chapter 1, I outlined some key forms of this interaction and intra-action. Centering the materiality of concepts is important for understanding mainstream practice as well as for understanding more radical forms of conceptual activism. Reports, discussions at meetings, speculative laws, art installations, placing where bodies can be and go, and building redesigns (such as of leisure center changing rooms) incorporated, depicted, and enacted conceptual imaginaries of gender and sex, and to different degrees sought or helped to accomplish them (although whether a policy or arts performance, for instance, represents gender in a specific way, or contributes to its accomplishment—which could mean shaping its accomplishment or being part of its accomplishment—also depends on how the concept of gender is understood; I explore this further in chapter 4 and Cooper 2024).

7. For an anthropological account of conceptual morphology, see Holbraad (2020, 518), who writes, "The morphological character of anthropological conceptualization comes down to . . . finding ways of expressing in conceptual form those parts of life that hold our anthropological interest by articulating the shapes in which they are configured."

8. Concern about sidelining legal sex generated a governmental review in 2024, by the then Conservative government, asking the public for "examples of policy or guidance in which public bodies—or organisations that advise public and private organisations—wrongly suggest that people have a legal right to access single-sex spaces and services according to their self-identified gender." "Call for Input: Incorrect Guidance on Single-Sex Spaces and Gender Self-Identification," UK Government, May 1, 2024, https://www.gov.uk/government/publications/call-for-input-incorrect-guidance-on-single-sex-spaces-and-gender-self-identification. The results of this review were reported on by the subsequent Labour government's Office for Equality and Opportunity, which suggested, "Approximately 10% of the guidance submitted had text or examples that seem to have misinterpreted the Act's single-sex spaces provisions." "Response to Call for Input on Single-Sex Spaces Guidance," UK Government, December 17, 2024, https://www.gov.uk/government/publications/response-to-call-for-input-on-single-sex-spaces-guidance/response-to-call-for-input-on-single-sex-spaces-guidance.

9. One complication to this narrative is the Supreme Court decision in *For Women Scotland Ltd v. The Scottish Ministers* [2025] UKSC 16. The downgrading of a Gender Recognition Certificate and focus on biological sex by the Court in this decision can be read as a form of decertification, albeit a conservative version, in which sex endures as a significant category but becomes one understood as a legally *recognized* fact rather than a

legally *created* fact. This judicially enacted form of decertification has generated significant currents since the decision was handed down in April 2025.

10. An alternative account, based on the discussion in chapter 3, approaches decertification as having mutated to become part of the cellular structure holding up opponents' political project, as a kind of "adversarial concept" (Perry-Kessaris 2023).

11. When concepts are hegemonic, this dance can be difficult to observe since the moves are plentiful, concurrent, and fully existent. However, counterhegemonic emergent concepts lend themselves to being approached in this way, since the moves are in formation. This makes it possible to trace how they combine and connect in different contexts.

12. For further discussion, see also Cooper and Renz 2016; Decoster 2024.

13. See also S. Hunter (2008, 520), who addresses the economy of concepts in relation to narratives of whiteness when she writes, "A core part of the institutionalization of whiteness is the production of whiteness and blackness as fetish objects, achieved by cutting them off from their histories of production; labour, circulation and exchange."

14. This book has explored three connected sites in which the production, acquisition, and use of such concepts have taken place: academic scholarship, play (including speculative lawmaking and political participatory art), and the institutionalization of revised concepts through law, administrative policies (such as the Census), and service provision. These sites identify diverse pathways through which counterhegemonic meanings (as well as hegemonic meanings), from gender self-identification to sex decertification, gender proliferation, gender abolition, and even sex realism (which moved between hegemonic and counterhegemonic status), got made, used, and held. Focusing on concepts' making, allocation, acquisition, and use as onto-epistemic phenomena foregrounds what is brought into being when gender is enacted as plural and mutable, as in an installation, speculative legal judgment, or access to a service.

15. Approaching agender, for instance, as a prefigurative form of enactment avoids the conceptual binarism established between gender as an imposed societal structure and gender as a voluntary choice. Instead, it recognizes that within an environment structured by the expectation that everyone has a gender (which, in Britain, primarily means identification as either a woman or man), people can live *as if* other options were possible. What this means and does is not predetermined and fixed, but it is also not rendered impossible by the presence of an institutionalized gender order. Atheism may provide a fruitful analogy—living as if one lacked a religion in a country, like Britain, that is still structured culturally, politically, and legally by the established status of the Church of England.

16. Different metacategories for gender may emerge through metaphoring, such as when gender is characterized as a language, grammar, performance, or institution—concepts that are more familiar to other contexts. Yet while some metacategories may appear figurative ones, imported to understand what gender is in new ways, this does not mean that their application is fictive, simply that the use of such metacategory concepts is a novel and unfamiliar one that may settle (or not), and that if it does settle, the meaning of the metacategory will also change or embrace multiple distinct meanings; for further discussion, see chapter 2. Metaphoring is also a way of recognizing *already existing* material cuts, joins, and practices as being part of a concept, where they are less attended to or unattended to through other conceptual metacategories.

17. Considerable political, organizational, and cultural work may go into establishing specific metacategories, such as "protected characteristics" in British equality law, which gives rise to sex, race, age, sexual orientation, and religion as broadly analogous legal umbrella categories, although their definition and the determination of member categories (e.g., what counts as a religion or race) operate in quite different legal ways; for further discussion, see Malleson 2018; Renz and Cooper 2022. In legal analogizing, the ideational content of concepts like sex, religion, sexual orientation, and race becomes reconfigured—some elements are deleted, others get centered; for instance, sexuality in equality law becomes, as sexual orientation, a matter of directionality; more specifically, it becomes a matter of directionality toward the "same," "opposite," or "either" sex (Equality Act 2010, s. 12). For a critical response to the analogizing logic used for social inequalities and the historical development of a "minority model" framework (for disability and race), see Frederick and Shifrer 2019. Within specific categories, further analogizing around a dominant template takes place, so religion in Britain has been understood in Christian terms (foregrounding conscience, faith-based association, and open admittance), a framework then applied to other "religions" with awkward consequences; e.g., see Danchin and Blond 2014; Herman 2011; Petty 2014.

18. Identifying concepts like sex, gender, and race as instances (or members) of another metacategory concept—whether that other concept is the equality concept of "protected characteristic" or instead "inequality," "social relation," or "identity"—can be a pragmatic and strategic act, imposing (or recognizing) a specific shared form for member concepts that could be understood (and arranged) in quite other ways. In selecting a metacategory, member concepts are gathered, split from others, and subsumed as instances of something else (a something else that is, in turn, a member concept of something else), in a process that gives rise to stories about how these metacategories came to be. This book too has participated in gathering and classification work through the language of institutionalization, inequalities, and social relations. But it has also drawn on dance as a different kind of connective form—one that tends toward horizontal modes of gathering, and that foregrounds proximity and connection between concepts rather than subordination to an overarching category. At the same time, dance does not presume what is near or far; it is less concerned with tracking already-established connections than with forging them, to observe what they express and do.

19. We might turn here to the concept of the monstrous as an (anti)classificatory device that prompts us to follow rather than preemptively pin down gender; see Sharpe 2010, 2017. Alex Sharpe (2017) describes the monstrous as excessive and unstable, challenging categorical divisions, uncontained by law, and as failing to hold a settled shape. While Sharpe considers the monstrous in relation to gender transgression, for our purposes here, the monstruous might relate to the concept of gender more generally, how it fails to be contained by form as it stretches and slides, incites fear and desire, intensifies, wanes, and advances as its conceptual shape evolves. At the same time, while the monstrous can identify that which is not named or recognized, once it appears it can then become integrated and normalized (Derrida 1995, 386–87); this might here involve new metacategorical shapes. On the association between the monstrous and stigmatized women within legal discourse, see M. Thomson 1997.

20. This does not require optimism or inculcating a hopeful attitude or affect. Acting *as if* one were hopeful can carry a hope that is not felt. I am reminded here of Amy Cohen and Bronwen Morgan's (2023, 1065) prefigurative modality of acting "anyhow and in case."

21. There are many examples of this process, but one described to me was the academic concept of "power geometry," associated with the geographer Doreen Massey, which got taken up and used during Hugo Chávez's presidency in Venezuela, as part of a twenty-first-century socialist agenda, to express how space instantiates relations of power and can also advance new spatialized relations. Doreen Massey (2009, 20) writes, "Here, then, a geographical concept is being put to positive political use. Indeed, as will be seen, part of what lay behind the proposal was an impressive recognition of the existence and significance, within Venezuela, of highly unequal, and thus undemocratic, power-geometries." Massey goes on to describe how the concept gained nuance and complexity through being taken up as a political tool and ambition in the Venezuelan context; for discussion of Massey's work, see Featherstone and Painter 2013.

References

Abers, Rebecca Neaera. 2019. "Bureaucratic Activism: Pursuing Environmentalism Inside the Brazilian State." *Latin American Politics and Society* 61 (2): 21–44.

Adams, David, and Michael Hardman. 2014. "Observing Guerrillas in the Wild: Reinterpreting Practices of Urban Guerrilla Gardening." *Urban Studies* 51 (6): 1103–19.

Adams, David, Michael Hardman, and Peter Larkham. 2014. "Exploring Guerrilla Gardening: Gauging Public Views on the Grassroots Activity." *Local Environment* 20 (10): 1231–46.

Afshary, Mohammad. 2018. "Prefiguring the Revolution: The Politics of Law and Lawyering in Egypt." PhD thesis, University of Kent.

Ahmed, Sara. 2020. *On Being Included: Racism and Diversity in Institutional Life*. Duke University Press.

Akbar, Amna A. 2022. "Non-Reformist Reforms and Struggles over Life, Death, and Democracy." *Yale Law Journal* 132:2497–577.

Anderson, Ben. 2023. "Forms and Scenes of Attachment: A Cultural Geography of Promises." *Dialogues in Human Geography* 13 (3): 392–409.

Appadurai, Arjun. 1988. *The Social Life of Things: Commodities in Cultural Perspective*. Cambridge University Press.

Appleton, Matthew. 2000. *A Free Range Childhood: Self Regulation at Summerhill School*. Foundation for Educational Renewal.

Arendt, Hannah. 1958. *The Human Condition*. University of Chicago Press.

Armstrong, John, and Alice Sullivan. 2023. "A Critical Analysis of Athena Swan as a Policy-Scoring Scheme." *British Educational Research Journal* 51 (1): 225–43.

Arnould, Eric J. 2022. "Ontology and Circulation: Towards an Eco-Economy of Persons." *Journal of Marketing Management* 38 (1–2): 71–97.

Asara, Viviana, and Giorgos Kallis. 2023. "The Prefigurative Politics of Social Movements and Their Processual Production of Space: The Case of the Indignados Movement." *Environment and Planning C: Politics and Space* 41 (1): 56–76.

Ashar, Sameer M. 2023. "Pedagogy of Prefiguration." *Yale Law Journal Forum* 132:869–903.

Assaf-Zakharov, Katya, and Tim Schnetgoke. 2021. "Reading the Illegible: Can Law Understand Graffiti?" *Connecticut Law Review* 53:117–53.

Atanasova, Aleksandrina. 2021. "Re-Examining Utopia in Contemporary Consumption: Conceptualization and Implications for Marketing." *Academy of Marketing Science Review* 11 (1): 23–39.

Azcárate, Matilde Córdoba. 2025. "Cultural Repertoires and a Beach Dispute in Southern California." In *Beach Politics: Social, Racial, and Environmental Injustice on the Shoreline*, edited by Setha Low, 40–63. New York University Press.

Ballakrishnen, Swethaa S. 2025. "Blasé: Deviant Lawyers and the Denial of Discrimination." *Law and Society Review* 59 (2): 324–55.

Banks, Robin, Alice Taylor, and Beth Goldblatt. 2024. "A Lounge of One's Own: Art, Gender, Discrimination and the Law." *Alternative Law Journal* 49 (3): 234–39.

Barad, Karen. 2003. "Posthumanist Performativity: Toward an Understanding of How Matter Comes to Matter." *Signs: Journal of Women in Culture and Society* 28 (3): 801–31.

Barad, Karen. 2007. *Meeting the Universe Halfway: Quantum Physics and the Entanglement of Matter and Meaning*. Duke University Press.

Barad, Karen. 2014. "Diffracting Diffraction: Cutting Together-Apart." *Parallax* 20 (3): 168–87.

Barad, Karen, and Daniela Gandorfer. 2021. "Political Desirings: Yearnings for Mattering (,) Differently." *Theory and Event* 24 (1): 14–66.

Bardhi, Fleura, and Giana M. Eckhardt. 2012. "Access-Based Consumption: The Case of Car Sharing." *Journal of Consumer Research* 39 (4): 881–98.

Barnes, Elizabeth. 2019. "Gender and Gender Terms." *Nous* 54 (3): 704–30.

Baron, Jane B. 2013. "Rescuing the Bundle-of-Rights Metaphor in Property Law." *University of Cincinnati Law Review* 82:57–102.

Barrett, Susan, and Colin Fudge, eds. 1981. *Policy and Action: Essays on the Implementation of Public Policy*. Methuen.

Bartley, Tim. 2003. "Certifying Forests and Factories: States, Social Movements, and the Rise of Private Regulation in the Apparel and Forest Products Fields." *Politics and Society* 31 (3): 433–64.

Bartoli, Isabella. 2025. "Social Externalism and the Implementation Challenge: Revising Socially and Politically Significant Terms." *Metaphilosophy* 56 (3–4): 389–406.

Bassi, Serena, and Greta LaFleur. 2022. "Introduction: TERFs, Gender-Critical Movements, and Postfascist Feminisms." *Transgender Studies Quarterly* 9 (3): 311–33.

Basten, Stuart. 2006. "From Rose's Bill to Rose's Act: A Reappraisal of the 1812 Parish Register Act." *Local Population Studies* 76:43–62.

Batagol, Becky, Kate Seear, Heli Askola, and Jamie Walvisch, eds. 2024. *The Feminist Legislation Project: Rewriting Laws for Gender-Based Justice*. Routledge.

Bateson, Gregory. 1972. *Steps to an Ecology of Mind: Collected Essays in Anthropology, Psychiatry, Evolution, and Epistemology*. Chandler.

Beckert, Jens. 2010. "Institutional Isomorphism Revisited: Convergence and Divergence in Institutional Change." *Sociological Theory* 28 (2): 150–66.

Belinsky, Zoe. 2019. "Gender and Family Abolition as an Expansive and Not Reductive Process." Medium, September 11. https://medium.com/@malkekvmachashayfele/gender-and-family-abolition-as-an-expansive-and-not-reductive-process-d933f1f71da2.

Belleri, Delia. 2021. "On Pluralism and Conceptual Engineering: Introduction and Overview." *Inquiry*, September 29. https://doi.org/10.1080/0020174X.2021.1983457.

Bem, Sandra Lipsitz. 1995. "Dismantling Gender Polarization and Compulsory Heterosexuality: Should We Turn the Volume Down or Up?" *Journal of Sex Research* 32 (4): 329–34.

Bennett, David. 2010. "Libidinal Economy, Prostitution and Consumer Culture." *Textual Practice* 24 (1): 93–121.

Bennett, David. 2016. *Currency of Desire: Libidinal Economy, Psychoanalysis and Sexual Revolution.* Lawrence and Wishart.

Benzer, Matthias. 2011. "Social Critique in the Totally Socialized Society." *Philosophy and Social Criticism* 37 (5): 575–603.

Berleant, Arnold. 2004. *Re-Thinking Aesthetics: Rogue Essays on Aesthetics and the Arts.* Routledge.

Bey, Marquis. 2021. "Trouble Genders: 'LGBT' Collapse and Trans Fundamentality." *Hypatia* 36 (1): 191–206.

Bey, Marquis. 2022. *Black Trans Feminism.* Duke University Press.

Bhambra, Gurminder K. 2015. "Citizens and Others: The Constitution of Citizenship Through Exclusion." *Alternatives* 40 (2): 102–14.

Bieszczad, Lilianna. 2022. "Can Arnold Berleant's Aesthetics of Engagement Be Applied to Conceptual Dance?" *AVANT* 12 (2): 1–14.

Biggs, Michael. 2024. "Gender Identity in the 2021 Census of England and Wales: How a Flawed Question Created Spurious Data." *Sociology* 58 (6): 1305–23.

Bittner, Amanda, and Elizabeth Goodyear-Grant. 2017. "Sex Isn't Gender: Reforming Concepts and Measurements in the Study of Public Opinion." *Political Behavior* 39:1019–41.

Black, Julia. 2001. "Decentring Regulation: Understanding the Role of Regulation and Self-Regulation in a 'Post-Regulatory' World." *Current Legal Problems* 54 (1): 103–46.

Black, Max. 1993. "More About Metaphor." In *Metaphor and Thought*, edited by Andrew Ortony, 19–41. Cambridge University Press.

Blandy, Sarah. 2021. "Narratives of Property and the Limits of Legal Reform in the English Leasehold System and Its Counterparts in Other Jurisdictions." In *Condominium Governance and Law in Global Urban Context*, edited by Randy Lippert and Stefan Treffers, 13–28. Routledge.

Bledsoe, Adam, Tyler McCreary, and Willie Wright. 2022. "Theorizing Diverse Economies in the Context of Racial Capitalism." *Geoforum* 132:281–90.

Blomley, Nicholas. 2003. "Law, Property, and the Geography of Violence: The Frontier, the Survey, and the Grid." *Annals of the Association of American Geographers* 93 (1): 121–41.

Blomley, Nicholas. 2005. "Flowers in the Bathtub: Boundary Crossings at the Public–Private Divide." *Geoforum* 36 (3): 281–96.

Blomley, Nicholas. 2011. "Cuts, Flows, and the Geographies of Property." *Law, Culture and the Humanities* 7 (2): 203–16.

Blomley, Nicholas. 2013. "Performing Property: Making the World." *Canadian Journal of Law and Jurisprudence* 26 (1): 23–48.

Blomley, Nicholas. 2014. "Disentangling Law: The Practice of Bracketing." *Annual Review of Law and Social Science* 10 (1): 133–48.

Bobel, Chris. 2007. "'I'm Not an Activist, Though I've Done a Lot of It': Doing Activism, Being Activist and the 'Perfect Standard' in a Contemporary Movement." *Social Movement Studies* 6 (2): 147–59.

Bogad, Larry. 2016. *Tactical Performance: Serious Play and Social Movements*. Routledge.

Bogost, Ian. 2016. *Play Anything: The Pleasure of Limits, the Uses of Boredom, and the Secret of Games*. Basic Books.

Bossy, Sophie. 2014. "The Utopias of Political Consumerism: The Search of Alternatives to Mass Consumption." *Journal of Consumer Culture* 14 (2): 179–98.

Bower-Brown, Susie. 2024. "Safeguarding? Critiquing Gender-Critical Discourse Around Gender Diversity at School." *Amicus Curiae* 5 (3): 429–47.

Brannigan, Erin. 2018. "Talking Back: What Dance Might Make of Badiou's Philosophical Project." *Performance Philosophy* 4 (2): 354–73.

Brannigan, Erin. 2021. "Choreography as Concept, Dancing as Material." *Performance Research* 26 (4): 24–31.

Bratich, Jack Z., and Heidi M. Brush. 2011. "Fabricating Activism: Craft-Work, Popular Culture, Gender." *Utopian Studies* 22 (2): 233–60.

Brown, Nik, and Sarah Nettleton. 2017. "'There Is Worse to Come': The Biopolitics of Traumatism in Antimicrobial Resistance (AMR)." *Sociological Review* 65 (3): 493–508.

Brown, Sandy, and Christy Getz. 2008. "Privatizing Farm Worker Justice: Regulating Labor Through Voluntary Certification and Labeling." *Geoforum* 39 (3): 1184–96.

Browne, Kath, and Catherine J. Nash. 2017. "Heteroactivism: Beyond Anti-Gay." *ACME: An International Journal for Critical Geographies* 16 (4): 643–52.

Browne, Kath, and Catherine J. Nash. 2023. "From Hegemonic to Where? The Public Spatialities of Shifting Positionings for Those Who Are Opposed to/Concerned About Socio-Legal Changes in Sexual and Genders." *Tijdschrift Voor Economische En Sociale Geografie* 114 (4): 271–88.

Browne, Sarah, and Jesse Jones. 2019. "Refusal First, Then Reimagination: Presenting the Burn in Flames Post-Patriarchal Archive in Circulation." In *Reimagining the State: Theoretical Challenges and Transformative Possibilities*, edited by Davina Cooper, Nikita Dhawan, and Janet Newman, 251–62. Routledge.

Bruun, Maja Hojer, Patrick Joseph Cockburn, Bjarke Skærlund Risager, and Mikkel Thorup, eds. 2018. *Contested Property Claims*. Routledge.

Buchter, Lisa. 2021. "Escaping the Ellipsis of Diversity: Insider Activists' Use of Implementation Resources to Influence Organization Policy." *Administrative Science Quarterly* 66 (2): 521–65.

Burgess, Alexis, and David Plunkett. 2020. "On the Relation Between Conceptual Engineering and Conceptual Ethics." *Ratio* 33 (4): 281–94.

Burton, Sarah, and Benjamin Bowman. 2022. "The Academic Precariat: Understanding Life and Labour in the Neoliberal Academy." *British Journal of Sociology of Education* 43 (4): 497–512.

Butler, Judith. 2004. *Undoing Gender*. Routledge.

Butler, Judith. 2015. "Performative Agency." In *The Limits of Performativity*, edited by Franck Cochoy, Martin Giraudeau, and Liz McFall, 10–24. Routledge.

Butler, Judith. 2025. *Who's Afraid of Gender?* Random House.

Byrnes, Andrew, and Gabrielle Simm, eds. 2018. *Peoples' Tribunals and International Law*. Cambridge University Press.

Calhoun, Craig, Dilip Gaonkar, Benjamin Lee, Charles Taylor, and Michael Warner. 2015. "Modern Social Imaginaries: A Conversation." *Social Imaginaries* 1 (1): 189–224.

Callon, Michel. 2010. "Performativity, Misfires and Politics." *Journal of Cultural Economy* 3 (2): 163–69.

Cantalamessa, Elizabeth Amber. 2021. "Disability Studies, Conceptual Engineering, and Conceptual Activism." *Inquiry* 64 (1–2): 46–75.

Cappelen, Herman. 2023. *The Concept of Democracy: An Essay on Conceptual Amelioration and Abandonment*. Oxford University Press.

Cappelen, Herman, and David Plunkett. 2020. "Introduction: A Guided Tour of Conceptual Engineering and Conceptual Ethics." In *Conceptual Engineering and Conceptual Ethics*, edited by Alexis Burgess, Herman Cappelen, and David Plunkett, 1–34. Oxford University Press.

Carlson, Åsa. 2010. "Gender and Sex: What Are They? Sally Haslanger's Debunking Social Constructivism." *Distinktion: Scandinavian Journal of Social Theory* 11 (1): 61–72.

Cass, Hilary. 2024. *Independent Review of Gender Identity Services for Children and Young People: Final Report*. https://cass.independent-review.uk/home/publications/final-report/.

Certeau, Michel de. 1984. *The Practice of Everyday Life*. Translated by Steven Rendall. University of California Press.

Chalmers, David J. 2025. "What Is Conceptual Engineering and What Should It Be?" *Inquiry* 68 (9): 2902–19.

Chatterton, Paul, and Andre Pusey. 2020. "Beyond Capitalist Enclosure, Commodification and Alienation: Postcapitalist Praxis as Commons, Social Production and Useful Doing." *Progress in Human Geography* 44 (1): 27–48.

Chatzidakis, Andreas, Gretchen Larsen, and Simon Bishop. 2014 "Farewell to Consumerism: Countervailing Logics of Growth in Consumption." *Ephemera: Theory and Politics in Organization* 14 (4): 753–64.

Chua, Hillary. 2023. "Consent to Treatment for Transgender Youth: The Next Chapter—*Bell & Anor v. The Tavistock and Portman NHS Foundation Trust & Ors*." *Modern Law Review* 86 (1): 214–25.

Clarke, Alan, and Allan Cochrane. 1989. "Inside the Machine: The Left and Finance Professionals in Local Government." *Capital and Class* 13 (1): 35–61.

Clarke, Jessica A. 2005. "Adverse Possession of Identity: Radical Theory, Conventional Practice." *Oregon Law Review* 84 (2): 563–654.

Clarke, Jessica A. 2015. "Identity and Form." *California Law Review* 103 (4): 747–840.

Clarke, Jessica A. 2019. "They, Them, and Theirs." *Harvard Law Review* 132:894–991.

Clarke, John. 2014. "Imagined, Real and Moral Economies." *Culture Unbound* 6 (1): 95–112.

Clarke, John. 2019a. *Critical Dialogues: Thinking Together in Turbulent Times*. Policy Press.

Clarke, John. 2019b. "Harmful Thoughts: Reimagining the Coercive State?" In *Reimagining the State: Theoretical Challenges and Transformative Possibilities*, edited by Davina Cooper, Nikita Dhawan, and Janet Newman, 213–30. Routledge.

Clarke, John. 2020. "Why Imagined Economies?" In *Imagined Economies—Real Fictions: New Perspectives on Economic Thinking in Great Britain*, edited by Jessica Fischer and Gesa Stedman, 17–34. Transcript.

Clarke, John. 2023. *The Battle for Britain: Crises, Conflicts and the Conjuncture.* Policy Press.

Cleaver, Frances. 2002. "Reinventing Institutions: Bricolage and the Social Embeddedness of Natural Resource Management." *European Journal of Development Research* 14 (2): 11–30.

Close, Samantha. 2018. "Knitting Activism, Knitting Gender, Knitting Race." *International Journal of Communication* 12:867–89.

Cohen, Amy J., and Bronwen Morgan. 2023. "Prefigurative Legality." *Law and Social Inquiry* 48 (3): 1053–82.

Cohen, Ed. 2009. *A Body Worth Defending: Immunity, Biopolitics, and the Apotheosis of the Modern Body*. Duke University Press.

Comaroff, Jean, and John L. Comaroff. 2001. "Naturing the Nation: Aliens, Apocalypse and the Postcolonial State." *Journal of Southern African Studies* 27 (3): 627–51.

Comor, Edward. 2011. "Contextualizing and Critiquing the Fantastic Prosumer: Power, Alienation and Hegemony." *Critical Sociology* 37 (3): 309–27.

Conklin, Edwin G. 1939. "Predecessors of Schleiden and Schwann." *American Naturalist* 73 (749): 538–46.

Connolly, William. 1993. *The Terms of Political Discourse*. Princeton University Press.

Connolly, William. 2002. *Identity, Difference: Democratic Negotiations of Political Paradox*. University of Minnesota Press.

Connolly, William. 2013. *The Fragility of Things: Self-Organizing Processes, Neoliberal Fantasies, and Democratic Activism*. Duke University Press.

Consalvo, Mia. 2009. "There Is No Magic Circle." *Games and Culture* 4 (4): 408–17.

Cook, Ian, and Tara Woodyer. 2012. "Lives of Things." In *The Wiley-Blackwell Companion to Economic Geography*, edited by Trevor J. Barnes, Jamie Peck, and Eric Sheppard, 226–41. Wiley-Blackwell.

Cooper, Davina. 1994. *Sexing the City: Lesbian and Gay Politics Within the Activist State.* Rivers Oram.

Cooper, Davina. 1995. *Power in Struggle: Feminism, Sexuality and the State.* New York University Press.

Cooper, Davina. 1996. "Institutional Illegality and Disobedience: Local Government Narratives." *Oxford Journal of Legal Studies* 16 (2): 255–74.

Cooper, Davina. 2013. "Public Bodies: Conceptualising Active Citizenship and the Embodied State." In *Beyond Citizenship? Feminism and the Transformation of Belonging*, edited by Sasha Roseneil, 112–37. Palgrave Macmillan.

Cooper, Davina. 2014. *Everyday Utopias: The Conceptual Life of Promising Spaces*. Duke University Press.

Cooper, Davina. 2016. "Enacting Counter-States Through Play." *Contemporary Political Theory* 15 (4): 453–61.

Cooper, Davina. 2017. "Prefiguring the State." *Antipode* 49 (2): 335–56.

Cooper, Davina. 2019a. *Feeling Like a State: Desire, Denial, and the Recasting of Authority*. Duke University Press.

Cooper, Davina. 2019b. "A Very Binary Drama: The Conceptual Struggle for Gender's Future." *Feminists@Law* 9 (1). https://doi.org/10.22024/UniKent/03/fal.655.

Cooper, Davina. 2020a. "Taking Public Responsibility for Gender: When Personal Identity and Institutional Feminist Politics Meet." *Feminists@Law* 10 (2). https://doi.org/10.22024/UniKent/03/fal.968.

Cooper, Davina. 2020b. "Towards an Adventurous Institutional Politics: The Prefigurative 'As If' and the Reposing of What's Real." *Sociological Review* 68 (5): 893–916.

Cooper, Davina. 2022. "What Does Gender Equality Need? Revisiting the Formal and Informal in Feminist Legal Politics." *Journal of Law and Society* 49 (4): 800–823.

Cooper, Davina. 2023. "Crafting Prefigurative Law in Turbulent Times: Decertification, DIY Law Reform, and the Dilemmas of Feminist Prototyping." *Feminist Legal Studies* 31 (1): 17–42.

Cooper, Davina. 2024. "Reconceptualizing the Real in the Struggle for Gender: From Gold Standard to Fragile Accomplishment." *Signs* 50 (1): 43–69.

Cooper, Davina. 2026. "Keeping Prefigurative Law in Play: Utopianism, Failure, and the Problem of Legal Sex." *Law and Social Inquiry*. Published online:1–27. https://doi.org/10.1017/lsi.2026.10139.

Cooper, Davina, Nikita Dhawan, and Janet Newman, eds. 2019. *Reimagining the State: Theoretical Challenges and Transformative Possibilities*. Routledge.

Cooper, Davina, and Robyn Emerton. 2020. "Pulling the Thread of Decertification: What Challenges Are Raised by the Proposal to Reform Legal Gender Status?" *Feminists@Law* 10 (2). https://doi.org/10.22024/UniKent/03/fal.938.

Cooper, Davina, Robyn Emerton, Emily Grabham, Han Newman, Elizabeth Peel, Flora Renz, and Jessica Smith. 2022. *Abolishing Legal Sex Status: The Challenge and Consequences of Gender-Related Law Reform*. Future of Legal Gender Project. https://www.kcl.ac.uk/law/research/future-of-legal-gender-abolishing-legal-sex-status-full-report.pdf.

Cooper, Davina, Robyn Emerton, Jessica Smith, Elizabeth Peel, Han Newman, Emily Grabham, and Flora Renz. 2023. "Future of Legal Gender: Survey and Interview Data, 2018–2022." Data collection. UK Data Service. https://reshare.ukdataservice.ac.uk/855476/.

Cooper, Davina, Emily Grabham, and Flora Renz. 2020. "Introduction to the Special Issue on the Future of Legal Gender: Exploring the Feminist Politics of Decertification." *Feminists@Law* 10 (2). https://doi.org/10.22024/UniKent/03/fal.937.

Cooper, Davina, and Didi Herman. 2013. "Up Against the Property Logic of Equality Law: Conservative Christian Accommodation Claims and Gay Rights." *Feminist Legal Studies* 21:61–80.

Cooper, Davina, and Didi Herman. 2020. "Doing Activism Like a State: Progressive Municipal Government, Israel/Palestine and BDS." *Environment and Planning C: Politics and Space* 38 (1): 40–59.

Cooper, Davina, and Flora Renz. 2016. "If the State Decertified Gender, What Might Happen to Its Meaning and Value?" *Journal of Law and Society* 43 (4): 483–505.

Cooper, Davina, and Flora Renz. 2023. "Introduction to Special Issue: Decertifying Legal Sex—Prefigurative Law Reform and the Future of Legal Gender." *Feminist Legal Studies* 31 (1): 1–16.

Cornelissen, Joep P. 2004. "What Are We Playing At? Theatre, Organization, and the Use of Metaphor." *Organization Studies* 25 (5): 705–26.

Cornelissen, Joep P. 2006. "Making Sense of Theory Construction: Metaphor and Disciplined Imagination." *Organization Studies* 27 (11): 1579–97.

Cosker-Rowland, Rach. 2023. "Recent Work on Gender Identity and Gender." *Analysis* 83 (4): 801–20.

Cowan, Sharon, Harry Josephine Giles, Rebecca Hewer, Becky Kaufmann, Meryl Kenny, Sean Morris, and Katie Nicoll Baines. 2021. "Sex and Gender Equality Law and Policy: A Response to Murray, Hunter Blackburn and Mackenzie." *Scottish Affairs* 30 (1): 74–95.

Craps, Stef. 2026. "Ecological Apologies: Reckoning with Grief, Guilt, and Multispecies Justice." *Environmental Politics* 35 (1): 31–49.

Cull, Matthew J. 2024. *What Gender Should Be*. Bloomsbury.

Cullen, Michael J. 1974. "The Making of the Civil Registration Act of 1836." *Journal of Ecclesiastical History* 25 (1): 39–59.

Cunningham, Naomi. 2021. "Submission and Compliance: Risks for Stonewall Champions." *Legal Feminist* (blog), February 1. https://www.legalfeminist.org.uk/2021/02/01/submission-and-compliance/.

Currah, Paisley. 2022. *Sex Is as Sex Does: Governing Transgender Identity*. New York University Press.

Currah, Paisley, and Lisa Jean Moore. 2009. "'We Won't Know Who You Are': Contesting Sex Designations in New York City Birth Certificates." *Hypatia* 24 (3): 113–35.

Daly, Helen L. 2015. "Sex, Vagueness, and the Olympics." *Hypatia* 30 (4): 708–24.

Danchin, Peter, and Louis Blond. 2014. "Unlawful Religion: Modern Secular Power and the Legal Reasoning in the JFS Case." *Maryland Journal of International Law* 29 (1): 419–80.

Davies, Margaret. 1994. "Feminist Appropriations: Law, Property and Personality." *Social and Legal Studies* 3 (3): 365–91.

Davies, Margaret. 2011. "Feminism and the Idea of Law." *Feminists@Law* 1 (1). https://doi.org/10.22024/UniKent/03/fal.9.

Davies, Margaret. 2020. "Can Property Be Justified in an Entangled World?" *Globalizations* 17 (7): 1104–17.

Davies, Margaret. 2021. "Re-Forming Property to Address Eco-Social Fragmentation and Rift." In *Posthuman Legalities: New Materialism and Law Beyond the Human*, edited by Anna Grear, Emille Boulot, Iván Darío Vargas-Roncancio, and Joshua Sterlin, 13–37. Edward Elgar.

Davies, Margaret, Lee Godden, and Nicole Graham. 2021. "Situating Property Within Habitat: Reintegrating Place, People, and Law." *Journal of Law, Property, and Society* 6:1–50.

De Jong, Sara, and Susanne Kimm. 2017. "The Co-Optation of Feminisms: A Research Agenda." *International Feminist Journal of Politics* 19 (2): 185–200.

Decoster, Ariël. 2024. "'POSTED: No Trespassing': On the Performativity of Property and Gender as Intertwined Social Practices of Power." *Social and Legal Studies* 34 (6): 881–95.

Dekeyser, Thomas. 2023. "Worldless Futures: On the Allure of 'Worlds to Come.'" *Transactions of the Institute of British Geographers* 48 (2): 338–50.

Dembroff, Robin. 2018. "Real Talk on the Metaphysics of Gender." *Philosophical Topics* 46 (2): 21–50.

Dempsey, Michelle Madden, and Matthew Lister. 2016. "Applied Political and Legal Philosophy." In *A Companion to Applied Philosophy*, edited by Kasper Lippert-Rasmussen, Kimberley Brownlee, and David Coady, 409–27. Wiley-Blackwell.

Derrida, Jacques. 1974. "White Mythology: Metaphor in the Text of Philosophy." Translated by F. C. T. Moore. *New Literary History* 6 (1): 5–74.

Derrida, Jacques. 1995. *Points . . . : Interviews, 1974–1994*. Translated by Peggy Kamuf et al. Stanford University Press.

Derrida, Jacques. 2001. "A Discussion with Jacques Derrida." *Theory and Event* 5 (1). https://doi.org/10.1353/tae.2001.0004.

Dietz, Chris. 2023. *Self-Declaration in the Legal Recognition of Gender.* Routledge.

DiMaggio, Paul J., and Walter W. Powell. 1983. "The Iron Cage Revisited: Institutional Isomorphism and Collective Rationality in Organizational Fields." *American Sociological Review* 48 (2): 147–60.

Dittmer, Jason. 2013. "Humour at the Model United Nations: The Role of Laughter in Constituting Geopolitical Assemblages." *Geopolitics* 18 (3): 493–513.

Diversity Solutions Consultancy. 2008. "Equality Impact Assessment Screening: 2011 Census, Development of Question on Sex/Gender." https://www.ons.gov.uk/file?uri=/census/2011census/howourcensusworks/howweplannedthe2011census/questionnairedevelopment/equalityimpactassessmentsforthe2011census/eiascreening sexandgendertcm77183984.pdf.

Duke-Williams, Oliver. n.d. "Census Explainer: Sexual Orientation and Gender Identity Questions." UK Data Service. Accessed December 4, 2025. https://ukdataservice.ac.uk/learning-hub/census/census-explainers/census-explainer-sexual-orientation-and-gender-identity-questions/.

Durham, Martin. 1991. *Sex and Politics: The Family and Morality in the Thatcher Years.* Macmillan.

Edwards, Jason. 2013. "Play and Democracy: Huizinga and the Limits of Agonism." *Political Theory* 41 (1): 90–115.

Edwards, Rosalind. 2022. "Why Do Academics Do Unfunded Research? Resistance, Compliance and Identity in the UK Neo-Liberal University." *Studies in Higher Education* 47 (4): 904–14.

Eklund, Matti. 2024. "Conceptual Engineering and Conceptual Innovation." *Inquiry*, July 31. https://doi.org/10.1080/0020174X.2024.2384066.

Emerton, Robyn. 2023. "'We're Not There Yet' but It's Not 'Pie-in-the-Sky': Legal Consciousness, Decertification and the Equality Sector in England and Wales." *Feminist Legal Studies* 31 (1): 95–120.

English, Kirstie Ken. 2025. "Binary Barriers: Representing Trans and Gender Diverse Populations in Censuses and Other Population Surveys." In *Second International Handbook on the Demography of Sexuality*, edited by Amanda K. Baumle and Zelma Oyarvide Tuthill, 165–85. Springer.

Enright, Máiréad. 2021. "The Touching Contract." *Paper Visual Art* 2:31–40.
Enright, Máiréad, and Tina Kinsella. 2023. "Legal Aesthetics in the Touching Contract: Memory, Exposure and Transformation." *Law, Culture and the Humanities* 19 (2): 297–319.
Escalante, Alyson. 2018. "Beyond Negativity: What Comes After Gender Nihilism?" Medium, March 15. https://alyesque.medium.com/beyond-negativity-what-comesafter-gender-nihilism-bbd80a5fc05d.
Fabius, Jeroen. 2012. "The Missing History of (Not) Conceptual Dance." In *Danswetenschap in Nederland*, vol. 7, edited by Merel Heering, Ruth Naber, Bianca Nieuwboer, and Liesbeth Wildschut, 99–111. Vereniging voor Dansonderzoek.
Fair, Hannah. 2022. "Playing with the Anthropocene: Board Game Imaginaries of Islands, Nature, and Empire." *Island Studies Journal* 17 (1): 85–101.
Fairbairn, Catherine, Doug Pyper, and Bukky Balogun. 2022. *Gender Recognition Act Reform: Consultation and Outcome*. House of Commons. https://researchbriefings.files.parliament.uk/documents/CBP-9079/CBP-9079.pdf.
Farran, Sue. 2016. "Graffiti Artists and Guerrilla Gardeners: Challenging Our Understandings of Property Law." In *Contributions to Law, Philosophy and Ecology*, edited by Ruth Thomas-Pellicer, Vito De Lucia, and Sian Sullivan, 192–211. Routledge.
Farran, Sue, and Rhona Smith. 2021. "Graffiti in a Time of Covid-19: Spray Paint and the Law." *King's Law Journal* 32 (1): 84–95.
Fauconnier, Gilles, and Mark Turner. 1998. "Conceptual Integration Networks." *Cognitive Science* 22 (2): 133–87.
Featherstone, David, and Joe Painter, eds. 2013. *Spatial Politics: Essays for Doreen Massey*. Wiley-Blackwell.
Feigenbaum, Anna. 2008. "Tactics and Technology: Cultural Resistance at the Greenham Common Women's Peace Camp." PhD thesis, McGill University.
Feraro, Shai. 2016. "Invoking Hecate at the Women's Peace Camp: The Presence of Goddess Spirituality and Dianic Witchcraft at Greenham Common in the 1980s." *Magic, Ritual, and Witchcraft* 11 (2): 226–48.
Ferreira, Nuno, Maria Federica Moscati, and Senthorun Raj. 2025. *Queer Judgments*. Counterpress.
Ferretti, Federico, and Harro van Lente. 2022. "The Promise of the Maker Movement: Policy Expectations Versus Community Criticisms." *Science and Public Policy* 49 (1): 18–27.
Finocchiaro, Peter. 2025. "Sexual Engineering: Conceptual Authority and the Gadfly Strategy." *Inquiry*, 1–27. https://doi.org/10.1080/0020174X.2025.2578647.
Fish, Julie, Andrew King, and Kathryn Almack. 2018. "Queerying Activism Through the Lens of the Sociology of Everyday Life." *Sociological Review* 66 (6): 1194–208.
FitzGerald, Maggie. 2023. "Rethinking the Political in the Pluriverse: The Ethico-Political Significance of Care." *Journal of International Political Theory* 19 (3): 252–68.
Fjællingsdal, Kristoffer S., and Christian A. Klöckner. 2019. "Gaming Green: The Educational Potential of Eco—a Digital Simulated Ecosystem." *Frontiers in Psychology* 10:2846. https://doi.org/10.3389/fpsyg.2019.02846.
Fletcher, Ruth. 2020. "Cheeky Witnessing." *Feminist Review* 124 (1): 124–41.
Franklin, Sarah. 2022. "Gender as a Proxy: Diagnosing and Resisting Carceral Genderisms." *European Journal of Women's Studies* 29 (Supplement 1): 132S–39S.

Frederick, Angela, and Dara Shifrer. 2019. "Race and Disability: From Analogy to Intersectionality." *Sociology of Race and Ethnicity* 5 (2): 200–214.
Freeman, Richard, Steven Griggs, and Annette Boaz. 2011. "The Practice of Policy Making." *Evidence and Policy* 7 (2): 127–36.
Fuad-Luke, Alastair. 2016. "Adjusting Our Metabolism: Slowness and Nourishing Rituals of Delay in Anticipation of a Post-Consumer Age." In *Longer Lasting Products: Alternatives to the Throwaway Society*, edited by Tim Cooper, 133–55. Routledge.
Gadamer, H. G. 1982. *Truth and Method.* Crossroad.
Gallie, Walter Bryce. 1955–56. "Essentially Contested Concepts." *Proceedings of the Aristotelian Society* 56:167–98.
Garforth, Lisa. 2025. "Climate and Failure: For a Weak Utopianism." *European Journal of Social Theory*, ahead of print, November 6. https://doi.org/10.1177/13684310251392829.
Garland, Fae, and Mitchell Travis. 2025. "Gendered Childhoods, Linear Sex Development and Unruly Temporalities." *Feminist Legal Studies* 33 (1): 1–28.
Gascoigne, Mollie. 2024. "Legal Sex Status: The Attitudes of Non-Binary People Towards Reform in England and Wales." *Legal Studies* 44 (2): 277–94.
Gayoye, Martha, Mateenah Hunter, Ambreena Manji, et al. 2021. "Feminist Judgments Projects at the Intersection." *Feminist Legal Studies* 29 (2): 251–61.
Geertz, Clifford. 2000. *Local Knowledge: Further Essays in Interpretive Anthropology.* Basic Books.
Gheaus, Anca. 2023. "Feminism Without 'Gender Identity.'" *Politics, Philosophy and Economics* 22 (1): 31–54.
Gibbons, Adam F. 2024. "Rational Conceptual Conflict and the Implementation Problem." *Inquiry* 67 (9): 3355–81.
Gibson-Graham, Julie Katherine. 1996. *The End of Capitalism (as We Knew It): A Feminist Critique of Political Economy.* University of Minnesota Press.
Gibson-Graham, Julie Katherine. 2008. "Diverse Economies: Performative Practices for 'Other Worlds.'" *Progress in Human Geography* 32 (5): 613–32.
Giddings, Seth. 2024. "Why Look at Toy Animals? Play, Protopolitics, and the Postnatural." *Cultural Politics* 20 (1): 60–74.
Gleeson, Jules Joanne. 2017. "Abolitionism in the 21st Century: From Communization as the End of Sex, to Revolutionary Transfeminism." *Blind Field: A Journal of Cultural Inquiry* 7. https://blindfieldjournal.com/2017/08/07/abolitionism-in-the-21st-century-from-communisation-as-the-end-of-sex-to-revolutionary-transfeminism/.
Glover, Robert W. 2012. "Games Without Frontiers? Democratic Engagement, Agonistic Pluralism and the Question of Exclusion." *Philosophy and Social Criticism* 38 (1): 81–104.
Goggin, Joyce. 2012. "Regulating (Virtual) Subjects: Finance, Entertainment and Games." *Journal of Cultural Economy* 5 (4): 441–56.
Goldberg-Hiller, Jonathan. 2023. *Law by Night.* Duke University Press.
Golder, Ben. 2025. "The Politics of Legal Form: An Essay on Subjunctive Jurisprudence." *Australian Feminist Law Journal*, May 6. https://doi.org/10.1080/13200968.2025.2486935.

Goldstein, Piotr. 2020. "Post-Yugoslav Everyday Activism(s): A Different Form of Activist Citizenship?" In *Activist Citizenship in Southeast Europe*, edited by Adam Fagan and Indraneel Sircar, 119–36. Routledge.

Goodman, Michael K. 2004. "Reading Fair Trade: Political Ecological Imaginary and the Moral Economy of Fair Trade Foods." *Political Geography* 23 (7): 891–915.

Goudet, Laura. 2024. "Quare Representations in Absentia: Non-Binary Black Characterization(s) in Video Games." *Popular Culture Studies Journal* 12 (1): 176–94.

Grabham, Emily. 2020. "Exploring the Textual Alchemy of Legal Gender: Experimental Statutes and the Message in the Medium." *Feminists@Law* 10 (2). https://doi.org/10.22024/UniKent/03/fal.950.

Grabham, Emily. 2023. "Decertifying Gender: The Challenge of Equal Pay." *Feminist Legal Studies* 31 (1): 67–93.

Grabham, Emily. 2025. "Parody Alternative Judgment: *For Women Scotland* [2025]." *Critical Legal Thinking* (blog), May 1. https://criticallegalthinking.com/2025/05/01/parody-alternative-judgment-for-women-scotland-2025/.

Graeber, David. 2011. "Consumption." *Current Anthropology* 52 (4): 489–511.

Gugerell, Katharina. 2023. "Serious Games for Sustainability Transformations: Participatory Research Methods for Sustainability—Toolkit #7." *GAIA—Ecological Perspectives for Science and Society* 32 (3): 292–95.

Gunn, Caitlin. 2019. "Black Feminist Futurity: From Survival Rhetoric to Radical Speculation." *Feral Feminisms* 9:15–20.

Gupta, Suman, Jernej Habjan, and Hrvoje Tutek, eds. 2016. *Academic Labour, Unemployment and Global Higher Education: Neoliberal Policies of Funding and Management.* Springer.

Guyan, Kevin. 2022. "Constructing a Queer Population? Asking About Sexual Orientation in Scotland's 2022 Census." *Journal of Gender Studies* 31 (6): 782–92.

Gyford, John. 1985. *The Politics of Local Socialism.* Allen and Unwin.

Hahner, Leslie A., and Scott J. Varda. 2014. "Yarn Bombing and the Aesthetics of Exceptionalism." *Communication and Critical/Cultural Studies* 11 (4): 301–21.

Hajer, Maarten, and Wytske Versteeg. 2019. "Imagining the Post-Fossil City: Why Is It So Difficult to Think of New Possible Worlds?" *Territory, Politics, Governance* 7 (2): 122–34.

Halley, Janet. 2006. *Split Decisions: How and Why to Take a Break from Feminism.* Princeton University Press.

Halsey, Mark, and Alison Young. 2006. "'Our Desires Are Ungovernable': Writing Graffiti in Urban Space." *Theoretical Criminology* 10 (3): 275–306.

Hamilton-Jones, Imogen, and Thomas de Groot. 2021. "For Amsterdam's Experiment in New Municipalism to Succeed, It Must Put Vague Terms into Practice." Minim, June 14. https://minim-municipalism.org/magazine/for-amsterdams-experiment-in-new-municipalism-to-succeed-it-must-put-vague-terms-into-practice.

Harris, Cheryl I. 1993. "Whiteness as Property." *Harvard Law Review* 106 (8): 1707–91.

Harris, Cheryl I. 2020. "Reflections on Whiteness as Property." *Harvard Law Review Forum* 134 (2020): 1–10.

Haslanger, Sally. 2000. "Gender and Race: (What) Are They? (What) Do We Want Them to Be?" *Noûs* 34 (1): 31–55.

Haslanger, Sally. 2020. "Going On, Not in the Same Way." In *Conceptual Engineering and Conceptual Ethics*, edited by Alexis Burgess, Herman Cappelen, and David Plunkett, 230–60. Oxford University Press.

Haveri, Minna. 2016. "Yarn Bombing—the Softer Side of Street Art." In *Routledge Handbook of Graffiti and Street Art*, edited by Jeffrey Ian Ross, 103–12. Routledge.

Heikkilä, Mia. 2022. "Boys, Weapon Toys, War Play and Meaning-Making: Prohibiting Play in Early Childhood Education Settings?" *Early Child Development and Care* 192 (11): 1830–41.

Hemmings, Clare. 2022. "'But I Thought We'd Already Won That Argument!': 'Anti-Gender' Mobilizations, Affect, and Temporality." *Feminist Studies* 48 (3): 594–615.

Henare, Amiria, Martin Holbraad, and Sari Wastell. 2007. *Thinking Through Things*. Routledge.

Herman, Didi. 2011. *An Unfortunate Coincidence: Jews, Jewishness, and English Law*. Oxford University Press.

Hey, David. 2011. "Kinder Scout and the Legend of the Mass Trespass." *Agricultural History Review* 59 (2): 199–216.

Higgs, Edward. 1996. "A Cuckoo in the Nest? The Origins of Civil Registration and State Medical Statistics in England and Wales." *Continuity and Change* 11 (1): 115–34.

Hines, Sally. 2020. "Sex Wars and (Trans) Gender Panics: Identity and Body Politics in Contemporary UK Feminism." *Sociological Review* 68 (4): 699–717.

Hines, Sally. 2025. "Hands Towards the Right: UK Gender–Critical Feminism and Right-Wing Coalitions." *Journal of Gender Studies* 34 (5): 699–715.

Hodges, Karen E. 2008. "Defining the Problem: Terminology and Progress in Ecology." *Frontiers in Ecology and the Environment* 6 (1): 35–42.

Højbjerre Larsen, Signe. 2021. "Parkour: Playing the Modern, Accelerated City." *Journal of the Philosophy of Sport* 48 (1): 26–44.

Holbraad, Martin. 2020. "The Shapes of Relations: Anthropology as Conceptual Morphology." *Philosophy of the Social Sciences* 50 (6): 495–522.

Holbraad, Martin, and Morten Axel Pedersen. 2017. *The Ontological Turn: An Anthropological Exposition*. Cambridge University Press.

Holzer, Lena. 2018. *Non-Binary Gender Registration Models in Europe: Report on Third Gender Marker or No Gender Marker Options*. Report for ILGA-Europe.

Holzer, Lena. 2019. "Sexually Dimorphic Bodies: A Production of Birth Certificates." *Australian Feminist Law Journal* 45 (1): 91–110.

Hong, Soonkwan, and Handan Vicdan. 2016. "Re-Imagining the Utopian: Transformation of a Sustainable Lifestyle in Ecovillages." *Journal of Business Research* 69 (1): 120–36.

Honig, Bonnie. 1993. *Political Theory and the Displacement of Politics*. Cornell University Press.

Honig, Bonnie. 1995. *Feminist Interpretations of Hannah Arendt*. Pennsylvania State University Press.

Honig, Bonnie. 2017. *Public Things: Democracy in Disrepair*. Fordham University Press.

Honig, Bonnie. 2021. *A Feminist Theory of Refusal*. Harvard University Press.

Horton, John, and Peter Kraftl. 2009. "Small Acts, Kind Words and 'Not Too Much Fuss': Implicit Activisms." *Emotion, Space and Society* 2 (1): 14–23.

Horton, John, and Peter Kraftl. 2018. "Rats, Assorted Shit and 'Racist Groundwater': Towards Extra-Sectional Understandings of Childhoods and Social-Material Processes." *Environment and Planning D: Society and Space* 36 (5): 926–48.
Huizinga, Johan. 1955. *Homo Ludens: A Study of the Play Element in Culture*. Beacon.
Hung, Holvert. 2017. "Formation of New Property Rights on Government Land Through Informal Co-Management: Case Studies on Countryside Guerilla Gardening." *Land Use Policy* 63:381–93.
Hunter, Rosemary, Clare McGlynn, and Erika Rackley. 2010. *Feminist Judgments: From Theory to Practice*. Bloomsbury.
Hunter, Shona. 2008. "Living Documents: A Feminist Psychosocial Approach to the Relational Politics of Policy Documentation." *Critical Social Policy* 28 (4): 506–28.
Hunter, Shona. 2012. "Ordering Differentiation: Reconfiguring Governance as Relational Politics." *Journal of Psycho-Social Studies* 6 (1). https://www.psychosocial-studies-association.org/wp-content/uploads/2017/01/ShonaHunterOrderingDifferentiation.pdf.
Hunter, Shona. 2015. *Power, Politics and the Emotions: Impossible Governance?* Routledge.
Ingold, Tim. 2007. "Materials Against Materiality." *Archaeological Dialogues* 14 (1): 1–16.
Jagoda, Patrick, Melissa Gilliam, Peter McDonald, and Christopher Russell. 2015. "Worlding Through Play: Alternate Reality Games, Large-Scale Learning, and *The Source*." *American Journal of Play* 8 (1): 74–100.
Jenkins, Katharine. 2016. "Amelioration and Inclusion: Gender Identity and the Concept of Woman." *Ethics* 126 (2): 394–421.
Jenkins, Katharine. 2023. *Ontology and Oppression: Race, Gender, and Social Reality*. Oxford University Press.
John, Nicholas A. 2013. "The Social Logics of Sharing." *Communication Review* 16 (3): 113–31.
Jones, Jane Clare. 2020. *The Political Erasure of Sex*. With Lisa Mackenzie. https://history.web.ox.ac.uk/files/political-erasure-sexfull-reportpdf.
Jorem, Sigurd. 2021. "Conceptual Engineering and the Implementation Problem." *Inquiry* 64 (1–2): 186–211.
Jorem, Sigurd, and Guido Löhr. 2024. "Inferentialist Conceptual Engineering." *Inquiry* 67 (3): 932–53.
Joubert, Tim. 2023. "Bridging Bureaucracy and Activism: Challenges of Activist State-Work in the 1980s Greater London Council." *Urban Studies* 60 (11): 2251–70.
Kane, Pat. 2011. *The Play Ethic: A Manifesto for a Different Way of Living*. Pan Macmillan.
Katyal, Sonia K. 2017. "The *Numerus Clausus* of Sex." *University of Chicago Law Review* 84 (1): 389–494.
Keenan, Sarah. 2010. "Subversive Property: Reshaping Malleable Spaces of Belonging." *Social and Legal Studies* 19 (4): 423–39.
Keenan, Sarah. 2014. *Subversive Property: Law and the Production of Spaces of Belonging*. Routledge.
Keenan, Sarah. 2017. "Smoke, Curtains and Mirrors: The Production of Race Through Time and Title Registration." *Law and Critique* 28:87–108.
Keenan, Sarah. 2019. "From Historical Chains to Derivative Futures: Title Registries as Time Machines." *Social and Cultural Geography* 20 (3): 283–303.

Keenan, Sarah. 2025. "Plants Against Property: Japanese Knotweed as Companion Species." *Theory, Culture and Society*, ahead of print, May 14. https://doi.org/10.1177/02632764251334369.
Keller, Evelyn Fox. 2002. *Making Sense of Life: Explaining Biological Development with Models, Metaphors, and Machines*. Harvard University Press.
Kemp, Tom. 2023. *Activism and the Detention of Migrants: The Law and Politics of Immigration Detention*. Taylor and Francis.
Ketterling, Jean. 2023. "'You Do It for the Good Times': Rival Feminist Readings of Torture and Kink in *Grand Theft Auto V*." *Feminist Media Studies* 23 (7): 3452–67.
Klag, Malvina, and Ann Langley. 2013. "Approaching the Conceptual Leap in Qualitative Research." *International Journal of Management Reviews* 15 (2): 149–66.
Köhler, Sebastian, and Herman Veluwenkamp. 2024. "Conceptual Engineering: For What Matters." *Mind* 133 (530): 400–427.
Koslow, Allison. 2022. "Meaning Change and Changing Meaning." *Synthese* 200: article 94. https://doi.org/10.1007/s11229-022-03563-8.
Kuang, R. F. 2022. *Babel: Or the Necessity of Violence: An Arcane History of the Oxford Translators' Revolution*. HarperCollins.
Lamble, Sarah. 2024. "Confronting Complex Alliances: Situating Britain's Gender Critical Politics Within the Wider Transnational Anti-Gender Movement." *Journal of Lesbian Studies* 28 (3): 504–17.
Lamble, Sarah. 2025. "Sexual Peril and Dangerous Others: The Moral Economies of the Trans Prisoner Policy Debates in England and Wales." *Sexualities* 28 (1–2): 492–513.
Lanari, Elisa. 2024. "Makeshift Activism and the Afterlives of Refugee Welcome in Covid-19 Italy." *Critique of Anthropology* 44 (2): 184–203.
Lansley, Stewart, Sue Goss, and Christian Wolmar. 1989. *Councils in Conflict: The Rise and Fall of the Municipal Left*. Springer.
Lastowka, F. Gregory, and Dan Hunter. 2004. "The Laws of the Virtual Worlds." *California Law Review* 92 (1): 1–73.
Law, John. 2004. *After Method: Mess in Social Science Research*. Routledge.
Law, John, and John Urry. 2004. "Enacting the Social." *Economy and Society* 33 (3): 390–410.
Lawford-Smith, Holly. 2022. *Gender-Critical Feminism*. Oxford University Press.
Layard, Antonia. 2020. "Property as Socio-Legal Institution, Practice, Object, Idea." In *Research Handbook on the Sociology of Law*, edited by Jiří Přibáň, 271–82. Edward Elgar.
Lee, James. 2023. "'Not Time to Make a Change'? Reviewing the Rhetoric of Law Reform." *Current Legal Problems* 76 (1): 129–72.
Lehdonvirta, Vili. 2005a. "Real-Money Trade of Virtual Assets: Ten Different User Perceptions." In *Proceedings of Digital Arts and Culture 2005 Conference (DAC 2005)*, 52–58. IT University of Copenhagen.
Lehdonvirta, Vili. 2005b. "Virtual Economics: Applying Economics to the Study of Game Worlds." Proceedings of the 2005 Conference on Future Play (Future Play 2005), Lansing, MI, October 13–15, 2005. SSRN. https://ssrn.com/abstract=1630302.
Lehner, Ace. 2022. "Trans Failure: Transformative Joy in Consumer Culture." *Cultural Politics* 18 (1): 95–115.

Leng, Mary. 2023. "Amelioration, Inclusion, and Legal Recognition: On Sex, Gender, and the UK's Gender Recognition Act." *Journal of Political Philosophy* 31 (2): 129–57.

Lepecki, André. 2004. "Concept and Presence: The Contemporary European Dance Scene." In *Rethinking Dance History: A Reader*, edited by Alexandra Carter, 170–81. Routledge.

Lepecki, André. 2006. *Exhausting Dance: Performance and the Politics of Movement.* Routledge.

Liboiron, Max, Manuel Tironi, and Nerea Calvillo. 2018. "Toxic Politics: Acting in a Permanently Polluted World." *Social Studies of Science* 48 (3): 331–49.

Lim, Hannah Yee Fen. 2010. "Virtual World, Virtual Land but Real Property." *Singapore Journal of Legal Studies* 2010:304–27.

Linstead, Stephen, and Alison Pullen. 2006. "Gender as Multiplicity: Desire, Displacement, Difference and Dispersion." *Human Relations* 59 (9): 1287–310.

Lipsky, Michael. 2010. *Street-Level Bureaucracy: Dilemmas of the Individual in Public Service.* Russell Sage Foundation.

Locke, Karen. 2007. "Rational Control and Irrational Free-Play: Dual-Thinking Modes as Necessary Tension in Grounded Theorizing." In *The SAGE Handbook of Grounded Theory*, edited by Antony Bryant and Kathy Charmaz, 565–79. SAGE.

Löhr, Guido. 2022. "Linguistic Interventions and the Ethics of Conceptual Disruption." *Ethical Theory and Moral Practice* 25 (5): 835–49.

Lombardo, Emanuela, and Petra Meier. 2022. "Challenging Boundaries to Expand Frontiers in Gender and Policy Studies." *Policy and Politics* 50 (1): 99–115.

Lorber, Judith. 2000. "Using Gender to Undo Gender: A Feminist Degendering Movement." *Feminist Theory* 1 (1): 79–95.

Loveday, Vik. 2018. "The Neurotic Academic: Anxiety, Casualisation, and Governance in the Neoliberalising University." *Journal of Cultural Economy* 11 (2): 154–66.

Macpherson, Crawford Brough. 1962. *The Political Theory of Possessive Individualism: Hobbes to Locke.* Oxford University Press.

Maeckelbergh, Marianne. 2011. "Doing Is Believing: Prefiguration as Strategic Practice in the Alterglobalization Movement." *Social Movement Studies* 10 (1): 1–20.

Maeckelbergh, Marianne. 2022. "Process-Time and Event-Time: The Multiple Temporalities of Prefiguration." In *The Future Is Now: An Introduction to Prefigurative Politics*, edited by Lara Monticelli, 204–16. Bristol University Press.

Malaby, Thomas M. 2007. "Beyond Play: A New Approach to Games." *Games and Culture* 2 (2): 95–113.

Malen, Betty. 2003. "Tightening the Grip? The Impact of State Activism on Local School Systems." *Educational Policy* 17 (2): 195–216.

Malleson, Kate. 2018. "Equality Law and the Protected Characteristics." *Modern Law Review* 81 (4): 598–621.

Mann, Joanna. 2015. "Towards a Politics of Whimsy: Yarn Bombing the City." *Area* 47 (1): 65–72.

Marchiori, Samuela. 2025. "Conceptual Affordances: (How) Should They Inform Conceptual Engineering?" *Synthese* 206: article 88. https://doi.org/10.1007/s11229-025-05161-w.

Marotta, Steve. 2021. "Making Sense of 'Maker': Work, Identity, and Affect in the Maker Movement." *Environment and Planning A: Economy and Space* 53 (4): 638–54.
Marsh, Dorota, and Martyna Śliwa. 2022. "Making a Difference Through Atmospheres: The Orange Alternative, Laughter and the Possibilities of Affective Resistance." *Organization Studies* 43 (4): 477–96.
Martin, Deborah G., Susan Hanson, and Danielle Fontaine. 2007. "What Counts as Activism? The Role of Individuals in Creating Change." *Women's Studies Quarterly* 35 (3/4): 78–94.
Martin, Emily. 1990. "Toward an Anthropology of Immunology: The Body as Nation State." *Medical Anthropology Quarterly* 4 (4): 410–26.
Martin, Patricia Yancey. 2004. "Gender as Social Institution." *Social Forces* 82 (4): 1249–73.
Massey, Doreen. 2009. "Concepts of Space and Power in Theory and in Political Practice." *Documents d'Anàlisi Geogràfica* 55:15–26.
McAuliffe, Cameron. 2012. "Graffiti or Street Art? Negotiating the Moral Geographies of the Creative City." *Journal of Urban Affairs* 34 (2): 189–206.
McDermont, Morag, Tim Cole, Janet Newman, and Angela Piccini, eds. 2020. *Imagining Regulation Differently*. Policy Press.
McDonald, Peter. 2014. "For Every To There Is a Fro: Interpreting Time, Rhythm, and Gesture in Play." *Games and Culture* 9 (6): 480–90.
McGovern, Alyce. 2019. *Craftivism and Yarn Bombing: A Criminological Exploration*. Springer Nature.
McKenna, Robin. 2018. "No Epistemic Trouble for Engineering 'Woman': Response to Simion." *Logos and Episteme* 9 (3): 335–42.
Mikkola, Mari. 2009. "Gender Concepts and Intuitions." *Canadian Journal of Philosophy* 39 (4): 559–83.
Mische, Ann. 2009. "Projects and Possibilities: Researching Futures in Action." *Sociological Forum* 24 (3): 694–704.
Misztal, Bronislaw. 1992. "Between the State and Solidarity: One Movement, Two Interpretations—the Orange Alternative Movement in Poland." *British Journal of Sociology* 43 (1): 55–78.
Mitchell, Timothy. 2008. "Rethinking Economy." *Geoforum* 39 (3): 1116–21.
Monticelli, Lara, ed. 2022. *The Future Is Now: An Introduction to Prefigurative Politics*. Bristol University Press.
Morales, Helen. 2013. "Aristophanes' Lysistrata, the Liberian 'Sex Strike,' and the Politics of Reception." *Greece and Rome* 60 (2): 281–95.
Morgan, Bronwen. 2024. "Institutional Design in Commons-Based Sharing Economies: Platform, Care and Place." *International Journal of Law in Context* 20 (4): 496–513.
Mottier, Véronique. 2008. "Eugenics, Politics and the State: Social Democracy and the Swiss 'Gardening State.'" *Studies in History and Philosophy of Science Part C: Studies in History and Philosophy of Biological and Biomedical Sciences* 39 (2): 263–69.
Mulcahy, Sean. 2021. "Dances with Laws: From Metaphor to Methodology." *Law and Humanities* 15 (1): 106–33.
Mulcahy, Sean, and Kate Seear. 2023. "A 'Tick and Flick' Exercise: Movement and Form in Australian Parliamentary Human Rights Scrutiny." *Dance Research Journal* 55 (3): 47–64.

Mulvey, Kelly Lynn, and Melanie Killen. 2015. "Challenging Gender Stereotypes: Resistance and Exclusion." *Child Development* 86 (3): 681–94.

Munasinghe, Amila, Thomas Cuckston, and Nick Rowbottom. 2021. "Sustainability Certification as Marketisation: Rainforest Alliance in the Sri Lankan Tea Production Industry." *Accounting Forum* 45 (3): 247–72.

Murray, Kath, and Lucy Hunter Blackburn. 2019. "Losing Sight of Women's Rights: The Unregulated Introduction of Gender Self-Identification as a Case Study of Policy Capture in Scotland." *Scottish Affairs* 28 (3): 262–89.

Mutersbaugh, Tad. 2002. "The Number Is the Beast: A Political Economy of Organic-Coffee Certification and Producer Unionism." *Environment and Planning A* 34 (7): 1165–84.

Mutersbaugh, Tad. 2005a. "Fighting Standards with Standards: Harmonization, Rents, and Social Accountability in Certified Agrofood Networks." *Environment and Planning A* 37 (11): 2033–51.

Mutersbaugh, Tad. 2005b. "Just-in-Space: Certified Rural Products, Labor of Quality, and Regulatory Spaces." *Journal of Rural Studies* 21 (4): 389–402.

Nachmanovitch, Stephen. 2009. "This Is Play." *New Literary History* 40 (1): 1–24.

Nado, Jennifer. 2021. "Conceptual Engineering, Truth, and Efficacy." *Synthese* 198 (Supplement 7): 1507–27.

Nado, Jennifer. 2026. "Re-Engineering Knowledge: A Case Study in Pluralist Conceptual Engineering." *Inquiry* 69 (1): 49–74.

Narotzky, Susana, and Niko Besnier. 2014. "Crisis, Value, and Hope: Rethinking the Economy: An Introduction to Supplement 9." *Current Anthropology* 55 (S9): S4–S16.

Nash, Catherine Jean, and Kath Browne. 2020. *Heteroactivism: Resisting Lesbian, Gay, Bisexual and Trans Rights and Equalities*. Bloomsbury.

Nedelsky, Jennifer. 1990. "Law, Boundaries, and the Bounded Self." *Representations*, no. 30, 162–89.

Neill, A. S. 1968. *Summerhill: A Radical Approach to Child Rearing*. Penguin.

Newman, Hannah J. H., and Elizabeth Peel. 2022. "'An Impossible Dream'? Non-Binary People's Perceptions of Legal Gender Status and Reform in the UK." *Psychology and Sexuality* 13 (5): 1381–95.

Newman, Janet. 2012. *Working the Spaces of Power: Activism, Neoliberalism and Gendered Labour*. Bloomsbury Academic.

Newman, Janet. 2019. "The Political Work of Reimagination." In *Reimagining the State: Theoretical Challenges and Transformative Possibilities*, edited by Davina Cooper, Nikita Dhawan, and Janet Newman, 19–36. Routledge.

Newman, Janet, and John Clarke. 2014. "States of Imagination." *Soundings* 57:153–69.

Nicholson, Daniel J. 2010. "Biological Atomism and Cell Theory." *Studies in History and Philosophy of Science Part C: Studies in History and Philosophy of Biological and Biomedical Sciences* 41 (3): 202–11.

Nicholson, Daniel J. 2019. "Is the Cell Really a Machine?" *Journal of Theoretical Biology* 477:108–26.

Noterman, Elsa, and Nicholas Blomley. 2024. "Children's Legal Geographies, and the 'Make-Believe' of Property." *Social and Legal Studies* 33 (2): 236–53.

Novac, Andreea. 2022. "On Bodies in Motion: New Perspectives in Contemporary Choreography." *Colocvii Teatrale* 12 (1): 186–93.

O'Brien, Erin, Hope Johnson, and Yu-An Murray. 2023. "Banning Indirect Boycotts: Contentious Interactions and the Role of the State in Marketplace Activism." *Business and Politics* 25 (4): 393–408.

O'Donnell, Jessica. 2020. "Militant Meninism: The Militaristic Discourse of Gamergate and Men's Rights Activism." *Media, Culture and Society* 42 (5): 654–74.

O'Grady, Alice. 2012. "Tracing the City—Parkour Training, Play and the Practice of Collaborative Learning." *Theatre, Dance and Performance Training* 3 (2): 145–62.

Olsson, Jan. 2009. "The Power of the Inside Activist: Understanding Policy Change by Empowering the Advocacy Coalition Framework (ACF)." *Planning Theory and Practice* 10 (2): 167–87.

Olsson, Jan, and Erik Hysing. 2012. "Theorizing Inside Activism: Understanding Policymaking and Policy Change from Below." *Planning Theory and Practice* 13 (2): 257–73.

ONS (Office for National Statistics). 2016a. *Census Transformation Programme: The 2021 Census: Assessment of Initial User Requirements on Content for England and Wales: Gender Identity Topic Report.* ONS. https://www.ons.gov.uk/file?uri=/census/censustransformationprogramme/consultations/the2021censusinitialviewoncontentforenglandandwales/topicreport03genderidentity.pdf.

ONS (Office for National Statistics). 2016b. *Census Transformation Programme: The 2021 Census: Assessment of Initial User Requirements on Content for England and Wales: Response to Consultation.* ONS.

Ozturk, Mustafa Bilgehan, Nick Rumens, and Ahu Tatli. 2025. "Diversity and Inclusion Practitioners and Non-Binary Employees in the UK: A Bourdieusian Analysis." *International Journal of Human Resource Management* 36 (7): 1191–214.

Pakes, Anna. 2019. "Can There Be Conceptual Dance?" *Midwest Studies in Philosophy* 44:195–212.

Pateman, Carole. 2002. "Self-Ownership and Property in the Person: Democratization and a Tale of Two Concepts." *Journal of Political Philosophy* 10 (1): 20–53.

Patton, Paul. 2006. "Mobile Concepts, Metaphor, and the Problem of Referentiality in Deleuze and Guattari." In *Metaphoricity and the Politics of Mobility*, edited by Maria Margaroni and Effie Yiannopoulou, 25–45. Brill.

Paxton, Naomi. 2024. "'When You Want a Thing Done, Get a Man to Do It!' Necessary Strategies of Presence and Absence in Suffrage Theatre and Performance." In *Women Experimenting in Theatre: Early Modern to Contemporary*, edited by Kate Aughterson and Deborah Philips, 103–25. Springer.

Pearce, Ruth, Sonja Erikainen, and Ben Vincent. 2020. "TERF Wars: An Introduction." *Sociological Review* 68 (4): 677–98.

Pedersen, Sarah. 2022. "'They've Got an Absolute Army of Women Behind Them': The Formation of a Women's Cooperative Constellation in Contemporary Scotland." *Scottish Affairs* 31 (1): 1–20.

Pedersen, Sarah. 2023. "'Believers in Biology': A Co-Ordinated Effort to Disrupt the 2022 Census." *Scottish Affairs* 32 (1): 1–18.

Peel, Elizabeth. 2025. "'Gender Debate' Discourse: Polarising, Bigoted, and Validating." In *Polarising Sexualities and Genders: Divisions, Differences and LGBTQIA+ Equalities*, edited by Kath Browne and Emily Kazyak, 119–36. Bloomsbury.

Peel, Elizabeth, and Hannah J. H. Newman. 2020. "Gender's Wider Stakes: Lay Attitudes to Legal Gender Reform." *Feminists@Law* 10 (2). https://doi.org/10.22024/UniKent/03/fal.953.

Peel, Elizabeth, and Hannah J. H. Newman. 2023. "'I Don't Think That's Something I've Ever Thought About Really Before': A Thematic Discursive Analysis of Lay People's Talk About Legal Gender." *Feminist Legal Studies* 31 (1): 121–43.

Perry-Kessaris, Amanda. 2023. "Living Methods for Living Law: Eugen Ehrlich Meets Bruno Latour Via Adversarial Exhibition Design." Prepared for Colloque Ehrlich: L'actualité de la pensée d'Eugen Ehrlich pour les méthodes empiriques du droit, Université Paris, September 22–23, 2022. SSRN. https://ssrn.com/abstract=4442665.

Perry-Kessaris, Amanda. 2026. "Activating Imagination to Promote Epistemic Justice: Speculations on an Island-Wide Citizens' Assembly for Cyprus." In *The Socio-Politics of Legal Design and Its Epistemic Consequences*, edited by Siddharth Peter de Souza and Joaquín Santuber. Hart.

Perry-Kessaris, Amanda, and Victoria Barnes. 2025. "Fantasy Legal Exhibitions." *Northern Ireland Legal Quarterly* 76 (2): 246–76.

Pettinicchio, David. 2012. "Institutional Activism: Reconsidering the Insider/Outsider Dichotomy." *Sociology Compass* 6 (6): 499–510.

Petty, Aaron R. 2014. "Faith, However Defined: Reassessing JFS and the Judicial Conception of Religion." *Elon Law Review* 6:117–50.

Petz, Marcus, Federico Bonelli, and Teppo Eskelinen. 2024. "Le Grand Jeu and the Potential of Money Games for Exploring Economic Possibilities." *Degrowth Journal* 2. https://doi.org/10.36399/Degrowth.002.01.01.

Philippopoulos-Mihalopoulos, Andreas. 2021. "Performing Metaphors." *Theory and Event* 24 (1): 268–93.

Phipps, Alison. 2025. "'Holding On' in a Crisis: Theorising Campus Sexual Violence Activism Within Precarious Labour Relations." *Feminist Theory* 26 (1): 63–82.

Pilon, Mary. 2015. "The Secret History of Monopoly: The Capitalist Board Game's Leftwing Origins." *Guardian*, April 11. https://www.theguardian.com/lifeandstyle/2015/apr/11/secret-history-monopoly-capitalist-game-leftwing-origins.

Pinder, Mark. 2022. "Is Haslanger's Ameliorative Project a Successful Conceptual Engineering Project?" *Synthese* 200: article 334. https://doi.org/10.1007/s11229-022-03803-x.

Pinder, Morgan. 2024. "Negotiating Anthropocentrism and Ecologies in Cozy Games." *Replay: The Polish Journal of Game Studies* 11 (1): 125–36.

Podosky, Paul-Mikhail Catapang. 2018. "Ideology and Normativity: Constraints on Conceptual Engineering." *Inquiry*, ahead of print, December 29. https://doi.org/10.1080/0020174X.2018.1562374.

Podosky, Paul-Mikhail Catapang. 2024. "Why Conceptual Engineers Should Resist Dialogical Individualism." *Topoi* 43 (5): 1671–84.

Pottinger, Laura. 2017. "Planting the Seeds of a Quiet Activism." *Area* 49 (2): 215–22.

Power, Marilyn. 2004. "Social Provisioning as a Starting Point for Feminist Economics." *Feminist Economics* 10 (3): 3–19.
Price, Laura. 2015. "Knitting and the City." *Geography Compass* 9 (2): 81–95.
Prinzing, Michael. 2018. "The Revisionist's Rubric: Conceptual Engineering and the Discontinuity Objection." *Inquiry* 61 (8): 854–80.
Pryke, Michael. 2007. "Geomoney: An Option on Frost, Going Long on Clouds." *Geoforum* 38 (3): 576–88.
Queloz, Matthieu, and Friedemann Bieber. 2022. "Conceptual Engineering and the Politics of Implementation." *Pacific Philosophical Quarterly* 103 (3): 670–91.
Quintana, Laura, Pablo Jaramillo, and Alhena Caicedo. 2022. "What's Up with Methodology? Faults, Experimentations, and Affective Displacements in the Reinventions of the Common." *Cultural Studies* 36 (4): 644–67.
Rai, Shirin M. 2024. *Depletion: The Human Costs of Caring*. Oxford University Press.
Ramshaw, Sara. 2023. "Law and Humanities: A Field Without a Canon." *Law, Culture and the Humanities* 19 (1): 77–88.
Rancière, Jacques. 1999. *Disagreement: Politics and Philosophy*. University of Minnesota Press.
Reay, Trish, and C. Robert Hinings. 2009. "Managing the Rivalry of Competing Institutional Logics." *Organization Studies* 30 (6): 629–52.
Reitan, Eric. 2001. "Rape as an Essentially Contested Concept." *Hypatia* 16 (2): 43–66.
Renz, Flora. 2019. "Fluctuating Intensities: Thinking About Gender Through Other Socio-Legal Categories." *SLSA Blog*, July 12. https://www.slsa.ac.uk/post/fluctuating-intensities-thinking-about-gender-through-other-socio-legal-categories.
Renz, Flora. 2023. "Gender-Based Violence Without a Legal Gender: Imagining Single-Sex Services in Conditions of Decertification." *Feminist Legal Studies* 31 (1): 43–66.
Renz, Flora. 2024. *Gender Recognition and the Law: Troubling Transgender Peoples' Engagement with Legal Regulation*. Taylor and Francis.
Renz, Flora, and Davina Cooper. 2022. "Reimagining Gender Through Equality Law: What Legal Thoughtways Do Religion and Disability Offer?" *Feminist Legal Studies* 30 (2): 129–55.
Reynolds, Andrew. 2007. "The Cell's Journey: From Metaphorical to Literal Factory." *Endeavour* 31 (2): 65–70.
Reynolds, Andrew. 2018. *The Third Lens: Metaphor and the Creation of Modern Cell Biology*. University of Chicago Press.
Rich, Jessica A. J. 2019. "Making National Participatory Institutions Work: Bureaucrats, Activists, and AIDS Policy in Brazil." *Latin American Politics and Society* 61 (2): 45–67.
Richardson, Janice. 2010. "Feminism, Property in the Person and Concepts of Self." *British Journal of Politics and International Relations* 12 (1): 56–71.
Richardson, Lizzie. 2015. "Performing the Sharing Economy." *Geoforum* 67:121–29.
Risberg, Annette, and Hervé Corvellec. 2022. "The Significance of Trying: How Organizational Members Meet the Ambiguities of Diversity." *Gender, Work and Organization* 29 (6): 1849–67.
Risman, Barbara J. 2004. "Gender as a Social Structure: Theory Wrestling with Activism." *Gender and Society* 18 (4): 429–50.

Rittich, Kerry. 2023. "Visibility and Value at Work: The Legal Organization of Productive and Reproductive Work: First Annual Lecture in the Laws of Social Reproduction, 18 August 2020." *Feminists@Law* 12 (2). https://doi.org/10.22024/UniKent/03/fal.1223.
Roberts, John M., and Colin Cremin. 2019. "Prosumer Culture and the Question of Fetishism." *Journal of Consumer Culture* 19 (2): 213–30.
Robertson, Morgan. 2012. "Measurement and Alienation: Making a World of Ecosystem Services." *Transactions of the Institute of British Geographers* 37 (3): 386–401.
Rogers, Nicole, and Michelle Maloney. 2014. "The Australian Wild Law Judgment Project." *Alternative Law Journal* 39 (3): 172–75.
Rogers, Nicole, and Michelle Maloney. 2022. "The Anthropocene Judgments Project: A Thought Experiment in Futureproofing the Common Law." *Alternative Law Journal* 47 (3): 173–78.
Romanienko, Lisiunia A. 2007. "Antagonism, Absurdity, and the Avant-Garde: Dismantling Soviet Oppression Through the Use of Theatrical Devices by Poland's 'Orange' Solidarity Movement." *International Review of Social History* 52 (S15): 133–51.
Roseneil, Sasha. 1995. *Disarming Patriarchy: Feminism and Political Action at Greenham.* Open University Press.
Roseneil, Sasha. 2000. *Common Women, Uncommon Practices: The Queer Feminisms of Greenham.* Cassell.
Rosiecka, Helena. 2021. "Methodology for Decision Making on the 2021 Census Sex Question Concept and Associated Guidance." UK Statistics Authority, February 10. https://uksa.statisticsauthority.gov.uk/publication/methodology-for-decision-making-on-the-2021-census-sex-question-concept-and-associated-guidance/.
Saguy, Abigail C., and Juliet A. Williams. 2024. "Too 'Full of Gender': How Activists Conceptualize the Promises and Pitfalls of Gender-Neutral Identity Documents." *Social Problems* 71 (4): 1247–61.
Salmenniemi, Suvi, Pilvi Porkola, and Hanna Ylöstalo. 2024. "Political Imagination and Utopian Pedagogy." *Critical Arts* 38 (4–5): 24–39.
Santarelli, Matteo. 2024. "Improving Concepts, Reshaping Values: Pragmatism and Ameliorative Projects." *Inquiry* 67 (3): 872–90.
Sargisson, Lucy. 2010. "Friends Have All Things in Common: Utopian Property Relations." *British Journal of Politics and International Relations* 12 (1): 22–36.
Saunders, Peter. 1984. "Rethinking Local Politics." In *Local Socialism? Labour Councils and New Left Alternatives*, edited by Martin Boddy and Colin Fudge, 22–48. Macmillan.
Saville, Stephen John. 2008. "Playing with Fear: Parkour and the Mobility of Emotion." *Social and Cultural Geography* 9 (8): 891–914.
Sawyer, Sarah. 2026. "Concept Pluralism in Conceptual Engineering." *Inquiry* 69 (1): 75–100.
Schneiberg, Marc, and Tim Bartley. 2008. "Organizations, Regulation, and Economic Behavior: Regulatory Dynamics and Forms from the Nineteenth to Twenty-First Century." *Annual Review of Law and Social Science* 4 (1): 31–61.
Schor, Juliet B., Connor Fitzmaurice, Lindsey B. Carfagna, Will Attwood-Charles, and Emilie Dubois Poteat. 2016. "Paradoxes of Openness and Distinction in the Sharing Economy." *Poetics* 54:66–81.

Schroeder, Richard A. 2010. "Tanzanite as Conflict Gem: Certifying a Secure Commodity Chain in Tanzania." *Geoforum* 41 (1): 56–65.
Schwarzbach, Natasha, and Ben Richardson. 2014. "A Bitter Harvest: Child Labour in Sugarcane Agriculture and the Role of Certification Systems." *UC Davis Journal of International Law and Policy* 21 (1): 99–128.
Seto, Theodore P. 2008. "When Is a Game Only a Game? The Taxation of Virtual Worlds." *University of Cincinnati Law Review* 77 (3): 1027–52.
Shah, Rita. 2022. "'This Ruins Lives': Using Monopoly© to Understand the Prison Industrial Complex." *Journal of Criminal Justice Education* 33 (3): 406–25.
Shapiro, Nicholas. 2015. "Attuning to the Chemosphere: Domestic Formaldehyde, Bodily Reasoning, and the Chemical Sublime." *Cultural Anthropology* 30 (3): 368–93.
Sharpe, Alex. 2010. *Foucault's Monsters and the Challenge of Law*. Routledge.
Sharpe, Alex. 2017. "Scary Monsters: The Hopeful Undecidability of David Bowie (1947–2016)." *Law and Humanities* 11 (2): 228–44.
Shaw, Deborah. 2023. "A Tale of Two Feminisms: Gender Critical Feminism, Trans Inclusive Feminism and the Case of Kathleen Stock." *Women's History Review* 32 (5): 768–80.
Shepard, Benjamin. 2009. *Queer Political Performance and Protest*. Routledge.
Shields, Rachel. 2015. "Ludic Ontology." *American Journal of Play* 7 (3): 298–321.
Simion, Mona. 2018a. "Epistemic Trouble for Engineering 'Woman.'" *Logos and Episteme* 9 (1): 91–98.
Simion, Mona. 2018b. "The 'Should' in Conceptual Engineering." *Inquiry* 61 (8): 914–28.
Sloterdijk, Peter. 2009. "Airquakes." *Environment and Planning D: Society and Space* 27 (1): 41–57.
Smith, Jess. 2023. *Law, Registration, and the State: Making Identities Through Space, Place, and Movement*. Routledge.
Smith, Thomas S. J. 2017. "Of Makerspaces and Hacklabs: Emergence, Experiment and Ontological Theatre at the Edinburgh Hacklab, Scotland." *Scottish Geographical Journal* 133 (2): 130–54.
Soaita, Adriana Mihaela. 2024. "Everyday Activism: Private Tenants Demand Right to Home." *Housing Studies* 39 (6): 1422–43.
Somers, Margaret R. 1995. "What's Political or Cultural About Political Culture and the Public Sphere? Toward an Historical Sociology of Concept Formation." *Sociological Theory* 13 (2): 113–44.
Spade, Dean. 2015. *Normal Life: Administrative Violence, Critical Trans Politics, and the Limits of Law*. Duke University Press.
Spiegel, Samuel J. 2015. "Contested Diamond Certification: Reconfiguring Global and National Interests in Zimbabwe's Marange Fields." *Geoforum* 59:258–67.
Statler, Matt, Loizos Heracleous, and Claus D. Jacobs. 2011. "Serious Play as a Practice of Paradox." *Journal of Applied Behavioral Science* 47 (2): 236–56.
Sterken, Rachel Katharine. 2020. "Linguistic Intervention and Transformative Communicative Disruptions." In *Conceptual Engineering and Conceptual Ethics*, edited by Alexis Burgess, Herman Cappelen, and David Plunkett, 417–34. Oxford University Press.
Stock, Kathleen. 2021. *Material Girls: Why Reality Matters for Feminism*. Hachette UK.

Stock, Kathleen. 2022. "The Importance of Referring to Human Sex in Language." *Law and Contemporary Problems* 85 (1): 25–45.
Stoker, Gerry. 1991. *The Politics of Local Government*. Bloomsbury.
Strathern, Marilyn. 1996. "Cutting the Network." *Journal of the Royal Anthropological Institute* 2 (3): 517–35.
Strick, James E. 2019. "Metaphors and Other Slippery Creatures." *British Journal for the History of Science* 52 (2): 345–52.
Strunz, Sebastian. 2012. "Is Conceptual Vagueness an Asset? Arguments from Philosophy of Science Applied to the Concept of Resilience." *Ecological Economics* 76:112–18.
Stubbs, Paul. 2018. "Slow, Slow, Quick, Quick, Slow: Power, Expertise and the Hegemonic Temporalities of Austerity." *Innovation: The European Journal of Social Science Research* 31 (1): 25–39.
Sullivan, Alice. 2021. "Sex and the Office for National Statistics: A Case Study in Policy Capture." *Political Quarterly* 92 (4): 638–51.
Sullivan, Sian. 2010. "'Ecosystem Service Commodities'—a New Imperial Ecology? Implications for Animist Immanent Ecologies, with Deleuze and Guattari." *New Formations* 69:111–28.
Sutton-Smith, Brian. 1997. *The Ambiguity of Play*. Harvard University Press.
Swain, Dan. 2019. "Not Not but Not Yet: Present and Future in Prefigurative Politics." *Political Studies* 67 (1): 47–62.
Swain, Dan. 2025. "Disaster Utopia and the State: Success, Failure and the Fear of Co-Option." *European Journal of Social Theory*, ahead of print, September 23. https://doi.org/10.1177/13684310251379192.
Thiele, Kathrin. 2014. "Ethos of Diffraction: New Paradigms for a (Post)Humanist Ethics." In *Diffracted Worlds—Diffractive Readings: Onto-Epistemologies and the Critical Humanities*, edited by Birgit M. Kaiser and Kathrin Thiele, 38–52. Routledge.
Thomasson, Amie. 2020. "A Pragmatic Method for Normative Conceptual Work." In *Conceptual Engineering and Conceptual Ethics*, edited by Alexis Burgess, Herman Cappelen, and David Plunkett, 435–58. Oxford University Press.
Thomasson, Amie. 2025. "Conceptual Engineering: When Do We Need It? How Can We Do It?" *Inquiry* 68 (9): 2993–3018.
Thomson, Kelly. 2020. "Slow Motion Revolution or Assimilation? Theorizing 'Entryism' in Destabilizing Regimes of Inequality." *Current Sociology* 68 (4): 499–519.
Thomson, Michael. 1997. "Legislating for the Monstrous: Access to Reproductive Services and the Monstrous Feminine." *Social and Legal Studies* 6 (3): 401–24.
Thorpe, Amelia. 2018a. "Pop-Up Property: Enacting Ownership from San Francisco to Sydney." *Law and Society Review* 52 (3): 740–72.
Thorpe, Amelia. 2018b. "'This Land Is Yours': Ownership and Agency in the Sharing City." *Journal of Law and Society* 45 (1): 99–115.
Thorpe, Amelia. 2020. *Owning the Street: The Everyday Life of Property*. MIT Press.
Thurlow, Claire. 2022. "From TERF to Gender Critical: A Telling Genealogy?" *Sexualities* 27 (4): 962–78.
Tickell, Andrew. 2022. "Gender Critical Litigation: Reconciling *Fair Play for Women* and *For Women Scotland*." *Edinburgh Law Review* 26 (3): 458–67.

Tilley, Christopher. 2002. "Metaphor, Materiality and Interpretation." In *The Material Culture Reader*, edited by Victor Buchli, 23–55. Routledge.
Tironi, Manuel. 2018. "Hypo-Interventions: Intimate Activism in Toxic Environments." *Social Studies of Science* 48 (3): 438–55.
Tønder, Lars. 2026. "Feeling the Trouble: Comic Politics in Times of Ecological Crises." *Environmental Politics* 35 (1): 50–67.
Torrance, David, and Doug Pyper. 2023. *The Secretary of State's Veto and the Gender Recognition Reform (Scotland) Bill*. UK House of Commons Research Briefing. https://researchbriefings.files.parliament.uk/documents/CBP-9705/CBP-9705.pdf.
Trammell, Aaron. 2020. "Torture, Play, and the Black Experience." *GAME: Games as Art, Media, Entertainment* 1 (9): 33–49.
Tsoukas, Haridimos. 1993. "Analogical Reasoning and Knowledge Generation in Organization Theory." *Organization Studies* 14 (3): 323–46.
Tunali, Tijen. 2020. "Humour as Political Aesthetics in Street Protests During the Political Ice Age." *European Journal of Humour Research* 8 (2): 129–45.
UK Government. 2018. *Help Shape Our Future: The 2021 Census of Population and Housing in England and Wales*. Cm 9745. https://assets.publishing.service.gov.uk/media/5c13e08aed915d0b9211b98d/Census2021WhitePaper.pdf.
Vachhani, Sheena J., Emma Bell, and Alexandra Bristow. 2025. "The Affective Micropolitics of Craftivism: Organizing Social Change Through the Minor Gesture." *Organization Studies* 46 (4): 525–47.
Vella, Kellie, Madison Klarkowski, Selen Turkay, and Daniel Johnson. 2020. "Making Friends in Online Games: Gender Differences and Designing for Greater Social Connectedness." *Behaviour and Information Technology* 39 (8): 917–34.
Verhoeven, Imrat, Michael Strange, and Gabriel Siles-Brügge. 2022. "The Dynamics of Municipal Contestation: Responses from Local Government to Perceived Policy Threats from Higher Authorities." *Policy and Politics* 50 (4): 587–604.
Vervoort, Joost M., Manjana Milkoreit, Lisette van Beek, Astrid C. Mangnus, David Farrell, Steven R. McGreevy, Kazuhiko Ota, Christoph D. D. Rupprecht, Jason B. Reed, and Matthew Huber. 2022. "Not Just Playing: The Politics of Designing Games for Impact on Anticipatory Climate Governance." *Geoforum* 137:213–21.
Viola, Tullio. 2019. "From Vague Symbols to Contested Concepts: Peirce, WB Gallie, and History." *History and Theory* 58 (2): 233–51.
Vivienne, Son, Benjamin Hanckel, Paul Byron, Brady Robards, and Brendan Churchill. 2021. "The Social Life of Data: Strategies for Categorizing Fluid and Multiple Genders." *Journal of Gender Studies* 32 (5): 498–513.
Vossen, Emma. 2018. "The Magic Circle and Consent in Gaming Practices." In *Feminism in Play*, edited by Kishonna L. Gray, Gerald Voorhees, and Emma Vossen, 205–20. Springer.
Walby, Sylvia. 2007. "Complexity Theory, Systems Theory, and Multiple Intersecting Social Inequalities." *Philosophy of the Social Sciences* 37 (4): 449–70.
Walby, Sylvia, and Karen A. Shire. 2024. *Trafficking Chains: Modern Slavery in Society*. Bristol University Press.
Waldman, Ari Ezra. 2024. "Opening the Gender Box: Legibility Dilemmas and Gender Data Collection on US State Government Forms." *Law and Social Inquiry* 49 (4): 2021–51.

Wang, Allegro. 2023. "(Im)possible Futures: Gender Hacking as Queer and Racial Futurity." *GLQ* 29 (3): 305–27.

Wedderburn, Alister. 2021. *Humour, Subjectivity and World Politics: Everyday Articulations of Identity at the Limits of Order*. Manchester University Press.

Wedlin, Linda. 2007. "The Role of Rankings in Codifying a Business School Template: Classifications, Diffusion and Mediated Isomorphism in Organizational Fields." *European Management Review* 4 (1): 24–39.

Weick, Karl E. 1998. "Introductory Essay—Improvisation as a Mindset for Organizational Analysis." *Organization Science* 9 (5): 543–55.

Weiss, Linda, and Elizabeth Thurbon. 2021. "Developmental State or Economic Statecraft? Where, Why and How the Difference Matters." *New Political Economy* 26 (3): 472–89.

Weiss, Margot. 2006. "Working at Play: BDSM Sexuality in the San Francisco Bay Area." *Anthropologica* 48 (2): 229–45.

Weiss, Margot. 2011. *Techniques of Pleasure: BDSM and the Circuits of Sexuality*. Duke University Press.

Welch, Christina. 2010. "The Spirituality of, and at, Greenham Common Peace Camp." *Feminist Theology* 18 (2): 230–48.

Weltman, Daniel. 2024. "What Do We Want? To Eliminate Gender! When Do We Want It? Later!" *Pacific Philosophical Quarterly* 105 (4): 510–40.

Werron, Tobias, Jelena Brankovic, and Leopold Ringel. 2024. "Theorizing Together." *Distinktion: Journal of Social Theory* 25 (2): 228–49.

Westbrook, Laurel, and Aliya Saperstein. 2015. "New Categories Are Not Enough: Rethinking the Measurement of Sex and Gender in Social Surveys." *Gender and Society* 29 (4): 534–60.

Wicker, Allan W. 1985. "Getting Out of Our Conceptual Ruts: Strategies for Expanding Conceptual Frameworks." *American Psychologist* 40 (10): 1094–103.

Williams, Juliet. 2026. "Solving for X: Gender Markers, the Law, and the Administrative State." *Signs* 51 (4): 881–907.

Williams, Miriam J. 2017. "Care-Full Justice in the City." *Antipode* 49 (3): 821–39.

Williams, Miriam J. 2020. "The Possibility of Care-Full Cities." *Cities* 98:102591. https://doi.org/10.1016/j.cities.2019.102591.

Williams, Miriam J. 2022. "Care-Full Food Justice." *Geoforum* 137:42–51.

Wittig, Monique. 1996. "The Category of Sex." In *Sex in Question: French Materialist Feminism*, edited by Diana Leonard and Lisa Adkins, 24–29. Taylor and Francis.

Wohlwend, Karen E. 2009. "Damsels in Discourse: Girls Consuming and Producing Identity Texts Through Disney Princess Play." *Reading Research Quarterly* 44 (1): 57–83.

Wohlwend, Karen E. 2012. "The Boys Who Would Be Princesses: Playing with Gender Identity Intertexts in Disney Princess Transmedia." *Gender and Education* 24 (6): 593–610.

Wolfe, Charles T. 2014. "The Organism as Ontological Go-Between: Hybridity, Boundaries and Degrees of Reality in Its Conceptual History." *Studies in History and Philosophy of Science Part C: Studies in History and Philosophy of Biological and Biomedical Sciences* 48:151–61.

Yates, Luke. 2021. "Prefigurative Politics and Social Movement Strategy: The Roles of Prefiguration in the Reproduction, Mobilisation and Coordination of Movements." *Political Studies* 69 (4): 1033–52.
Yuen, Felice C., and Susan M. Shaw. 2003. "Play: The Reproduction and Resistance of Dominant Gender Ideologies." *World Leisure Journal* 45 (2): 12–21.

Index

Acquisition: category membership, 83–84; open invitation, 184n39; relationship to making, 85
Activism, 20; conceptualization, 99; image of, 100–101; partisanship, 190n32; public bodies undertaking, 99, 101, 188nn17–18, 199n4; quieter, 189n21; slow, 191n40. *See also* Conceptual activism
Afshary, Mohammad, 48, 51
Agender, 201n15
Ahmed, Sara, 176–77n19
Anderson, Ben, 113–14
Anti-Discrimination Act 1998 (Australia), 141
Antigender, 164n10
Apology, 55
Arendt, Hannah, 196n38
Asara, Viviana, 166n31
Ashar, Sameer, 48
Attachments, 48, 49, 113–15, 118, 175n6, 188n10

Babel, 1
Ballakrishnen, Swethaa, 45, 56, 62, 178n30
Barad, Karen, 34–35, 170n12, 171n19, 181–82n19
Barbershop, 139
Barnes, Victoria, 182n23
Baron, Jane, 191n38
Bateson, Gregory, 125
Beliefs, as property, 114, 119–20
Belinsky, Zoe, 88
Bem, Sandra, 87, 88
Bennett, David, 67
Besnier, Niko, 92
Bey, Marquis, 55, 177n21
Bhambra, Gurminder, 51, 53, 62, 147, 178n31
Birth certification, 17, 37, 39–41, 69, 80, 170n11, 172n27, 183n31
Black, Julia, 186n56
Black, Max, 176n11
Blandy, Sarah, 52
Blomley, Nicholas, 131, 135
Bogost, Ian, 130, 195n26
Bragg v. Linden Research, Inc, 196n43
Brannigan, Erin, 48
Browne, Kath, 47, 55, 158
Browne, Sarah, 138, 177–78n24, 186n60, 197n51
Butler, Judith, 167n39

Cantalamessa, Elizabeth, 9–10, 27, 170n16
Cappelen, Herman, 170n13
Care, 53
Care-full: activism, 119; governance, 102; public bodies, 107–13
Category membership, 40, 69, 80–85. *See also* Census 2021 for England and Wales; Concept; Decertification; Gender; Sex
Census 2011 for England and Wales, sex question guidance, 37
Census 2021 for England and Wales, 24–25, 28, 36–44; conflict, 36–44; definition of gender, 36, 38; definition of sex, 36, 40–41, 170n11; gender identity, 42–43; gender question, 38–39; judicial review of, 40–41; outcome, 41–43; resistant play, 138–39; sex realists, 40; sex question, 37–43; trans respondents, 37, 39

Certeau, Michel de, 177n23
Certification: as constitutive, 84; sex realism, 82; use of, 89; value of, 82–83. *See also* Decertification
Chalmers, David, 26, 27, 29, 58
Clarke, Jessica, 30
Clarke, John, 71, 175n2, 168n46
Cohen, Amy, 51, 53, 192n43, 203n20
Commodification, 71
Common sense, 102–7
Concept: aid, 51–55, 64, 151; boundaries, 57, 62; cell, 61–64; Census sex, 64–65; conflict, 36, 142, 160–61, 171–72n24; countercurrents, 59–60; current, 59–61, 152; dance moves, 144–45, 158–60, 180n40, 182n19; disorganization of, 156; economy, 153–55, 156; expressed, 34; force of, 151; form, 19, 53; gardening, 58; ideational, 3, 31; imagining, 31–35, 46; invented, 178n26; lens, 54; maintenance work of, 63; materiality, 3, 31–35, 46, 55, 150–51, 160, 200n6; metacategories, 155–57; morphology of, 150–57; occupied, 57; parameters of, 33; played with, 125; realized, 12, 44, 170–71n18, 176–77n19; vague, 26, 110, 191nn35–36; world, 55–59
Conceptual activism: academic, 46, 51–55, 66, 68–93; conservative, 16, 148; materiality, 163n5; methods, 14–18, 157–61; play, 122–23; policy practice, 187n7; prefigurative, 147; varieties of, 147–48. *See also* Concept
Conceptual engineering, 9, 26–33; challenges, 29–30, 169nn8–9; critique of, 31–33; law and, 30
Conceptual guerilla gardening, 58–59
Conceptual meaning, 8–14, 25; create, 69; imagined and materialized, 32–35; negative, 12–13; propertied, 37. *See also* Concept
Conceptual methods, 47–51. *See also* Concept
Conceptual ontology, 47–49. *See also* Concept
Conceptual politics, 9, 15, 25. *See also* Concept
Conceptual prefiguration, 10–14; common sense, 103; critical, 12–13, 147. *See also* Concept
Consalvo, Mia, 193n7
Conservative conceptual activism, 16, 148
Cook, Ian, 121
Counterhegemonic meanings, 34; *See also* Concept; Conceptual prefiguration
Craftivism, 75
Critical institutional play, 75. *See also* Play
Cull, Matthew, 88, 186n58
Currah, Paisley, 176n14

Dance, 17, 19; concepts and, 144, 158–60; conceptual dance partners, 74; conceptual device, 90; conceptual moves, 65–66; decertification, 74
Data, 17
Davies, Margaret, 134
Decentralizing regulatory categories, 85
Decertification, 13–14, 17, 19; conceptual cell, 152–53; conceptual current, 152; conceptual world, 151–52; definition of, 68; legislative proposal, 76–79; objections, 68, 77–78, 185n46, 185n49; plausible reform, 75; play, 140; rationale, 68; regulatory change, 69, 79–85; research data, 76; slow activism, 116
Deformalization, 79. *See also* Decertification
Dembroff, Robin, 11, 169n6
Dempsey, Michelle, 12
Deregulation. *See* Decertification; Regulation
Derrida, Jacques, 167n36
Disability, 52
Diverse economies, 73. *See also* Economy

Economy: acquiring, 72; concept of, 19; conceptual, 153–55; gender, 91; making, 71–72; reimagined, 70–74, 92; responsibility, 85; use, 72. *See also* Certification; Decertification
Edwards, Rosalind, 182n27
Enright Máiréad, 138, 197n51
Equality law, property in beliefs, 132

Fair Play for Women, 40–41
Fair Play for Women Ltd v. Registrar General for Scotland, 169–70n11, 172n26
Fast activism, 116
Feminist judgments projects, 75
Fitzgerald, Maggie, 177n20
Fletcher, Ruth, 55, 62
For Women Scotland Ltd v. The Scottish Ministers, 2, 98, 137, 200–201n9
Free-running, 195n28; the state, 133
Future of Legal Gender, 17, 180n2

Gandorfer, Daniela, 34
Gaonkar, Dilip, 175n5
Garforth, Lisa, 160

Geertz, Clifford, 103, 106
Gender: abolition, 87–88, 149, 164n16, 186n58; acquisition-use, 91; categories, 80–81, 87; common sense, 118; conceptual economy of, 86, 153–54; denationalization, 87; diversity, 4–6, 86, 104, 149, 163n4; economic dance, 89; economy and, 70; institution, 8, 117–18, 165nn26–27, 187n7; living as, 184nn42–43; made, 84, 91; materialization of, 118; metacategories, 155–57; metaphoring, 201n16; ontology of, 170–171n18; overcoming of, 88, 149–50; overproduction, 88; play, 136–42; plurality, 111; proliferation, 86; property, 86, 153, 164n12; quality of subjects, 91; realism, 97; spectrum, 104–5; use of, 86–88; valued, 6. *See also* Decertification; Sex
Gender-(as)-diversity, 4–6, 104, 149, 163n4; Census, 24; common sense, 104, 107; decertification, 89, 90–91, 97–98; policies, 109, 110; slow activism, 116
Gender-critical: beliefs, 119; caselaw, 165n20; feminism, 4–5, 7, 149, 164n9; free-running, 133; litigation, 98, 113–14; sex registration and, 82. *See also* Census 2021 for England and Wales; Common sense; Decertification; Public bodies
Gender identity: census, 172–73n34; multiple, 85; production of, 184n41; property, 132
Gendering, society, 84
Gender-neutral policies, 102, 108
Gender politics, 6–8; contested terminology, 37–43, 102–6, 108–11
Gender-realism, 97; common sense, 103, 106–7
Gender Recognition Act 2004 (UK), 7, 81, 184n43
Gender Recognition Certificate, 40
Gender recognition law reform, 78; consultations, 80
Gheaus, Anca, 87
Gibbons, Adam, 36, 38
Gibson, Katherine, 15
Gibson-Graham, J. K., 15, 19, 73, 181n17
Giddings, Seth, 127
Golder, Ben, 139
Governance rationalities, common sense, 103–4
Graham, Julie, 15
Greenham Common Women's Peace Camp, 193n12
Guerilla gardening, 58–59
Gunn, Caitlin, 14

Hajer, Maarten, 1
Halsey, Mark, 195n28
Haringey Council (London borough), 96
Harris, Cheryl, 164n12, 196n37
Haslanger, Sally, 23, 167n37, 169nn6–7
Holbraad, Martin, 47, 170n17, 200n7
Honig, Bonnie, 77, 156
Horton, John, 116
Huizinga, Johan, 193n13
Hunter, Shona, 201n13

Ingold, Tim, 59
Institution: approach, 8; gender as, 117–18
Intimate activism, 99

Jeffrey, Craig, 55, 175n6
Jones, Jane Clare, 38, 171n22
Jones, Jesse, 138, 177–78n24, 186n60, 197n51
Jorem, Sigurd, 169n9

Kaechele, Kirsha, 141
Kallis, Giorgos, 166n31
Keenan, Sarah, 130, 132
Keller, Evelyn Fox, 176n11
Kemp, Tom, 57, 59, 166n32
Klag, Malvina, 15
Köhler, Sebastian, 178n29
Koslow, Allison, 30, 169n9
Kraftl, Peter, 54, 116, 175n8
Kuang, R. F., 1

Ladies Lounge, 140–41, 198nn58–62
Lanari, Elisa, 188n12
Land acknowledgment, 55
Langley, Ann, 15
Lau, Jason, 140–41
Lau v. Moorilla Estate Pty Ltd, 198n58
Law: play and, 139–41; public services, 105; sex and, 105. *See also* Decertification; Gender-critical: litigation
Legal category reform, 79–85
Legal dramas, 16
Legal gender, 68. *See also* Decertification
Legal meanings, materialization, 69
Legal sex, 65, 69. *See also* Decertification
Lehner, Ace, 139

Liboiron, Max, 115
Linstead, Stephen, 88
Lister, Matthew, 12
Litigation, 7
Local government, 95–96, 102, 103–6; balance, 109; community, 108; power, 101

Mackenzie, Lisa, 38, 171n22
Maeckelbergh, Marianne, 116
Magic circle, 143
Maker movement, 75
Marsh, Dorota, 196n33
Massey, Doreen, 203n21
Materiality: of concept, 150–51, 160, 163n5; relationship to imagining, 32–35
McDermont, Morag, 56, 60–61, 64, 66
Meaning. *See* Concept
Metacategories, 201–2nn16–18. *See also* Concept
Metaphor, 49–50
Methods, 46–51, 69–71; conceptual activism, 14–16, 47–47, 69, 157–61; decertification and economy, 68, 70–71, 76–77, 91–92; interviews, 17, 47–48; play-oriented, 123–24; policy practice, 97–98, 101–2. *See also* Dance
Mind-to-world, 29, 31
Mona (Hobart), 140–41
Monopoly, 194nn19–20
Moorilla Estate Pty Ltd v. Lau, 198nn58–59
Morgan, Bronwen, 35, 49, 175n4, 177n22, 192n43, 198n1, 203n20

Nachmanovitch, Stephen, 121, 125
Nado, Jennifer, 26, 27–28
Narotzky, Susana, 92
Neoliberalism, 71
Newman, Hannah, 200n5
Newman, Janet, 52, 53, 57, 60, 175n7, 176n9
Nicholson, Daniel, 179n35
Nonbinary identity: legal recognition, 199n5; public policy, 104; public provision, 189–90n26
Noterman, Elsa, 131

Office for National Statistics (ONS), 23–24
Orange Solidarity, 193n12
Overcoming gender, 88, 149–50. *See also* Gender

PARK(ing) Day, 131–32
Pedersen, Morten Axel, 47, 170n17
Pedersen, Sarah, 138–39, 164n13, 174n51, 200n5
Perry-Kessaris, Amanda, 55, 62, 64, 158, 182n23
Philippopoulos-Mihalopoulos, Andreas, 49
Play, 20–21; aid, 130; conceptual activism and, 122–23, 142, 143; currents, 131–33; definition of, 124–25; free-running the state, 133; gender, 136–42; graffiti, 130; magic circle, 126, 143, 154; pleasure, 128; power, 126–27, 129; property, 123, 127–35; satire, 126; touch, 138; trespass, 130; twisty, 142–44; unpredictability, 142; value, 124–26
Play Anything: The Pleasure of Limits, the Uses of Boredom, and the Secret of Games, 130
Playworlds, 128–30
Plunkett, David, 170n13
Pluriverse, 177n20
Podosky, Paul-Mikhail Catapang, 31
Policy practice: activism, 118; gender, 118; materialization, 187n6. *See also* Public bodies
Positive action, 80
Power geometry, 203n21
Prefiguration, 10–14; common sense and, 103; conceptual activism, 147, 199nn3–4; conceptual methods, 17; conservative, 167n38; politics, 166n31
Prefiguring economy, 70, 72–74. *See also* Economy
Prinzing, Michael, 51
Proctor, Alice, 195n29
Progressive conceptual activism, 148. *See also* Conceptual activism; Prefiguration
Property: bundle of rights/ sticks, 183–84n38, 191n38; children, 131; counterhegemonic norms, 135; currents, 130–31; games, 194nn17–23; governance and, 134; graffiti, 130; institution, 192n2; play, 123, 127–35; pleasure, 128; reimagined, 72; repurposed, 131–33; shared, 52; speculative law, 78–79
Prosumption, 181n12. *See also* Economy
Protected characteristics, 155, 202n17
Protection, as gendered concept, 63
Public bodies: activism, 99, 101, 188nn17–18, 199n4; balance, 108–10; best practice, 105–6; common sense, 103; gender, 97–98;

good sense, 117; organizational gender work, 110
Pullen, Alison, 88

R (Fair Play for Women Ltd) v. UK Statistics Authority, 40–42
R (JHRW) v. Leicester City Council, 188–89n20, 190n29
R (Smith) v. The Chief Constable of Northumbria Police, 190n31
Rai, Shirin, 53, 54, 178n25
Regulation, 60–61, 69, 84, 85. *See also* Certification; Decertification
Renz, Flora, 52, 178n32, 179n37
Reynolds, Andrew, 50, 179n35
Romanienko, Lisiunia, 193n12
Rosiecka, Helena, 40

Santarelli, Matteo, 31
Saville, Stephen, 133
Sawyer, Sarah, 29, 30
Scottish Census, 38
Second Life, 129; property, 194n22
Self-identification, 81
Seto, Theodore, 194n20
Sex: categories, 24, 80; certification, 80; Census question, 36–43; data collection, 172n31; definition, 4, 28, 83; embodiment, 5; nativism, 4–5, 63, 109; ontology, 171n18; quality of subjects, 91; scrutiny, 82. *See also* Decertification; Gender; Sex realism
Sex Matters, 42
Sex realism, 5–7, 28, 106, 149; Census and, 36, 44; decertification, 77, 89–90; free-running, 133; public policy, 113. *See also* Gender-critical
Sex registration, 40, 82, 90. *See also* Certification; Decertification
Shapiro, Nicholas, 60
Sharpe, Alex, 202n19
Shields, Rachel, 124
Simion, Mona, 168n6
Śliwa, Martyna, 196n33
Slow activism, 115–17, 118, 191n40
Soft decertification, 97. *See also* Decertification
Speculative law, 17, 76–79; play, 140. *See also* Decertification; Play
State: activism, 100, 189n21; conceptual revision, 29–30, 57–58, 166–67n35; withdrawal, 85. *See also* Public bodies; Regulation
Stock, Kathleen, 14, 167n41
Strick, James, 62
Sullivan, Alice, 28, 40, 173n41
Summerhill School, 135; freedom at, 179–80n38; laws, 178–79n33

Thomasson, Amie, 23, 29
Thomson, Michael, 202n19
Thorpe, Amelia, 53–54, 55, 132, 196n34
Tironi, Manuel, 99
Touching Contract, The, 138, 141
Trade union, gender approach, 103, 106, 110, 111
Trammell, Aaron, 193n15
Transgender: opposition to, 112–13; policies, 106, 109; politics, 5–6, 11
Troubled attachments, 113–14, 119
Troublesome concepts, play and, 154. *See also* Concept

UK Statistics Authority, 40

Vagueness: concepts, 26, 110, 191nn35–36; public policy categories, 110
Veluwenkamp, Herman, 178n29
Versteeg, Wytske, 1
Vossen, Emma, 193n15

Wedderburn, Alister, 136
Weiss, Margot, 127, 193n10
Williams, Juliet, 200n5
Williams, Miriam, 53, 56, 190–91n33
Withdrawal, 185n45; regulatory frameworks and, 79
Wittig, Monique, 167n37
Woman: concept, 62–63; definition, 5, 167n37; self-identification, 103. *See also* Gender; Sex
Women's services, certification, 77, 83. *See also* Decertification; Public bodies
Woodyer, Tara, 121
World-to-mind, 29–30, 31, 84

Yarn-bombing, 139, 140, 197n54, 198n63
Young, Alison, 195n28

www.ingramcontent.com/pod-product-compliance
Lightning Source LLC
LaVergne TN
LVHW102200101026
849957LV00026B/240
9781478039280